RESOURCES FOR TEACHING

A WORLD OF IDEAS

ESSENTIAL READINGS
FOR COLLEGE WRITERS

FIFTH EDITION

Lee A. Jacobus
University of Connecticut

BEDFORD BOOKS Boston

For information, write: Bedford Books, 75 Arlington Street, Boston, MA 02116
(617-426-7440)

0–312–16705–9

Instructors who have adopted *A World of Ideas: Essential Readings for College Writers*, Fifth Edition, by Lee A. Jacobus as a textbook for a course are authorized to duplicate portions of this manual for their students.

PREFACE

This book is designed for first-year college English instruction in basic composition, the level at which I use these essays for my own students. I am well aware of the problems involved in trying to teach something other than writing while teaching writing. We usually ask our students to read compositions while they are learning to write them, and I have found that using essays by significant writers is one of the best ways to help students to write and keep writing. I do have to teach the essays, it is true. And I am sure that you, too, will have to address class time to a discussion of each of the essays you choose to teach. But I am convinced that it is important time spent well. I find it exhilarating to discuss Freud, Arendt, and Darwin with first-year college students. They sense these are writers that they ought to know. And because they feel that way, I find it easier to hold their attention and show them how to learn about writing—while learning about other things—from a discussion of the prose before them.

These *Resources* are arranged in three sections. The first section includes discussions of all forty-one readings in *A World of Ideas* and provides additional writing suggestions to supplement those in the book. The second section consists of sentence outlines; each selection is outlined in order that the main ideas stand out clearly. You should feel free to photocopy and hand out these sentence outlines to students as an aid to understanding. (I am grateful to Carol Verburg, Ellen Troutman, Ellen Darion, and Mike Hennessy for preparing the sentence outlines.) The third section includes alphabetically arranged bibliographies of all of the writers represented in the book. If students wish to read more by and about these writers, you may want to distribute photocopies of these as well. Finally, I include in an appendix two student papers written in response to essays in *A World of Ideas*. You might want to use these as models or as prompts for discussion.

This manual is designed not to get in your way. I can't pretend to explain these essays the way you should explain them to your class. Students are all so different that no two discussions of, say, Machiavelli, are ever the same. Even principal areas of focus change from discussion to discussion. Therefore, you probably will not want to use all of the materials—discussion topics, writing assignments, sentence outlines, and bibliographies—for each essay that you teach. But you may appreciate knowing that all these options are available, particularly if some of the essays turn out to be more difficult than you thought.

Using this book with first-year students implies that we respect their native intelligence. The Brunerian hypothesis—that students who are treated as if they were geniuses will perform as such—may not withstand the proof of experience, but I have found that even the most difficult students in an average class labor successfully to derive benefit from assignments on this kind of material. Not every first-year class can handle this approach. I have had extensive experience in remedial English and understand some of the reading problems that even an average class contains. Yet I have been warmed by the enthusiasm my students have shown for the approach I recommend here. Granted, one must work hard to help them understand the ideas and grasp the basic rhetorical principles that they must apply. But I find the work is well rewarded.

One genuine reward is the quality of class discussions. I am pleased with the ways my students will pursue lines of argument or implications of a thought and then try to make sense of the essays they have read. I find, for instance, that it is very interesting to discuss Machiavelli's questions concerning ends and means, particularly in a world in which the justification of certain means is still a primary subject.

Another reward of this approach is the belief that I am contributing to the education of beginning students. Because most composition classes demand that some reading material be used for discussion and models of good writing, I consider it important to provide the best there is. In this case, the best thinkers, talking about some of the most vital ideas of all time, represent the best stimuli and models for writing. It is surprising to see how each of these authors does provide a model.

Whether the essay posits an argument, employs image or metaphor, or examines a single idea from many points of view, it remains a model with teaching potential for beginning students. Contemporary journalistic essays of the sort that appear in most anthologies available today are easy and fun reading for my students. But they are also insubstantial in many cases and often do not really offer the kind of model for writing that is truly useful. Most of the essays I describe—by Joan Didion, Tom Wolfe, E. B. White, Joseph Wood Krutch, and other fine writers—fascinate the reader because of their style. It is not the invention or the organization that stands out. It is style. And style is the one element that first-year students simply cannot learn from such models. These students can learn in their first semester how to use methods of development to help invention. They can also learn about argumentation, narrative, and other organizational principles. But they cannot hope to imitate or learn directly from a mature polished style. That comes only with time. Meanwhile, the kinds of essays included here have a great deal to offer beginning students of writing. I have tried to make the going as simple as I can to maintain morale and give students the chance to make the most of this valuable opportunity.

CONTENTS

Contents

EVALUATING IDEAS
AND
WRITING ABOUT IDEAS

Evaluating Ideas

The first section of the text, "Evaluating Ideas," treats the question of critical reading. I know that some of the essays in this book are not easy for many students to read, and the sentence outlines for each of the selections are available at the end of the manual to help students cope with demanding material during the first difficult stages. Reports travel to me from great distances as well as from teaching assistants down the hall about how students begin to learn to read these essays well. I have heard that students in two-year colleges as well as four-year colleges of all kinds are able to master the material. It takes time, but student confidence eventually builds, and class discussions help many people learn to read critically.

You might include some opportunity for students to read aloud in your first experiments with the text in class. I recommend beginning with the Machiavelli, in part because it is so accessible and in part because most students hold strong opinions on the issues that Machiavelli raises. I have never been disappointed using this essay.

Begin with paraphrasing in order to gain a sense of the extent to which your students understand the immediate meaning of what they are reading. Then proceed to the level of questioning. Encourage students to develop questions from the text, and then show them how some of the questions can be developed and how implications can be widened by applying questions to various kinds of experience.

I have divided the stages of critical reading into five relatively obvious and traditional steps:

1. Prereading
2. Annotating
3. Questioning
4. Reviewing
5. Forming your own ideas

I have been around long enough to know that few if any students will actually follow these five steps— or let's say few will follow all of them. But that is no reason to ignore them. I think that annotating and questioning are the two most important, and I observe my class early in the term to ensure that students are marking up the margins of their books. Many students resist writing in books, so a good lesson or two can help them. I would suggest you photocopy a few pages of your own text and show them how it is done.

Underlining a text is important for later recall, but I also think that writing commentary in the margin is even more so. You might mention points that seem obvious to teachers but not to students: when you comment on a passage in class, the students should mark it for future examination. If the passage is important enough to comment on, then surely it is important enough to be remembered.

Suggestion

Give your students a chance to annotate the rest of the Machiavelli in class, and have them break into groups of three and discuss with one another the ways in which they annotated passages. They can learn fairly quickly from one another, especially if you provide them with initial suggestions and advice.

The kinds of questions that emerge out of annotating depend on many factors, but you will probably find related questions for discussion in your class. It helps to select a few questions that were developed by your own students and then offer them for examination by the class. You can remind your students that in their discussion they are carrying on a dialogue with the text, with one another, and with you. And that dialogue is a model for critical thinking.

1

FORMING YOUR OWN IDEAS

I hope it is clear from "Evaluating Ideas" that one of my principal purposes is to help students develop some ideas of their own. I do not want them to be passive receptors when they are reading these writers. I know from the experience of reading student responses from all over the country that many students fiercely disagree with some of these authors. I have added some authors in this fifth edition that will provoke even more disagreement. But controversy notwithstanding, it is essential that students be given the opportunity to initiate their own thoughts and their own responses to the ideas in this text. I want students to be participants in the quest for truth. For that reason, I end this section with a stimulus to thought. The point of this book is to encourage students to think on an intellectual level that is worthy of them.

Writing About Ideas

The material on "Writing About Ideas" and the sample essay that offers one way to approach Machiavelli appear in the text on page 769, after the selections. It continues the discussion of Machiavelli that is begun at the front of the book in "Evaluating Ideas." If you choose, you could assign both sections of this material at the same time. Or you could wait for students to read one or two of the selections and then assign the section titled "Writing About Ideas."

You know best what kinds of essays or responses you want from your students after they have read some of this material. I have found that I can direct my students toward writing that is personal and revealing or toward writing that is more formal and objective. Some of the suggestions for writing invite a personal response, and for certain students, this is the best kind of response. But for other students, a more reasoned and detached response might be desirable. What kind of response to aim toward lies with you, and the text is flexible enough to allow you to decide.

I have suggested in earlier versions of this manual that you hold some discussions with your students about your expectations and discuss openly with them what their expectations in the course are and what kind of writing they feel they need to do. I feel that self-expressive writing is appropriate for some students, but I also feel that most students at the first-year level should attempt less self-expressive writing and practice instead writing that asks them to reason well, to think clearly, and to work with ideas that are mature and demanding. For that reason, you will find that most of the assignments direct students toward a kind of writing that is similar to the material they are reading—discursive, demanding, thoughtful, and rooted in the universal human experience.

Suggestions

1. Hold an open discussion with your students on why they ought to write about these essays instead of just discuss them. Ask them what they think the difference is, for example, between writing an essay and taking an examination on Karen Horney's selection. I think you will be able to uncover some interesting attitudes and help your students understand the differences between these two processes.

2. In the course of discussing an essay—the Machiavelli should do nicely—you might ask your students to make some observations about the author's tone or attitude toward the audience. These are important issues, and discussing them at an early stage can help you clarify some points. You can also explore with your students the kinds of choices they can make to control tone and use it to their best advantage.

3. It may be dangerously subjective—but also exceptionally human—to ask your students to comment on what they think about the author they are working with. How much of Machiavelli comes through and in which passages? Or you may prefer to ask your students to decide on the attitude the authors assume. For example, is Lao-tzu cynical? Is Machiavelli cynical? What about Jefferson or Arendt? Or Douglass, King, and Marx?

4. Spend some time in your class discussions on the question of what students might write about. Suggest topics as they occur to you, and ask other students to recommend and refine topics for essays. The virtue of this approach is that it encourages students to start thinking about writing topics early on, which in turn motivates them as they read.

GENERATING TOPICS FOR WRITING

You may regard the suggestions for writing at the end of the selections as a last resort for your students. But people tell me that the suggestions work. In fact, when I asked one user of the book what I could do to improve it, she recommended only that I include more suggestions for writing, which this edition does accomplish.

My students come up with ideas as they discuss the essays, but many also rely on the suggestions for writing and the questions that I intend for stimulating class discussion. Most students appreciate these suggestions and sometimes produce surprisingly varied papers based on what they choose.

Thinking Critically: Asking a Question

Education consists largely of learning how to ask the right questions. It is very important to point out that the authors in the text are often answering questions in their essays. Freud questions the function and significance of our dreams; Horney questions whether Freud may have misunderstood the sexuality of women. The questions posed based on Machiavelli's essay are only a fraction of those that could be asked.

Suggestions

1. Ask your students to come up with as many more questions as there are in the text. None of these questions is actually developed into an essay in the "Introduction," but all are indirectly relevant. Coming up with more questions can be very useful in discussing how to find ideas for writing. You might use some of the questions as vehicles for your students' writing.
2. This is a good place to develop thesis statements and to discuss the ways in which a thesis statement emerges from questions. I have decided in this edition to omit the discussion of the thesis sentence because it really needs the fuller treatment only found in a full-scale rhetoric text. If you use this book with a rhetoric text, you can introduce such material as is relevant.
3. Go over some sample arguments in class. When I do this, I usually link them with the methods of development (see text p. 774) and show how each method of development can yield an appropriate thesis statement from the same or similar concerns. Students need drilling in this, and no matter how many times you go over it, you will find students proposing theses that are too broad, too narrow, or too obvious for an essay. Sometimes no thesis statement at all will surface. If you feel this is important, you should allow some time for it in the opening days of the course.

Working up questions on the text is a good beginning exercise in class. You can begin by proposing some questions and then show how they can be answered in an essay. To me, the important issue is to teach how to raise questions of depth and complexity. I try to steer students away from any questions that require too simple a response. If the question is deep enough, the student will need to think carefully, and that will help produce an essay that might even surprise the student. This has happened often to me and it is rewarding.

I ask two basic types of questions. One kind limits itself to the author of the material and to what might be called internal issues. That means dealing with the way an author works with an idea by articulating a concept and then examining it. Other questions examine life and experience outside the text. You probably will want to stress one kind of question on some occasions and another kind on others.

Using Suggestions for Writing

In addition to suggestions for writing after each selection, there are more suggestions in this manual. I often take one of the suggestions from the manual, photocopy it for the class, and use it to discuss possible strategies for essay topics. This helps students become accustomed to the approaches that you will find in the "Suggestions for Writing."

One tip for the first papers is not to let them be too long. I am particularly finicky about the first set of papers. I urge even my best students to write no more than three pages, but I really think two pages for the first paper is acceptable. That way you can go over the paper in detail and inform your students about what kind of performance you expect. If you review the first papers carefully, you should have a better experience with the second papers.

Developing Ideas in Writing

Methods of Development

Users of earlier editions will recognize my reference to methods of development as allusions to many common topics. The use of definition, comparison and contrast, causal analysis, and discussion of circumstances can be important initial issues for most students. I work with my students very closely on these matters, and I find that it helps them think more clearly and write more confidently.

If you agree with me about the usefulness of studying these methods of development, especially as such methods are evident in the authors in the text, then I suggest that you try my approach of having your students develop single-paragraph essays guided by one of the methods of development. I often ask my students, once they have gotten used to thinking in terms of the methods of development, to write an essay using each method in turn. That is the structure of the sample essay at the end of the chapter.

Suggestions

1. Assign the class the job of writing a single paragraph using any one of the methods of development. Give your students a choice to ensure some variety in your reading. Be sure to ask them to identify at the beginning of the essay which method they are using. If you would prefer that everyone use the same method of development, try causal analysis or analysis of circumstance. Or for one that is less difficult, try definition, which is important for freshmen.
2. Assign a one-paragraph essay, but do not allow students to identify the method they used. Read some aloud in class (or photocopy them), and see if the class can identify them.
3. Like the sample essay, request an essay that uses a different method of development in each paragraph.

This type of assignment may not appeal to you. However, you will see that it serves the important purpose of connecting the act of writing to the act of reading the essays in a way that is helpful for improving your students' writing. I feel that these methods of invention can be learned from watching how good writers work, even when the writers are formidable thinkers. The final result is that your students think much more about how they write something. Not only should their writing styles improve, but their thoughts about the subject at hand should deepen. The suggestions I have made have produced some probing essays and also give those students who are the most problematic writers approaches they never knew before. Often such students show the most rapid progress.

Sample Essay

Give your students a chance to go over the sample essay with you. You may find it contains elements that you do not want your students to repeat. If so, give the essay a thorough critique. Your students will want to critique it on their own terms, and they should be given a chance to do so.

Suggestion

I make an agreement with my students. They hand in their essay on time, and I grade it and give it back in the next meeting. This helps build morale. Students know how well they did almost immediately, and I know what needs to be done to have them writing at the level I think appropriate for them. The reward for turning in the essay on time is that if the student truly underperforms, I permit the student to resubmit the revised essay for a better grade. This works.

My most helpful practice is to photocopy some samples from my students' work and offer critiques of them in class. The rule is that no one knows whose work is being discussed, and there is to be no cruel or nasty criticism. Everything is directed toward the goal of writing better. Students are impressively helpful to each other. They become good editors, make good suggestions for revision, and develop a keen eye that extends to the examination of their own work. In one way this makes their writing part of the subject matter of the entire course. I have not found a faster way to improve student writing than this. Naturally, I make sure every student contributes at least one sample in these "publications" and usually two or three. I choose a wide range, from excellent to good to not-so-good writing samples for them to read.

HOW MANY ESSAYS TO ASSIGN?

Judging from my mail, this is impossible to answer. One student from Tufts University wrote me a long letter at the end of the summer after his freshman year. He had used the book and said that he had been assigned only six essays. During the summer he had read all the other essays except one, and he simply wanted to tell me how much they meant to him. Some instructors used ten to fourteen of the essays. Many looked for essays that related to each other in some way. For those of you who are interested in possible pairings, see "Suggested Pairings of Essays," which follows the syllabus.

A Sample Syllabus

What follows is the syllabus I used when I last taught the course. Modified to include some of the new essays that are now in the fifth edition, it presently reflects the way I am teaching the course. I know it's a workout. I'm often exhausted after class, and I know that I could get by without having the students read so many essays. But the truth is that I enjoy all of these essays so much that I wish we could read more. The only way to do that is to eliminate assignments in the rhetoric text. In any event, I make sure that I read each essay in the book over a two-semester period.

But as I said, the response to this book has been such that any number of users will have totally different experiences. You must gauge how hard you want your students to work and how hard they can work. Set your own pace, knowing that whatever you read, you will be working with rewarding ideas.

The following is an actual syllabus—warts and all.

ENGLISH 105   COMPOSITION   **LEE A. JACOBUS   XT2570**
Class meets: JHA 407   Office hours: JHA 410
FALL 199-
T–Th: 9:30–11:00   T–Th: 9:15–9:30, 11:00–12:00

The basic purpose of this course is for you to master the fundamentals of rhetoric while also confronting the ideas of some of the most important writers in Western culture.

Your responsibilities will include reading the assignments carefully and generating from them appropriate essays that test your thinking and help craft your writing.

TEXTS: Lee A. Jacobus, *A World of Ideas*, 5th ed. (Boston: Bedford Books, 1997). I have most recently taught the book with my own rhetoric text, *Writing as Thinking* (Macmillan), but before that I used some of the other well-known rhetoric texts.

ESSAYS: *Format.* Your essays will be typewritten on standard 8-1/2- by 11-inch paper. Leave a margin of 1-1/2 inches on the left for my comments. The essays will be given to me on their due date. Their length may vary from assignment to assignment, but one important point is that they should be as short as you can humanly make them. Essay length will be about three pages at first and then will escalate to a maximum of eight pages (but only when I give the word).

ESSAYS: *Style.* We will practice what rhetoricians call the *plain style*, which means that you ought to aim for the simplest, most direct, unadorned, and unaffected style possible. As a guide, you should think in terms of short sentences, averaging twenty words or so. Your paragraphs should have a clear topic with every subsequent sentence growing naturally from your intentions regarding its development. Your paragraphs ought to be relatively short (five to eight sentences) and structured with a clear plan. Style is to be thought of as an instrument to achieve clarity of expression. Your vocabulary should be jargon-free and designed to inform and not to impress.

ASSIGNMENTS: The pattern throughout the course will be for you to hand in essays on Tuesday. We will discuss some of your essays on the following Thursday as well as new readings that have been assigned. The Tuesday essay will usually be on a subject involving your reading of the selection assigned for discussion on Tuesday.

Sept. 6	Tuesday:	Introduction to rhetoric
Sept. 8	Thursday:	Read: Jacobus, "Evaluating Ideas," pp. 1–10.
		Read: RHETORIC, "Invention and Rhetoric," pp. 00–00.
Sept. 13 1st essay due.	Tuesday:	Read: Lao-tzu, "Thoughts from the *Tao-te Ching*," and Machiavelli, "The Qualities of the Prince," pp. 17–49.
		ASSIGNMENT: Write a brief essay on a topic chosen from those at the end of the essays.
Sept. 15	Thursday:	Read: Rousseau, "The Origin of Civil Society," and Jefferson, "The Declaration of Independence," pp. 51–80.
		Read: RHETORIC, pp. 000–000.
Sept. 20 2nd essay due.	Tuesday:	Read: Douglass, "From *Narrative of the Life of Frederick Douglass, an American Slave*," pp. 107–121.
		Or read Thoreau, "Civil Disobedience," pp. 123–148.
		ASSIGNMENT: Write a brief essay using Douglass or Thoreau as your source.
Sept. 22	Thursday:	Read: RHETORIC, "Argument," pp. 000–000.
Sept. 27 3rd essay due.	Tuesday:	Read: King, "Letter from Birmingham Jail," pp. 151–171.
		ASSIGNMENT: Write an essay using the principles of argument we have discussed.
Sept. 29	Thursday:	Read: Simone de Beauvoir, "From *The Second Sex*," pp. 173–186.
Oct. 4	Tuesday:	Read: Adam Smith, "Of the Principle of the Commercial or Mercantile System," pp. 192–206.
Oct. 6	Thursday:	Read: Marx, "The Communist Manifesto," pp. 209–234. Prepare to discuss some of the topics mentioned at the end of the essay.
Oct. 11 4th essay due.	Tuesday:	Read: Reich, "Why the Rich Are Getting Richer and the Poor, Poorer," pp. 251–268.
		ASSIGNMENT: Write an essay using a topic provided for Reich's essay.
Oct. 13	Thursday:	Read: Dawkins, "All Africa and Her Progenies," pp. 447–469.
Oct. 18	Tuesday:	Read: Darwin, "Natural Selection," pp. 395–412.
Oct. 20	Thursday:	Read: Kaku, "A Theory of the Universe?," pp. 431–447.
Oct. 25 5th essay due.	Tuesday:	Read: Plato, "The Allegory of the Cave," pp. 275–286.
		ASSIGNMENT: Choose a topic for an essay on nature.
Oct. 27	Thursday:	Read: Maimonides, "On the Limits of Man's Intellect," pp. 289–304.
		Read: RHETORIC, "Informative Writing," pp. 000–000.
Nov. 1	Tuesday:	Read: Freud, "From *The Interpretation of Dreams*," pp. 307–318.
Nov. 3	Thursday:	Read: Jung, "The Personal and the Collective Unconscious," pp. 321–334.
Nov. 8 6th essay due.	Tuesday:	Read: Horney, "The Distrust Between the Sexes," pp. 337–351.
		ASSIGNMENT: Choose a topic for an essay on the mind.
Nov. 10	Thursday:	Read: Cabeza De Vaca, "From *La Relación*," pp. 497–508.
Nov. 15	Tuesday:	Read: Benedict, "The Pueblos of New Mexico," pp. 511–526.
Nov. 17	Thursday:	Read: Aristotle, "Tragedy and the Emotions of Pity and Fear," pp. 681–696.
Nov. 22 7th essay due.	Tuesday:	Read: Woolf, "Letter to a Young Poet," pp. 731–799.
		ASSIGNMENT: Choose from among the suggestions for writing, and examine the issues that inform any of these last four essays.

THANKSGIVING

Nov. 29	Tuesday:	Read: Buddha, "Meditation: The Path to Enlightenment," pp. 569–587.
Dec. 1	Thursday:	Read: Muhammad, "From the Koran," pp. 617–626.
Dec. 6	Tuesday:	Read: Teresa, "The Raptures of St. Teresa," pp. 629–639.
Dec. 8 8th essay due.	Thursday:	ASSIGNMENT: Write an essay that uses both principles of argumentation and principles of research.
Dec. 13	Tuesday:	Read and discuss an essay of your choice.

NOTE: Prompt completion of essays is crucial in this course. If you feel you cannot keep the pace we have set, you probably shouldn't take the course. Naturally, sickness or family problems may slow you down now and then. See me if you have a *real* problem. All late essays, except those made late by *real* problems, will suffer a severe grade reduction.

HINT: The RHETORIC should be regarded as a reference book. I have asked you to read selected portions, but it is useful for a great many things. For one, the question of how to write sentences and paragraphs is described in detail in "Sentences" (pp. 000–000) and "Paragraphs" (pp. 000–000). Questions of connotation and metaphor are treated on pp. 000–000. Techniques for the research paper, which will be required in many future courses, are mentioned in "Writing the Research Paper," pp. 000–000. "Writing About Literature," pp. 000–000, will come in handy next semester for your second English course. The point is that this book is likely to be a resource for you throughout college. Perhaps it will be useful thereafter as well.

Completed essays are due on the following dates:

1   September 13
2   September 20
3   September 27
4   October 11
5   October 25
6   November 8
7   November 22
8   December 8

SUGGESTED PAIRINGS OF ESSAYS

Many instructors look for useful connections between two or more essays; if you are interested in trying that approach, you might consider the following groupings. In "Suggestions for Writing" following each selection, the "Connections" items also make concrete suggestions for pairings.

1. Machiavelli and Jefferson (or Marx). The understanding of how ends and means are related as well as of justice in government expands in these pairings.
2. Jefferson and Rousseau. Trace the influence of Rousseau in Jefferson.
3. Machiavelli, Arendt, and Jefferson (or even Marx) read together will produce some interesting insights. The questions of oppression and striking out for freedom as well as the question of maintaining power are very strong here.
4. Lao-tzu and Machiavelli are powerful contrasts in terms of how they address taking action in government.
5. Smith, Galbraith, and Reich offer an interesting progression. The issue of poverty contrasts with the issue of the freedom of the individual to pursue wealth.
6. Marx and Smith offer a good chance to talk about the growth of wealth and materialism.
7. Freud and Jung are a natural pairing, since there is potential conflict between their theories regarding the sources of psychological forces and the nature of the unconscious—personal or collective.
8. Horney can be teamed with any of these male psychologists as a way of exploring the question of whether there is a female psychology apart from Freud's imaginings.
9. Douglass and Thoreau. Obedience and disobedience, just laws and unjust laws: these work well together.
10. King and Thoreau. King was influenced by Thoreau's essay.
11. Maimonides and Kaku. Both postulate limits to the intellect.
12. De Beauvoir, Mead, and Horney. All three are interesting as feminists.
13. Gardner and Maimonides. They are a good contrast.
14. Bacon, Darwin, and Gould. These three may be compared in many ways—in terms of method and intellectual procedure, in terms of scientific premises, in terms of social impact. Any combination of these works well.

15. Dawkins and Gould. They are especially interesting to compare for the ways in which they write. They are both good writers writing on complex and difficult subjects.
16. Nietzsche and Benedict. They are a natural pairing because of the way Benedict develops Nietzsche's idea of the Apollonian and Dionysian in American Indian culture.
17. Herodotus, Cabeza de Vaca, and Geertz. These three make a natural grouping because of their concern for how we can understand people of another culture.

This list omits a few names from the table of contents but not because I could not find a place for them. Rather, I emphasize many obvious pairings, as well as some I did not mention in the above list, in the "Connections" questions in the "Suggestions for Writing" following each selection in the text. Playing with the essays in the fashion above, whether in an essay or in your own assignments, is likely to point up the richness of the material.

GOVERNMENT

The five selections in Part One focus on how government shapes itself in response to the interests of the people governed. They discuss realities and ideals. They examine social orders designed to achieve many goals such as stability, strength, and peace. But in some times and places the social order impinges on the rights of individuals. The authors in this part all wrestle with the challenge of satisfying individual needs while ensuring a strong social order.

LAO-TZU

Thoughts from the *Tao-te Ching* (pp. 17–31)

The Book of Tao is difficult for most Westerners to understand, and it is risky to offer freshmen this selection as their first text in a discussion of politics. The author, moreover, is reputedly interested less in political issues than in issues that govern individual life. Taoism in its earliest forms conflicted with Confucian thought, much of which originated from Confucius's own desire to be a public officer and a politician. Confucius was concerned with public life and with the virtues essential to serving the people properly. Lao-tzu is said to have mocked Confucius when they met and berated Confucius for his pride. Although the meeting may simply be legend, the way of Tao does represent a much more personal philosophy than Confucianism.

For Lao-tzu, for example, the evil doer should be met with good. Confucius, however, says that the evil doer should be met with justice and the doer of good should be met with good. Confucius's doctrine seems, at least to Western minds, much more worldly, practical, and responsive to the realities in which we live.

I am indebted to Michael Bybee of the University of Oregon, who has used a previous edition of this book with his students. Bybee compared human nature as it is reflected in Lao-tzu and Machiavelli's discussions of power and the state and questioned what makes a group of people cohere into a society.

Lao-tzu's text, odd and difficult as it may seem at first, works well with students. They use it to develop ideas of their own, to respond to Lao-tzu's ideas, and to explore issues that are of considerable importance to them. The conflict between the materialism of our culture and the metaphysical views that Lao-tzu promotes is quite palpable to many undergraduates. My experience is that most students are pragmatic, interested in succeeding in the material world and in being well paid when they receive their degrees, but are also susceptible to idealist viewpoints and have an interest in spiritual values. If you are fortunate enough to teach some students who are attracted by an idealistic outlook, your class discussions may blossom with exciting moments.

What may surprise you is how much discussion may be distilled from small segments of the text. For example, the order of "best" rulers in paragraphs 4 to 6 is well worth consulting. In any class discussion, students will find many examples of leaders that fit each of the categories.

If you assign the Lao-tzu and Machiavelli selections together, you should stimulate lively debate. For most of my students, Machiavelli holds great appeal. It is wonderful to see them interpret the conflict between these two writers' positions.

SUGGESTIONS FOR CLASS DISCUSSION

1.   What are Lao-tzu's views of human nature? Does he seem cynical or optimistic about human nature?

2. What are the chief values that Lao-tzu seems to hold dear? Some are peace, love, wisdom, and benevolence. See how many others your students can find.
3. Ask your students if they would feel comfortable living in a state that is governed in the way Lao-tzu recommends. What problems do they envision a modern American might face?

SUGGESTIONS FOR BRIEF ESSAYS

1. What kinds of individuals would have a difficult time living in the kind of state that Lao-tzu regarded as most desirable? Which individuals would find such a state most compatible to their way of life?
2. Taoism has developed into a religion. What religious qualities mark the selection? What qualities are clearly not religious? Is there a conflict between the two? Is it surprising that a book such as the *Tao-te Ching* should now be regarded as religious?
3. What is the role of the military in the state that Lao-tzu praises? How important would the military be, and who would serve in the armies? Which verses indicate the importance of the military? What do they say?

SUGGESTIONS FOR LONGER ESSAYS

1. Examine the way popular advertising in any medium demonstrates the truth of Lao-tzu's contention that "there is no disaster greater than not being content." Show how advertising makes it impossible for anyone who is its victim to be content. What is the result of advertising's success in making people discontented?
2. Choose a text or series of texts that you feel are especially difficult for you to accept as appropriate for either the state or the individual. Examine them in enough detail so that you show why you could not easily accept what they recommend. What would happen to our society if the recommendations were put into effect?
3. Write a series of verses in imitation of Lao-tzu, giving what you feel are the loftiest and wisest principles you can offer on the operation of the state and the proper behavior of its citizens. Use the form that appears in the selections—short declarative sentences that imply more than they say explicitly, verses that include several sections, ideals that can be put into action.
4. Consult the entire *Tao-te Ching*, and collect texts that shed light on what Lao-tzu means by "the way." Consider what recommendations he makes for achieving enlightenment, what enlightenment seems to mean, and how likely you feel it would be to achieve what he recommends. What illumination does the rest of the text provide for Lao-Tzu's political views?
5. How would Lao-tzu critique the society in which you live? What would he recommend to you as worthwhile behavior, and what would he condemn? Would you feel it possible to argue against his critique and maintain a worthwhile and virtuous path of behavior for yourself?

SENTENCE OUTLINE: See p. 77 of this manual.

BIBLIOGRAPHY: See p. 140 of this manual.

NICCOLÒ MACHIAVELLI

The Qualities of the Prince (pp. 33–49)

The original Italian for "qualities," *virtù*, connotes not only strength and force of personality but also fortune, destiny, and ingrained luck. The term is complex and deserves some opportunity for examination. This excerpt from *The Prince* is one of the most popular selections in *A World of Ideas*, and it is among the easiest to teach. Students seem ready to accept much of what Machiavelli says as being essentially practical and often necessary. One of the best opening gambits is to ask students how they evaluate Machiavelli's advice in terms of its likelihood to produce a successful government.

The question of ends and means—whether the means a prince uses will justify his ends, assuming they are high-minded—is central to this selection, although the original Italian is not entirely clear in establishing such a clear-cut distinction. Nonetheless, it is worthwhile to probe the question with your students, asking them if there are conditions under which it is appropriate to say that the political means can justify a political end. The writing assignments in the text center on this question because it is both important and clearly essential to an understanding of Machiavelli.

Another interesting question to ask concerns the term "wise princes," which Machiavelli uses near the end of the essay (para. 28). What would a wise prince be? Would that be a prince who has paid close attention to Machiavelli? Indeed, would a prince who paid very close attention to Machiavelli be a good prince? Or would that prince be merely a successful prince? You might ask your students if they think a distinction can be made between the two terms or if indeed a good prince must then be a successful prince.

Machiavelli's social structure assumed a noble class of citizens from which would arise the prince. But he also assumed the existence of "the masses," and he does not entirely write them off. It is worthwhile to examine the text with an eye toward what Machiavelli says about the people and their relation to the prince. He is concerned that they feel content and that they not hate the prince. It is useful to make some comparisons between Machiavelli's views and those of Lao-tzu and Rousseau.

Ultimately, the question is that of government. What kind of government does Machiavelli feel is most desirable? What does government seem to mean in the Renaissance Italy of his day? Is it relevant to our concepts of government today?

SUGGESTIONS FOR CLASS DISCUSSION

1. Can the desired qualities of the prince be taught, or are they inherent? Does genetics or the environment produce these qualities?
2. Is the prince really like our modern politicians? I last read over this material at a time when the newspapers were filled with statements from politicians that seemed to come right out of the passage. Ask your students to look through news magazines or newspapers—and do the same if you can—for evidence that Machiavelli's ideas are still current.
3. One of the chief points I raise in discussing this piece is the question of ends and means. First-year college students can grasp this concept easily, and they are often direct enough and innocent enough (if you will) to make the discussion interesting. The phrase "one must consider the final result" in paragraph 24 hedges things a bit. You may want to point out that the original Italian is *si guarda al fine* and that it is often translated as "we must often look to the end." Translators using "result" are concerned that we not get too deeply into an ends-and-means tangle, but the fact is we have been doing just that for centuries. You will find that your students will warm to an examination of this issue. You also will find that later essays (Rousseau's concern for the social contract, Jefferson's declaration and break from England, Douglass's attitude toward slavery and his freedom, and King's explanation of his means and the desired ends) will richly reward a careful discussion of this concept here.

SUGGESTIONS FOR BRIEF ESSAYS

1. Define the terms *ends* and *means*, and explain why they are important.
2. Compare Machiavelli's advice with the behavior of a politician—past or present.
3. Under what political circumstances might the ends justify the means? (This could be seen as a trap, but it nonetheless is a stimulating topic.)

SUGGESTIONS FOR LONGER ESSAYS

1. Research Machiavelli's life, and compare his actions with the advice he gives here. Did he have the qualities of a prince?
2. Machiavelli advises the prince to study history and reflect on the actions of great men. Would you support such advice? Machiavelli mentions a number of great leaders in his essay. Which leaders would you recommend that a prince study? Do you think Machiavelli would agree?
3. Look up the term *Machiavellian* in an unabridged dictionary or encyclopedia. From reading this essay, do you feel that the definition is warranted? Do you feel it is a distortion of what Machiavelli really means?

4. In an essay titled "The Qualities of the Politician," give your own advice to the politician of your choice. Use Machiavelli's rhetorical technique of sharply focused, brief paragraphs on a single subject that usually contrast two kinds of behavior, as well as his technique of the aphorism. Be sure to use Machiavelli's categories so that you are sure to cover the full range of activities pertinent to political life.

5. What form of government would Machiavelli feel is most stable and desirable? Base your answer on an analysis of the recommendations Machiavelli gives his prince. Consider his views of individuals in society and their roles and responsibilities in regard to the prince. What governments of today might satisfy Machiavelli's demands for the way the state should operate?

SENTENCE OUTLINE: See p. 79 of this manual.

BIBLIOGRAPHY: See p. 140 of this manual.

JEAN-JACQUES ROUSSEAU
The Origin of Civil Society (pp. 51–71)

The fact that Rousseau influenced the Romantics may be of some use to you in beginning a discussion of this piece. He represents some of the innovative thinking that stimulated late eighteenth-century philosophers concerning alternatives to traditional forms of government. Beginning in the early seventeenth-century in England, questions had been raised about the ways in which the monarchy was to be served or was to serve. Rousseau was instrumental in producing an atmosphere in which ideals of democracy were at least tenable and in some circles fashionable. When he began writing *The Social Contract*, the Philosophes, dominant thinkers in France, held that the monarchy could behave despotically if the goal was to produce good behavior in its citizens. Rousseau seems to have believed that there was an essential goodness in people and that a despotic ruler was undesirable no matter what his or her goals. Thus, the problem of ends and means figures in Rousseau's thinking as it does in Machiavelli's.

Perhaps Rousseau's most romantic belief was in liberty as a value to be held above all. The question of what freedoms the individual forgoes in committing to a social contract is sometimes complex to consider, since it seems on the surface that the individual "alienates" his freedoms when he joins the civil polity. Maurice Cranston, in his introduction to *The Social Contract*, explains that what "Rousseau is saying is that instead of surrendering their liberty by the social contract, they convert their liberty from independence into political and moral freedom, and this is part of their transformation from creatures living brutishly according to impulse into men living humanly according to reason and conscience."

The abstract concepts of political and moral freedom are important to consider with your students. It is also important to ask what freedoms people give up—and which people give them up—when they accept a social polity such as the one we live in. Likewise, it is important to discuss what freedoms the individual gains in the social contract.

Discussing the relationship of equality and democracy might be useful, but before doing so, I usually try to give students some idea of the kind of government under which Rousseau lived. The reigns of Louis XV (1715–1774) and Louis XVI (1774–1792) were shabby imitations of that of the "Sun King," Louis XIV (reigned 1643–1715). The worst conservatism took hold, and the government avoided the reforms that might have forestalled the French Revolution, which Rousseau never lived to see. If some students have a background in the Revolution, you might give them a chance to say what they think about Rousseau's contribution. You might also point to Wordsworth and Shelley as democrats influenced by Rousseau.

Ultimately, I think, your energies will probably be devoted to helping your students define for themselves what Rousseau has in mind by the social contract. Further, your efforts will probably be largely involved with distinguishing between natural law and civil law or natural man and civil man. You also will find yourself examining the concept of liberty and the concept of government as Rousseau seems to be establishing it.

SUGGESTIONS FOR CLASS DISCUSSION

1. It would be good to discuss the use of analogy in this piece. Aristotle warned that analogy was useful only when the "fit" between the two elements compared was more or less exact. Discussing this analogy's appropriateness should help your students understand their responsibility in constructing their own analogies—something they all do anyway.

2. One of the most fruitful subjects of class discussion might prove to be Rousseau's comparison of the family to the state. You might go into the reasons why Rousseau makes this comparison—particularly why he considers the king to be a surrogate father and the country his family. The thought is comforting but unreal. Ask if anyone's family is run on the model of a government, using, for instance, democratic or autocratic methods.

3. It is important to raise the question of people voluntarily yielding their freedom in order to enter into a compact with leaders who will govern on their behalf. This is a complex and controversial concept that should stimulate discussion. How could people actually do what Rousseau postulates in the first compact? Ask your students if they think it reasonable that government could have begun this way. You might want to distinguish between a people's consciously entering into a contractual compact and their making a compact subconsciously or by implication. Ask your students what their relationship is to their government. What kind of compact exists?

SUGGESTIONS FOR BRIEF ESSAYS

1. What is a compact drawn between a people and their government? What are its qualities?
2. Compare the natural state with the civil state. Which is preferable?
3. Is the family a necessary antecedent to government, or is government a necessary antecedent to the generally accepted structure of the family?
4. Is it possible to have a natural state today? What would it be like, and what would make it possible (or impossible)?

SUGGESTIONS FOR LONGER ESSAYS

1. Choose the most significant idea Rousseau presents in his essay. Explain why it is significant and to whom. Further, defend your choice as if you were speaking to someone who disagreed with you.
2. Rousseau talks about primitive societies. What do you imagine is the governmental situation in most primitive societies? How does your view compare with Rousseau's?
3. What form of government would Rousseau approve of today? Describe briefly the kind of rulers, the kind of institution, and the behavior of the governed that would most please him. Does any such government exist? Could it exist?

SENTENCE OUTLINE: See p. 80 of this manual.

BIBLIOGRAPHY: See p. 145 of this manual.

THOMAS JEFFERSON

The Declaration of Independence (pp. 73–80)

Jefferson was specifically invited to write this declaration because other members of the Continental Congress had been impressed by his style. John Adams and Benjamin Franklin worked and reworked the document until it was "scored and scratched like a school boy's exercise." In the original version, Jefferson attacked the slave trade, but in the revision that attack was omitted. A number of other interesting items were removed or changed as well.

The question of style is important in analyzing this piece because most students are familiar with its content and can be persuaded to look closely at style. Jefferson said, "I did not consider it any part of my charge to invent new ideas, but to place before mankind the common sense of the subject, in terms so plain and firm as to command their assent." The introduction to the piece talks about some stylistic issues, and you may wish to raise others. The use of parallel structure can become wearing, especially in contemporary prose, but it is valuable to use this piece to show how it can work and be effective. Naturally, it is important to remind students that the style of this piece was designed to ensure it was memorable and effective in argument.

The content of the Declaration is important, too. The list of causes needs examination to see whether any one of them is so overwhelmingly important that individuals ought to be willing to fight and die for it even today. It may be that some students feel that none of these causes is worth dying for, either now or in Jefferson's time. If you get such a reaction, it would be worth pursuing it to see exactly what your students' views on the subject are.

In view of Jefferson's concerns for the law, it is also interesting to examine the list of causes to see which of them pertain to laws either rigged or ignored for the benefit of the monarch. Paragraph 22, "abolishing the free System of English Laws," is interesting on this account. The next paragraph concerns the abolishing of laws that the colonists established for themselves. The relationship of laws imposed from without and laws conceived from within is of special interest as well. Of course, as Jefferson reveals in paragraph 25, the monarch has also waged war against the colonies, and that fact colors some of what Jefferson says in the document.

SUGGESTIONS FOR CLASS DISCUSSION

1. Define the range of the colonies' complaints against the crown.
2. Examine the document for seeds of democracy and republicanism. The members of the Congress were generally landed and patrician, and it is worthwhile to ask what made them different from their aristocratic overseers in England.
3. Stimulate a discussion of style. Mention Jefferson's concern for common sense, and see if your students agree that he achieved it.
4. If possible, have some students scan the opening sentences to determine their rhythms. If they can't, do it for them. Explain that some of the power of the document depends on the stately rhythms of the prose. This aspect of style is important to communicate to students.
5. Raise the question of Jefferson as a slaveholder and the value, in light of that, of his attitudes toward independence. Jefferson was a reluctant owner of slaves and opposed to its practice, but he did not free his slaves. Does his position as a slaveholder invalidate the Declaration? Does it invalidate the Revolutionary War?

SUGGESTIONS FOR BRIEF ESSAYS

1. How does the document seem to define *independence*? Use this definition as a basis for your own. To what extent does your definition of independence agree with or differ from Jefferson's?
2. By means of researching the background of the American Revolution, establish the political antecedents of the Declaration and what its consequences were thought to be.
3. What are the most important circumstances that brought the colonies to the point of rebellion?

SUGGESTIONS FOR LONGER ESSAYS

1. The Declaration was written after the first year of the American Revolution. What would be some of the reasons for writing such a document if the colonies were already in battle? To whom could it be useful? Consider its effect both in England and in the colonies.
2. Refer to Machiavelli's concerns for the way things turn out—the relationship between ends and means. What does the declaration imply about the justification of rebellion to achieve the ends of independence? Do you feel confident that the means of rebellion—involving war, civil disorder, injustice, and death—can be justified by the end of independence? Do you feel that Jefferson thought these particular means were justified by the ends he had in mind? How would he have regarded Machiavelli's advice?

3. Analyze Jefferson's list of causes. Group them into three or four categories (economic, military, civil, religious, and so on), and discuss at least one in each category as a way of explaining what the category is. If you can compare one category with another, decide which of the categories Jefferson felt was most important and why.

SENTENCE OUTLINE: See p. 81 of this manual.

BIBLIOGRAPHY: See p. 137 of this manual.

HANNAH ARENDT

Ideology and Terror: A Novel Form of Government (pp. 83–101)

Hannah Arendt is well known for her obscurity, but this is not an obscure piece. Its difficulties, if we can call them such, lie first with the fact that it refers to what was, for her and for others living in the 1940s and 1950s, a painful living fact—that totalitarian governments seemed to threaten the entire world with their influence. Your students will vary as to what they know about the Nazi and Stalinist governments, about Mao and the Chinese communists, or about the governments of smaller, less threatening nations. You might spend some time explaining that the governments of Germany and Russia exercised power in such a way as to maintain a constant reign of terror. They founded their regimes on rigid ideas about race and history that permitted them to authorize the mass killings of races they deemed to be inferior, such as Jews, gypsies, homosexuals, and more. The Russians killed millions of its own citizens of specific classes, such as the five million kulaks, or well-to-do farmers, Stalin killed in the 1930s, in the name of history.

Arendt's point in the beginning of her essay is that totalitarianism is a relatively new form of government and did not exist in ancient times. She may be correct, but a close look at Nero's Rome and the Rome that continued the persecution of Christians might shed some corrective light on that claim. Certainly, though, Arendt's main point is worth examining in detail. She claims that modern totalitarian governments operate from a basic premise that is rooted in what they assert are ineluctable laws, such as the law of evolution or the law of the withering away of the classes. Once these "laws" are in place, everything else follows.

Another of her main points is that once these laws are accepted and their "logic" in place, the responsibility of the individual to behave morally along traditional lines is abolished. Rather, the behavior of the group, pressing the logic to its conclusion, is what matters. As she says in paragraph 7, "Totalitarian lawfulness . . . applies the law directly to mankind without bothering with the behavior of men." It is worth developing this idea with your students, since it concerns the responsibilities of citizens in a government to behave in a moral fashion. Some of our most difficult problems in examining the behavior of ordinary people in Germany and Russia concerns the ways in which they supported anti-Semitism and the genocide of their own citizens. Ordinary people did so with no thought to their own guilt because the inexorable laws they followed exonerated them. These "scientific laws" worked on their own, sweeping the people along with them.

Another potential difficulty is the fact that this is Chapter 13 (the final chapter) in a long study of totalitarianism. The three primary sections of the book are Part 1, Antisemitism; Part 2, Imperialism; and Part 3, Totalitarianism. The book is essentially historical. Its first section examined anti-Semitism as racism, showing its early connection to politics. The second part continues its concern with racism, with such titles as "Race-Thinking Before Racism" and "Race and Bureaucracy." The connection between racism and totalitarianism is one of the most original and most important parts of Arendt's discussion of politics. I feel it is essential to examine it in detail with students.

SUGGESTIONS FOR CLASS DISCUSSION

1. Bring the question of racism and politics into play early in your discussions. See what views your students hold on this matter.
2. Connect anti-Semitism with racism, and see how many forms of racism your students can identify. Ask them which forms of racism they see as most susceptible of political manipulation.
3. Ask your students to define the qualities of totalitarianism that lead Arendt to suggest that it is a novel form of government. Direct them toward an analysis of the "laws" totalitarian governments declare as the premise of their "logic."
4. In what ways might certain street gangs be considered totalitarian in their beliefs and behavior? What makes them so? Be as specific as possible.

SUGGESTIONS FOR BRIEF ESSAYS

1. Clarify the distinction with which Arendt begins paragraph 8: "At this point the fundamental difference between the totalitarian and all other concepts of law comes to light."
2. What is "totalitarian lawfulness" (para. 7)?
3. What distinctions does Arendt make between tyranny and totalitarianism? Do you agree with her?
4. What contemporary institutions exist that might lead toward a totalitarian system in or near your own environment? What are the dangers of such institutions? Are they perceived as being dangerous for the right reasons?

SUGGESTIONS FOR LONGER ESSAYS

1. Beginning with paragraph 13, Arendt discusses terror. Her concept of terror is complex and needs clarification. What do you see as the primary purposes of terror for the totalitarian government? How does it work, and what are its ultimate effects? Is terror aimed at a limited population within the state?
2. After having done some research on either Nazi Germany or the Stalin years of Russian communism, describe the methods and results of the totalitarian state? How does such a state differ from the republicanism Rousseau imagined? How does it differ from the political institutions you know from personal experience?
3. How would government in a totalitarian state differ from that in a democratic state that was free of racism or specious theories of history? What would the role of government be in a totalitarian state. What would politicians do? What is government's job in such a state? How does terror help the government achieve its ends?
4. How does Arendt see the law functioning in a healthy republican state? How does she see it functioning in a tyranny? How does she see it functioning in a totalitarian state? As much as possible, establish her views on the law.
5. Why are ideologies essential to the growth and development of a totalitarian state? What is a typical ideology that might contribute to totalitarianism? Are you aware of ideologies that hold sway today that might be capable of spawning new totalitarian states? Establish the details and specifics of any such ideology and suggest what its outcome—should it be widely accepted—would be.

SENTENCE OUTLINE: See p. 82 of this manual.

BIBLIOGRAPHY: See p. 129 of this manual.

PART TWO

JUSTICE

The four essays in Part Two concentrate on issues of justice, especially in situations in which the laws seem to fly in its face. This is particularly true in the case of slavery in the United States when Frederick Douglass and Henry David Thoreau lived, and of segregation when Martin Luther King, Jr. lived. Simone de Beauvoir was an adult when France finally granted the right to vote to women, and she was ardent in her defense of justice for women on all fronts.

FREDERICK DOUGLASS

From *Narrative of the Life of Frederick Douglass, an American Slave* (pp. 107–21)

Douglass's narrative is an accessible document that needs little preparation or background. Among the fascinating aspects of the excerpt here are the portraits of people, slave and free, who are part of Douglass's life. He records very carefully their views and attitudes and reveals his own as he writes. His new mistress, Mrs. Auld, was a northerner who married and moved to Maryland to take up the life of the slave holder. Her original occupation, weaving, is a coincidental metaphor for creating a life, weaving a fate. Douglass constantly reminds us of the tenderheartedness of this woman but also shows that slavery makes her as sinister as those who were born into slave-holding families. Douglass was an especially fair-minded man, active in movements toward freedom of many people. He died just after attending a meeting on women's suffrage on February 20, 1895. During his life he was sometimes criticized for having married a white woman in 1884, after his first wife died. When he was confronted by his critics, he said simply that his first wife was the color of his mother and his second wife was the color of his father.

SUGGESTIONS FOR CLASS DISCUSSION

1. What were Douglass's expectations of his new mistress? What surprised him, and why was he surprised? Did his mistress seem to have a clear idea of what it meant to be the mistress of a slave? How was she affected by learning to be a slave holder?
2. Do you think Douglass's views about the power of learning are still persuasive today? Can it still be advantageous for people to deny others the right to an education? Do all oppressed people feel that education is a key to freedom?

SUGGESTIONS FOR BRIEF ESSAYS

1. Douglass learned his letters by observing the markings on pieces of timber used in building a boat (para. 12). Explain the symbolism in his observations. To what extent was literacy like a boat to him?
2. Reading becomes the pathway to freedom for Douglass, and he determines to learn to read despite his master's efforts to stop him. To what extent is Douglass right about finding the pathway to freedom? Is his insight still useful to us? Does the experience of discontentment that Douglass felt contribute positively to improving the lot of those enslaved?
3. Why is Douglass so disturbed over the fate of his grandmother after the death of Master Andrew? What had his grandmother meant to the slave owners? How did they treat her in her old age? What would Douglass have rather had her fate be?

17

SUGGESTIONS FOR LONGER ESSAYS

1. Douglass tells us about a period in his life marked by change and growth. How did the changes contribute to his determination to secure his freedom? What political lessons does Douglass learn, and how does he impart them to us?
2. To a large extent Douglass tells us about the degrading effects that slavery had on white slave holders. What evidence does Douglass give us for the changes that take place in slave holders? Consider the evidence of the proper behavior of a slave as implied in the opening of the essay. What political realities does Douglass reveal that would affect the behavior of those in power? What effect does power have on those who hold it?
3. Tell a story in the first person of your relationship with people who hold power over you legally. Tell your story in such a way as to reveal the political realities that affect both you and those with power. To what extent is your situation similar to Douglass's?

SENTENCE OUTLINE: See p. 84 of this manual.

BIBLIOGRAPHY: See p. 133 of this manual.

HENRY DAVID THOREAU

Civil Disobedience (pp. 123–48)

One of the most important concepts to emphasize in discussing this essay is the question of conscience. It is often said that Thoreau is the conscience of the nation, and it is worth having students hash out just what that might mean. It helps to give some background for the term, including the etymological implications of knowing what is within us, within our hearts. The religious tradition Thoreau draws upon is avowedly Puritan, figuring prominently in the works of Calvin and especially in the prose and poetry of Milton, which Thoreau surely knew well. The implication of such a consideration is that the individual must reign foremost and always act according to what the individual knows is right. This was Milton's view; he was a champion in the eyes of later revolutionaries of conscience. Translating this concept into contemporary terms is not difficult. Consider the Nazi trials at Nuremberg where individuals were held accountable for following Hitler's orders, or the atrocities in Vietnam, or the current stockpiling of nuclear weapons. The contemporary examples proliferate.

It is also helpful to mention something about the Fugitive Slave Act of 1850, which was designed to enforce the already existing Fugitive Slave Law of 1793. The act was designed to tame those Northerners who expressed open hostility to slavery and who had been operating the highly efficient Underground Railway, which spirited slaves away from the South and into safety in Canada. Anyone who helped or harbored a slave anywhere in the nation was subject to a $2,000 fine. This amount was a small fortune in 1850. The fact is that Northern states resented the law and passed counterlaws—the Personal Liberty Laws, which had the effect of nullifying the act. In border states, however, it ought to be mentioned that the act was enforced even during the early years of the Civil War.

Students might be led to see the significance of having to capitulate to laws that are clearly unjust, immoral, and inhuman by reflecting on how they themselves would act if they had to deal with a law such as the Fugitive Slave Act.

SUGGESTIONS FOR CLASS DISCUSSION

1. What does it mean to say "That government is best which governs least" (para. 1)?
2. Thoreau says "That government is best which governs not at all" (para. 1). What does he mean by this? Do you agree?
3. In paragraph 2, Thoreau says about the government: "*It* does not keep the country free. *It* does not settle the West. *It* does not educate." Is this still true? Is Thoreau's view of government accurate? What exactly does government do?

SUGGESTIONS FOR BRIEF ESSAYS

1. In paragraph 11 Thoreau says "All voting is a sort of gaming." What does he mean by this? Is this true? What is the gaming aspect of voting? Why is Thoreau so harsh about voting? (Remember that in his time only men had the vote.)
2. Thoreau mentions a "wise minority" in paragraph 16. What does he mean by this? Is it possible to have a wise minority in the sense that he describes? If there is such a minority, what should government do? What should the wise minority do? How would a wise minority be likely to behave?

SUGGESTIONS FOR LONGER ESSAYS

1. Compare the government of Thoreau's day with that of our own. How much are they alike? What specific qualities do the governments have in common? How do they differ? Do you believe that the United States government has improved since Thoreau's time? Do you think Thoreau would retract some of the things he says if he were alive today?
2. What do you think Thoreau means by "conscience"? According to Thoreau, what should the role of conscience be in government? Is it possible for a government to act out of conscience? If a government did act out of conscience, how would it act? Does our government act out of conscience? Does any government that you know of act out of conscience?
3. What do you think Thoreau's attitude toward school segregation would be, whether it were voluntary or forced by circumstances? Would the difference be important to him in his analysis? Do you think Thoreau would approve of affirmative action laws that grant preferential treatment to minorities in matters of college admission and job appointments? Would he think such programs are just or unjust?

SENTENCE OUTLINE: See p. 85 of this manual.

BIBLIOGRAPHY: See p. 147 of this manual.

MARTIN LUTHER KING, JR.

Letter from Birmingham Jail (pp. 151–71)

One of the intriguing qualities of this piece stems from its being a letter. I like to talk about the letter as a form—however vague that concept is. I usually bring in some other letters, such as passages from the letters of Paul in the Bible and letters from a collection called *The World's Great Letters*, edited by M. Lincoln Schuster (Simon and Schuster, 1940). I read letters by Beethoven, Leonardo da Vinci, and others. I try to point out to my students that letter writing is important, that it is one of the forms that they will continue to use long after they've left the classroom, and that it is not just a catch-as-catch-can enterprise.

Beyond this, I try to emphasize King's concern with the issues of ends and means. He felt that the means could taint the desired ends. He emulated Mahatma Gandhi—a figure we must introduce to our students—who insisted on passive resistance and whose methods freed an entire nation. I also emphasize that King remained nonviolent despite repeated acts and threats of violence against him. Finally, there is the question of law again. King's views on how we should react to unjust laws are worth careful examination.

SUGGESTIONS FOR CLASS DISCUSSION

1. Discuss the question of what one does when one must face an unjust law. What are the real choices? What are the moral imperatives?
2. If you want to talk about this piece of writing as a model of the letter, ask your students what they have learned about how to write a letter. What could they actually do better now that they have looked closely at this model?

3. King worked very hard on behalf of African-American people in the South. It is useful to see in the letter the extent to which he expressed concern for one race over another. To what extent is this a "nonracial" document?

SUGGESTIONS FOR BRIEF ESSAYS

1. Examine the letter for details that permit you to define the nature of "Birmingham society" during King's lifetime.
2. Examine one of St. Paul's letters in the Bible (see the suggestions in Writing Assignment 5 in the text, p. 170), and analyze the effectiveness of King's use of the topic of testimony.
3. Which method of development is dominant in King's letter? Choose one, and then defend your choice by showing how often it is used.

SUGGESTIONS FOR LONGER ESSAYS

1. Write a letter from the clergy addressed by Martin Luther King, Jr. How would they respond to his letter, given the positions they have already held? How could they counter the reasoned argument King presents? What references from the Bible could they use? As a hint, you can rely on a concordance to locate uses of the concept of the law in the Bible.
2. King's letter is profoundly rational, reasonable, and logical. However, the letters in the Bible are often passionate and emotional as well as rational. Which sections of King's letter are emotional? What is the difference in style between the emotional and rational passages? Which is more impressive? Which is easier to emulate?
3. King says that to defy or evade the law is to invite anarchy (para. 20). Look up *anarchy* in a good dictionary or an encyclopedia. Would anarchy be less or more desirable than the conditions that existed in Birmingham?

SENTENCE OUTLINE: See p. 86 of this manual.

BIBLIOGRAPHY: See p. 139 of this manual.

SIMONE DE BEAUVOIR

From *The Second Sex* (pp. 173–86)

Some of your students will be familiar with Beauvoir, but most will not. It may not be important to discuss with them her relationship with Jean-Paul Sartre. There was widespread disappointment when Deirdre Bair's biography detailed the ways in which Beauvoir winked at Sartre's behavior as well as the ways in which she sometimes abandoned her own goals on his behalf. Beauvoir's friends may have misunderstood her relationship with Sartre, or they may not have been privy to Beauvoir's feelings. In any event, it is clear that by 1949 she was ready to write one of the most influential and lasting feminist treatises. I do not think it is obvious that she distances herself from women, as early critics, including Elizabeth Hardwick, said. The problem may be in part with the translation, which took H. M. Parshley, a retired professor of zoology at Smith College, four years to finish. He was an expert on the science of reproduction, and his choice as translator tells us something about the way the original publisher, Knopf, thought of the book. Both Parshley and Alfred Knopf felt the book was too long and too repetitious, and Parshley excised some portions, which annoyed Beauvoir immensely. However, she never tried to revise the English version because she was very pleased with the royalties that it brought her.

The question of style is interesting to consider from our perspective. Some critics interpret her style as feminist in that it avoids the directness and argumentative structure of male writing. If that is a reasonable point of view, then it will be obvious why Parshley and Knopf (who accused Beauvoir of "verbal diarrhea") had trouble with it. The style is not tailored but rather relaxed expatiation. The repetition is accumulative and often very effective. You might even dare ask your students if they can contrast Beauvoir's style with that of some of the male writers in this book and decide whether they can describe her style as feminist.

Sometimes, one should note, Beauvoir is inconsistent or contradictory. She says at one point that men and women are separate economic castes. However, she had said much earlier "Never have women constituted a separate caste, nor in truth have they ever as a sex sought to play a historic role" (para. 1). Some feminists might not agree with this view.

One of the most interesting approaches to this work is to review the position of women at different times in history, according to Beauvoir, and then to compare them with your students' perceptions of women today. You might have your students list the statements that still apply to the condition of women as they perceive it. This might lead to a discussion of the degree of change that the fifty years since the book's inception have seen.

SUGGESTIONS FOR CLASS DISCUSSION

1. Examine the claim that because they are "tied down in their situation" that women "can hardly take a hand in affairs in other than a negative and oblique manner" (para. 4). Have students gather examples of the women who have taken a hand in current affairs in both positive and negative ways.
2. Beauvoir discusses the rights of the married woman in her early paragraphs. Do the circumstances Beauvoir describes still prevail? Do married women have a place in society that is denied to unmarried women?
3. Are there any modern female "oddities" (para. 5) who have taken on the role of heroine? Do they support Beauvoir's views?

SUGGESTIONS FOR BRIEF ESSAYS

1. In paragraph 4 Beauvoir says that women's voices have been "silent when it comes to concrete action." Examine the context of that statement and decide whether or not she is correct.
2. Beauvoir tells us that Joan of Arc is one of those women who are "exemplary figures" rather than historical agents" (para. 5). Examine the life of Joan, and decide whether or not she had a distinct role in history—or was she primarily ornamental in a man's world?
3. About Rosa Luxemburg and Marie Curie, Beauvoir says: "They brilliantly demonstrate that it is not the inferiority of women that has caused their historical insignificance: it is rather their historical insignificance that has doomed them to inferiority" (para. 5). Explain what Beauvoir means, then take a stand on whether or not she is correct in her assumption. Are there other examples that help clarify your views?

SUGGESTIONS FOR LONGER ESSAYS

1. Beauvoir says that the period we live in is a period of transition. Has the period since 1949 been a positive period for feminists? With reference to women's place in history, how have women progressed since Beauvoir wrote this piece? Be specific and refer to important women in enough detail to make your case.
2. In paragraph 10, Beauvoir considers "the lot of peasant women" in enough detail to communicate what she sees as their daily routine and their circumstances. Although it is difficult to generalize about any group of women—and we have no peasant class about which to speculate—describe what you feel is the lot of a given group of women whom you know at first hand.

21

That may be a group of undergraduate women, women with children, women with jobs, women of leisure, women athletes, or any other group that interests you.

3. Men still hold a "privileged place" (para. 16) in economic life. Try to clarify what that means in today's terms. Do men still win better jobs? Do they still earn higher pay? Do they have special perks because they are men? Do women still have a hard time breaking into the economic inner circle? What makes it possible to assert these views? How, after the changes in laws and the changes in attitudes of the last fifty years, is it possible that women should still lag behind men in important economic areas?

SENTENCE OUTLINE: See p. 88 of this manual.

BIBLIOGRAPHY: See p. 131 of this manual.

PART THREE

WEALTH

These are four stimulating, approachable essays, and they introduce your students to some important names in economics. Adam Smith (be sure to point out that the twentieth-century writer using this name is paying homage to the eighteenth-century writer, who wrote this essay) is a lucid writer whose views should illuminate much of the question of what wealth consists of. Your students' views on what exactly constitutes wealth should be interesting for you to examine. Karl Marx discusses the abuses of capital and proposes a communistic scheme that would benefit all people. In light of what Hannah Arendt says, you might examine the ways in which Marx treats the question of inevitability in the march of history. John Kenneth Galbraith discusses poverty, the other side of wealth. His examination of the phenomenon demonstrates that we know much less about it than we should. Robert Reich, who held a cabinet position in Bill Clinton's first term, examines a continuing problem—the disparity between the rich and poor in the United States. The idea of wealth concerns all these writers. I'm sure it concerns our students as well.

ADAM SMITH

Of the Principle of the Commercial or Mercantile System (pp. 193–206)

This is a challenging essay. When *The Wealth of Nations* was published, David Hume, a close friend of Smith, read it with interest and told him that it deserved a wide audience but, because it was reasoned so closely, was not likely to get much readership at all. Smith's publisher, Strahan, was surprised that the sales were larger "than I could have expected from a work that requires much thought and reflection (qualities that do not abound among modern readers)." Therefore, it is clear that some time has to be spent explaining some key ideas.

Smith's emphasis is on money, but your students should know that this selection comes very late in his volume, after he has examined the value of labor, corn (in England's case this would be wheat), and goods. He has made some effort to normalize the value of money on the cost of labor, since in his time it was relatively stable. He sees a number of problems with money as the chief measure of wealth. However, by the time he reaches near the end of his book he becomes more and more easy with the idea that wealth is measured by money. Your students may wonder why this was a struggle for him.

One of the important themes in this selection is Smith's interest in foreign trade. He quotes Thomas Mun, whose book on foreign trade was published posthumously but was written in a period of enormous social and economic upheaval in England. It was Mun who made the most intelligent analyses of the concept of the balance of trade, and his thoughts are still current in modern concepts of foreign trade. England's subsequent success in foreign trade is one of Smith's reasons for looking on it so favorably. His efforts in this piece are to clarify the basis of the mercantile system, which is in many ways the system of economics we take for granted in a capitalist nation.

SUGGESTIONS FOR CLASS DISCUSSION

1. It is important to talk about capital here and compare, if your students read it, *The Communist Manifesto* with Smith's essay. The comparison of tone, of style, and of basic concerns should help your students begin to see the strengths and limits of Smith's argument.
2. Smith points out that the Spanish thought gold and silver represented wealth, while the Tartars thought cattle represented wealth. He ends his discussion by saying the Tartars may have been closer to the truth. What does he mean? Do you agree?

3. It is instructive to point out that one reason that Smith's work was so quickly and happily accepted is that he said what people wanted to hear—that selfishness is one way to increase the wealth and bounty of the nation. Rampant capitalists were then free to conduct business as usual with no regard to the consequences of practices that harmed the social structure. It is not an accident that another Scotsman, Andrew Carnegie, found Smith's views quite congenial.

4. The entire question of social values in modern terms needs to be raised in class. What kind of social conscience does Smith have? Students are likely to find Smith saying just what they want to hear, so some kind of social responsibility needs to be introduced into the discussion as a matter of balance. This may arise when you examine the observation that the merchant can worry only about his own profit and not about the consequence to his nation. Today, even the concept of nation may be too narrow to satisfy the most idealistic of students.

SUGGESTIONS FOR BRIEF ESSAYS

1. What is the modern counterpart of gold and silver money? Is paper money any less effective as currency than metal money? What is money? How can it be a modern measure of wealth?

2. Is there any modern equivalent for the Tartars' measure of wealth? Is there anything in modern society as fundamentally valuable as cattle was to Gengis Khan?

3. How can a student hope to accumulate capital? What methods would work? In Smith's time, and for a century and a half afterward, huge fortunes were being made by industrious individuals. Is it possible today to amass considerable wealth? How? Is the key to becoming wealthy in being industrious?

SUGGESTIONS FOR LONGER ESSAYS

1. Examine Adam Smith's social conscience. Compare his essay with Karl Marx's *Communist Manifesto*. Which of these writers is more aware of the conditions under which people actually labor? Is either more concerned with the larger questions of social value and human values of life? How does Smith express his concern for the well-being of humanity? Are his views likely to produce a more or less human environment than Marx's views?

2. Analyze the following quotation from paragraph 4: "Others admit that if a nation could be separated from all the world, it would be of no consequence how much, or how little money circulated in it. The consumable goods which were circulated by means of this money, would only be exchanged for a greater or a smaller number of pieces; but the real wealth or poverty of the country, they allow, would depend altogether upon the abundance or scarcity of those consumable goods." If this is true, what are the implications for using money as the basis of wealth in such a country? If it is true, why would an open program of foreign trade alter the conditions Smith set up in this example? Would it be a good thing for a nation with an adequate supply of consumable goods to be "separated from all the world"?

3. In paragraph 15 Smith says that "if the materials of manufacture are wanted, industry must stop. If provisions are wanted, the people must starve. But if money is wanted, barter will supply its place." He then suggests that credit could stand in for money and, further, that paper money could stand in for "real" money. We have depended entirely on paper money in the last several decades, and in some cases we depend on numbers written in checking and savings books and in stock and pension reports. How does that situation affect the measure of wealth?

SENTENCE OUTLINE: See p. 89 of this manual.

BIBLIOGRAPHY: See p. 146 of this manual.

KARL MARX
The Communist Manifesto (pp. 209–34)

Most students are familiar enough with the author and title of this work that little preparation is needed before discussing what Marx has to say. You might point out by way of background that Marx is redefining communism for his time (and ours). The ideal of communism had been well accepted in his time as rooted in certain religious teachings stressing equal sharing of property and equal work. Robert Owen's 1825 experiment in New Harmony, Indiana, was based on his visionary socioeconomic theories developed in England, but it was also typical of many such experiments in the United States. Most famous in literary history was Brook Farm in West Roxbury, Massachusetts (1841–1847), started by the Rev. George Ripley. Most experiments of this sort were devised for religious or spiritual purposes, and all were severely limited in size. Some screened those who wanted to be admitted.

Marx is notable for his materialism—which is to say his lack of concern for religious or other special spiritual values. For him communism is not a spiritual adventure; it is an economic necessity. The inevitability of communism is one of the key points to be raised in discussing the *Manifesto*. Marx developed the view that in the sweep of history, communism in his time is as inevitable as was the end of feudalism. He regarded his social science concepts as scientific in their certainty. If your students have read Hannah Arendt, you will want to focus on this point and see how your students react to Marx's ideas in light of how they later were put to use.

SUGGESTIONS FOR CLASS DISCUSSION

1. Marx attempts to clarify communism for his audience. You might ask your students what they think his audience's views were. What did people living in the midnineteenth century think about communism? What do your students think of it today?
2. You should be able to develop a useful discussion based on the impressions your students have of communism after reading the *Manifesto*. You might consider how contemporary Chinese communism compares with what Marx proposes.
3. I think it useful to talk about the question of spiritual values. What is the role of religion in Marx's view? You might bring up his famous observation, "Religion is the opium of the people" (from the introduction to *Critique of the Hegelian Philosophy of Right*, 1844). See if the class can take a stand on Marx's communism as being devoid of religious values.
4. One important line of discussion should concern the failure of communism in the Soviet bloc. Some of your students will know something about the pains that have been suffered by communist nations in trying to convert to a market economy.

SUGGESTIONS FOR BRIEF ESSAYS

1. Define *proletarian* for our time. Begin with Marx's definition (footnote 4), and move on to your own.
2. Speculate on what the antecedent social and economic conditions of Europe made *The Communist Manifesto* an important and influential document. Why was it written?

SUGGESTIONS FOR LONGER ESSAYS

1. Comment on Marx's rhetorical strategies in the second section. Does he deal fairly with all the objections against communism? What audience does he assume for his writing? When you have finished reading this section, are you sympathetic or antagonistic toward him? Because he feels communism is historically inevitable, why would he want to convince us of anything in regard to it?
2. Establish Marx's views of the family (refer to paras. 98–104). What does he recommend as its proper structure? Do you feel today's family is structured in more or less the same way it was structured in Marx's time? Do you approve of his suggestions for change?

3. Do you think Marx would agree with Machiavelli's views on the degree to which the desired ends would justify undesirable means? How far will Marx go to achieve communism? Does he seem to sympathize with Machiavelli's general advice?

4. What might Marx have said in response to Adam Smith's essay? How would he have attacked it? Write an essay from Marx's point of view dealing with the principal ideas in Adam Smith's essay.

SENTENCE OUTLINE: See p. 90 of this manual.

BIBLIOGRAPHY: See p. 141 of this manual.

JOHN KENNETH GALBRAITH

The Position of Poverty (pp. 237–49)

This essay is important because it is the only essay in Part Three to explore the condition of the poor. Galbraith exhibits a social conscience combined with a good understanding of economics. One of the things that I try to focus on is the general attitude students have toward poverty in America and the feelings they have toward the poor. Welfare reform in the last years of the twentieth century implies that the public's attitude is very different from what it was in midcentury, and it is worth discussing your students' sense of how the nation feels about the poor. Galbraith points out that the poor are degraded and that the result is that those who are well off hold the poor in contempt. This may be an unconscious feeling, and it helps to explore the issue with your students. Sometimes students are surprised by their own feelings.

The students' status as college students inevitably colors the discussion. And the student from the affluent suburbs will hold different views from the student from the city projects. Such differences of opinion and feeling should be a source of excitement in your classes discussing these issues.

An interesting point raised by Galbraith is that the poverty-stricken constitute a minority in the population today. It is a large minority but nonetheless a minority. In times past, the minority was the rich. Such a condition definitely makes the problem of dealing with poverty very difficult simply because the wealthy majority holds the impoverished minority in contempt. The old question, "I made it, why can't they?" is all too commonly heard. Galbraith's observation regarding this change should be stressed.

To prepare a good discussion, refer to the current *Statistical Abstracts* for an update on the income figures offered in paragraphs 6 and 7. The differences in the figures reflect both the progress that has been made by social programs and the damage that has been done to that progress by inflation. You might also watch for editorials or other current commentary on the plight of the poor in order to reveal the current attitudes of the press or government. The whole question of what the government is currently doing about poverty ought to be of immense interest to all students.

The question of cause and effect is important in the context of this essay, too, because the effects of poverty are felt by everyone. On the one hand, there is the rising toll in taxes required by our welfare programs. On the other hand, there is the rising prison population making the construction of new prisons a necessity for the first time in generations. Much crime is rooted in poverty, if not caused by it, and thus all members of society are affected by poverty.

Finally, one subject for class discussion probably should be the question of what our society ought to do about poverty. The fight against poverty is conducted by amateurs without power; however, all citizens are amateurs, and most of us feel as if we have relatively little power. But we all have the power of the vote, and such a discussion might help your students decide how they wish to use that power when they have the chance. An exploration of these issues is a good contribution toward an important social cause. The question of whether private resources or government resources ought to be used to rid the country of poverty is central and should be addressed.

SUGGESTIONS FOR CLASS DISCUSSION

1. Define "insular poverty" (para. 10) by referring to specific islands of poverty that you either know firsthand or have heard about.
2. What are the characteristics of insular poverty?
3. Do you agree with what Galbraith says in paragraph 20: "The corrupting effect on the human spirit of unearned revenue has unquestionably been exaggerated as, indeed, have the character-building values of hunger and privation"?
4. What do you think Galbraith means when he says, "The concern for inequality and deprivation had vitality only so long as the many suffered while a few had much" (para. 19)?
5. Clarify what you regard as the effects of poverty on our society. What effects has poverty had on you personally?

SUGGESTIONS FOR BRIEF ESSAYS

1. Galbraith admits that increased output cured the general condition of poverty when most of the population was poor. Explain why increased output cannot cure the poverty of those who remain poor.
2. Examine Galbraith's suggestions for how to cure case poverty and insular poverty. Do you feel that they will work if his suggestions are carried out as he recommends? His discussion of the cures for poverty begins in paragraph 20.
3. Galbraith blames our poverty on the nation's "insufficient investment in the public sector" (para. 25). Is this true? What evidence have you to support your view? How could America invest more in people? Why should it do so?

SUGGESTIONS FOR LONGER ESSAYS

1. One of Galbraith's most basic premises is that America is now an affluent society. Examine in detail the society that you know for the purposes of validating or contradicting that assertion. Is America an affluent society? What are the signs of affluence? What qualifies as affluence? What are the results of affluence?
2. In paragraph 22 Galbraith admits that it is impossible to cure poverty by giving those who need it the basic income that would support a decent lifestyle. Do you agree with him? If you do not agree, how do you propose to ensure that those who need it will get the basic income they need? If you agree, how then should we proceed? What should we do to guarantee a minimum level of income for the poor? Is it possible to achieve that goal?
3. One important question that Galbraith never mentions is the obligation that the affluent have toward the poor. Do you feel that those with affluence should make special efforts to help those who remain in poverty? What kinds of efforts should they make? Why should anyone think that the affluent are obligated to help the poor? Is it reasonable for the affluent to feel that people's poverty is their own fault?
4. In discussing the causes of insular poverty, Galbraith cites the "homing instinct" (para. 12) as a possible factor. Examine the concept of the "homing instinct," and, relying on your own experiences and observations, qualify it as a possible cause of insular poverty. Why would it be a cause of poverty rather than a cause of wealth? Do the wealthy exhibit a similar "homing instinct"? Do people you know exhibit it? What seem to be its causes and its consequences?

SENTENCE OUTLINE: See p. 92 of this manual.
BIBLIOGRAPHY: See p. 135 of this manual.

ROBERT B. REICH

Why the Rich Are Getting Richer and the Poor, Poorer (pp. 251–68)

I did not choose this piece because Reich was an economic guru for the Clinton administration but because I found the arguments and analyses in *The Work of Nations* to be compelling and worth examining. One thing I try to explain to students is that their training in language, writing, rhetoric, and explication of texts prepares them to think in ways that will eventually be valuable to them in the marketplace. Many students insist on graduating as pharmacists, electrical engineers, accountants, or some other such calling. They have a sense of security when they enter the job market. However, English majors or history majors (and physics majors, too) enter a job market with no clear sense of their worth. Reich's discussion of the symbolic analysts provokes students into revaluing their education. I find it useful to get them thinking in terms of the future job market and its relation to their college preparation.

Reich is, however, a controversial figure. Despite his conciliatory skills, he sometimes sparks criticism. He has been attacked for being cavalier with figures and facts. Some commentators have pointed out his looseness with detail and his ability to overstate a position based on relatively little information. Such complaints began more than fifteen years ago, and they may have prompted Reich to exert the kind of care he displays in this essay. Students may wonder why he footnotes so many details, when other economists rarely do. The answer is almost certainly that he wishes to defend himself against attackers.

It also has been said that he has changed his views on a number of important issues. For example, in earlier books, he has been less than kind toward Japanese corporations, reminding people that no matter how much money they may bring in locally, they still owe little to the community and ultimately send their wealth home to Japan. In this book, however, he insists that the nationality of the corporation is essentially less important than its contribution to the local economy. Several of his positions have changed since he began writing, but rather than seeing that as a problem, I regard it as a symptom of his willingness to rethink his views. In any event, it is either evidence of inconsistency or growth, and we may decide on our own terms.

One amusing detail regarding Reich's use of the metaphor of the boats and the tide is the fact that at Dartmouth he was the outstanding cox in crew. It was the sport that ultimately qualified him for the Rhodes fellowship. He was probably thinking less of that, however, than of the stock market cliché that says when the tide comes in all the boats rise—a description of an expanding economy.

Underlying all the careful analysis of routine, in-service workers, and the symbolic analysts, however, is the fear that Reich may be totally correct. If so, the implications for a stratified society are rather depressing. If the educational system remains as it is, the inevitability of the breach between the poor and the rich is potentially disastrous. One of the questions I like to pose to students is how we may avoid such extreme polarization.

SUGGESTIONS FOR CLASS DISCUSSION

1. In what ways does the potential for a split between the very rich and the very poor have serious social consequences in the United States?
2. What changes in education will be needed in order to avoid a society in which workers are rigidly stratified?
3. To what extent is it true that "your real competitive position in the world economy is coming to depend on the function you perform in it" (para. 1)? Do you feel this will be true for the foreseeable future? Or are things about to change?
4. With which economic group does Reich show sympathy?
5. What role will labor unions take in the economy of the future?

SUGGESTIONS FOR BRIEF ESSAYS

1. If you have personal experience of companies moving because they sought cheaper labor, describe what you feel the most important effects of such a move are.
2. What do you feel is the best educational preparation for doing well in a global economy such as we now enjoy? Describe that education beginning with preschool experience.
3. Reich defines three kinds of workers—routine producers, in-person workers, symbolic analysts. Are there any more kinds of workers? If so, describe them and their economic fate in terms similar to those Reich uses. Is their "boat" rising or sinking?

SUGGESTIONS FOR LONGER ESSAYS

1. If Reich is correct, there will be very few genuine opportunities in the new economy for people who drop out of secondary school. It seems clear that unless education is radically overhauled immediately, there will be many more dropouts than there are jobs for dropouts. What will be the long-range effects of such a condition?
2. To what extent is it the government's responsibility to provide jobs to people who would otherwise not be able to get them? For example, should the government provide jobs for routine workers if their opportunities dry up? What arguments favor or oppose such a proposal?
3. Should successful symbolic analysts be taxed disproportionately in order to provide social security and services to routine and in-person workers who earn much less? What impact would increased taxes have on symbolic analysts? Reich says they would probably want to work even if they did not make huge sums of money. If that were true, would they not be willing to pay extra taxes in order to secure social stability?
4. Are the distinctions that Reich describes similar to the class differences that Karl Marx focuses on in *The Communist Manifesto*? If they are, would any of Marx's suggestions be effective in providing an equitable distribution of wealth among the groups Reich defines?

SENTENCE OUTLINE: See p. 93 of this manual.

BIBLIOGRAPHY: See p. 144 of this manual.

PART FOUR

MIND

The six essays in this section vary in difficulty. The Maimonides piece on the limits of the human intellect is one of the most difficult in the book, although the introduction is designed to pull the main points of the discussion into focus. The discussion below will help as well. On the other hand, the essay by Howard Gardner, on multiple intelligences, is one of the easiest to understand in the entire book. The selections from Freud and Jung are challenging but not especially problematic for most students. The selection from Karen Horney is one of the most popular among users of the fourth edition. These essays describe the qualities of the mind, the limits of the mind, the nature of the unconscious, the gender-related issues of psychosocialization, and the problems associated with connecting our ideas of intelligence to a single model.

PLATO

The Allegory of the Cave (pp. 275–86)

It is probably best to begin with the essentialist nature of Plato's thought. Students are fascinated by Plato's ability to develop his argument so fully from the limits of his allegory. Students will often agree that the senses can be erroneous reporters of fact. But it is also worth pressing the point to stress what Kant and many later philosophers observed—that it is impossible to know about the world except in terms of its appearances to the senses. If the senses are unreliable at times, then so is our knowledge of the world. I point out that Plato and other Greeks described the observable details of things and experience in terms of accidents. What we see is accidental to an object. But as a way of postulating a reality underlying the accidents of experience, Plato had to conceive an essence. Students find this puzzling, and many of them want to get on with the common-sense business of daily life. The question persists: how can we ever know the essential nature of things? Well, first, we have to suspect that there is one. The people continuing in their everyday round are like those chained to Plato's wall. I remind my impatient students of that and watch their reaction.

Frankly, the entire question of the value of sensory experience is one that fascinates students, and it should help make your classroom discussion exciting and perhaps even frenetic. Oftentimes, when discussing Plato, I might need to attend closely to the class, helping to select ideas that could be made into successful essays. My students perform best when they react intensely.

SUGGESTIONS FOR CLASS DISCUSSION

1. Raise the issue of what it is we know when we rely on our senses. Is sensory knowledge as unreliable as Plato thinks?
2. Are we materialistic when we praise sense perception? What are the alternatives to any such materialism rising from overvaluing (or solely valuing) sense experience?
3. If we could perceive the world beneath sense experience, what would it be like?
4. I often ask my students to choose a sense that they do not already have and add it as a sixth sense that cannot be a merger of any of the five. It has to be new—not smelling, seeing, or hearing from a great distance. If nothing else, this exercise helps them begin to realize how hemmed in we are by our senses—particularly when I point out the ultimate similarity of touch, taste, and odor, three of the five senses that constitute virtually one sense with three "flavors."

SUGGESTIONS FOR BRIEF ESSAYS

1. Using Plato's cave as your basic reference, define *allegory*. Include a discussion of its usefulness and its effects along with a description of its nature.
2. Plato opens by talking about the extent to which we are enlightened. What is the effect on our enlightenment of the allegory he presents? What does an understanding of the allegory cause us to realize about ourselves?
3. What general human situation fits the circumstances that the prisoners in Plato's cave experience?
4. How successful is Plato's allegory for describing our awareness of how the mind works? How does it jibe with human experience?

SUGGESTIONS FOR LONGER ESSAYS

1. Consider whether Socrates is right when he says, "The truth is that the State in which the rulers are most reluctant to govern is always the best and most quietly governed, and the State in which they are most eager, the worst" (para. 61). Try to formulate a series of questions that might cast some light on this issue. Try to structure your essay in dialogue form.
2. In paragraphs 49 through 52, Socrates discusses a "clever rogue" whose mind is in the service of evil. He suggests that if circumstances were otherwise, the rogue might serve the good. What does this example say about Socrates's view of human nature and its relationship to education? Is personality a fixed thing? Is it fluid? What might affect it? Are Socrates's views on human nature and the personality modern or antiquated?
3. Write a new dialogue in which Socrates discusses a subject of keen importance to you or your friends. Include yourself as a speaker in the dialogue and any student friends you like. Try to make your dialogue sound as Platonic as possible.

SENTENCE OUTLINE: See p. 95 of this manual.

BIBLIOGRAPHY: See p. 143 of this manual.

MOSES MAIMONIDES

On the Limits of Man's Intellect (pp. 289–304)

This selection was brought to my attention by Shoshana Milgram Knapp, a professor who used an earlier edition of *A World of Ideas*. She supplemented the book with a number of photocopied essays, including the Maimonides selection (with an added chapter). Her view was that the piece was of special value to Jewish students, but its relevance is certainly universal. My interest in the piece centers on the epistemological issues: How much can we know? What can't we know? Maimonides is important for insisting on limitations to knowledge, but some of those limitations center on the reduced capacities of individuals as well as on the appropriate times for learning. Our thinking today is following some similar paths, and for that reason the piece is especially useful.

But it is also useful for its revelation of medieval attitudes toward education and who should be educated. Maimonides sees that only a small number of people are capable of learning, and such a fact—because for him it is a perceived fact—is not difficult for him to live with. I am interested in the approach modern universities take to the general education of masses of students. Clearly, our universities and colleges do not take Maimonides's position. But that does not invalidate what he has to say. His basic point is that preparatory studies are necessary in order to lay a foundation for later work. To a considerable extent, the educational philosophy of *A World of Ideas* follows that view. The essays in this book are important and basic—if occasionally difficult. They are prolegomena to an advanced education.

You may want to examine some of the basic issues in the essay, such as the moral requirements Maimonides sees for the advanced student. We do not emphasize those requirements in many colleges— but they are central to some. You might examine your students on their views concerning the moral requirements of a good education. I need hardly remind us of the potentials for abuse in law, medicine, and the sciences, all of which require higher education. Your students should have a reaction to the suggestion that they attend to moral issues as preliminary to advanced studies.

Maimonides's rhetoric is very useful to examine because what he does is easily understood and easily applied by students. He quotes liberally from important sources. He uses analogies—similes and metaphors—to make his points more tangible and pragmatic. And he relies on enumeration to structure the argument. All these are devices that the ordinary student can emulate, and all of them work as well today as they did in 1190.

SUGGESTIONS FOR CLASS DISCUSSION

1. Begin with an examination of the limits of the intellect as Maimonides sees them. How many of his limits do your students agree with? Do they see other limits that he does not mention?
2. Ask students if they think it true that "A boundary is undoubtedly set to the human mind which it cannot pass" (para. 2). What evidence do students have for the existence of such a boundary?
3. What is the relationship of physical perception to mental perception? Ask your students if they are convinced that the relationship Maimonides sets up is reasonable. What is mental perception?
4. Pursue the question of the moral education of the individual. It will open up interesting avenues of discussion.

SUGGESTIONS FOR BRIEF ESSAYS

1. Examine paragraphs 5, 6, and 7 concerning the fate of one who studies too much. From your own experience, can you validate Maimonides's claims?
2. What are some of the more important limits to human reason that you can use to validate Maimonides's views of the limits of the intellect? Do people recognize the limits and respect them, or do they ignore them and press onward with inquiries? What is the difference? What are your recommendations for respecting limits of the intellect?

SUGGESTIONS FOR LONGER ESSAYS

1. Examine Alexander Aphrodisius's "three causes that prevent men from discovering the exact truth" (para 2); the first is arrogance, the second is the difficulty of the subject, and the third is ignorance. The first and last are qualities of the individual. Is the second a quality of the subject to be studied? What about "habit and training," the fourth cause Maimonides adds? How is that also of serious importance in preventing people from knowing the truth?
2. In paragraph 11, Maimonides tells us the Torah (the first five books of the Bible) "speaks the language of man." In other words, it is human in scale and scope and intelligible for the young, women, and the common people. What do those books have to say about the limits of the intellect? Are they speaking the "language of man"?
3. Maimonides discusses the "privileged few" as those who attain perfection "after due preparatory labor" (para. 18). Can such a distinction be made among people getting an education today? Are the privileges deserved or undeserved? Do they attain perfection—and if so, what kind? Do you feel such a fact is democratic? Is one who earns distinction by hard labor then elitist? Does such a person deserve special recognition or special privileges?

SENTENCE OUTLINE: See p. 96 of this manual.

BIBLIOGRAPHY: See p. 141 of this manual.

SIGMUND FREUD

From *The Interpretation of Dreams* (pp. 307–18)

One of the good things about this passage is that Freud's writing is clear and approachable. He is strongly convinced of his view that dreams are wish fulfillments, and he has collected a number of pieces of evidence from associates, patients, and family members. This evidence is easy to relate because everyone understands what a dream is and most of us have spent a good deal of time either telling people our dreams or hearing about their dreams. Freud does offer some subcategories of fulfillment dreams. One of them is the dream of contingency—where usually the individual is responding to a physical need, such as thirst, the example Freud offers. Another is the "fulfilled fear" dream, which presents a situation that may be unpleasant but that satisfies a psychic need.

You may either disagree with my suggestion that the mountain metaphor functions as I think it does—or you may wish to push the metaphor further by including the detail of the path in the first paragraph. I certainly see Freud as offering us intellectual peaks to scale but at the same time as offering us the appropriate path that will take us to the top. For me these metaphors are powerful. I connect them with the metaphoric method of Maimonides, and I see many connections intellectually with Maimonides. You may see even more that you would like to develop. I mention one or two below, but you might want to pursue the question of what can be known about it or the limits of the intellect in relation to dreams. One area where this is especially interesting concerns the dreams of animals. Is it possible that we will never know what animals dream? That may be a clear example of the limits of the human intellect.

On the other hand, one interesting issue concerns the fact that the mind is at work concocting dreams even when it is unconscious. The implication of the mind as both conscious and unconscious is explored by Freud throughout his work, of course, but this is a clear example of the interdependence of the conscious and unconscious mind (speaking as if there were two aspects of the mind).

SUGGESTIONS FOR CLASS DISCUSSION

1. Begin with asking whether or not Freud convinces your students that dreams represent wish fulfillments. See how many different points of view you can evoke in the discussion. Remember, however, that not all wish fulfillments are for good things: some represent fulfillments of fear.
2. Open up a discussion of the specific dreams your students have. Gather a number of examples, and open up the possibility of an interpretation of some of the dreams. Be sure to ask the student who has the dream to analyze it.
3. Freud says that dreams can be "inserted into the chain of intelligible waking mental acts" (para. 1). Explore what Freud seems to mean by this statement.

SUGGESTIONS FOR BRIEF ESSAYS

1. Write out one of your more interesting dreams. If possible, choose a dream that is clearly an example of a wish fulfillment dream. Try to make it as detailed as possible.
2. Write a brief essay establishing that the dreams of animals will always be unknown to humans and that the inability to know such dreams represents a clear example of the limits of human knowledge. You may refer to Moses Maimonides.

SUGGESTIONS FOR LONGER ESSAYS

1. Describe a dream that is definitely not a wish fulfillment dream. Offer a detailed analysis that shows that it could not be a wish fulfillment dream. If possible, find examples from other people of similar non–wish fulfillment dreams. Make a case for dreams not necessarily being wish fulfillment dreams.

2. With reference to Freud's letter to Fliess (August 6, 1899) ("Freud's Rhetoric," text p. 309), examine this selection for its use of metaphors. Not only does he embed the metaphor of the walk and the path and the high prospect from which everyone can see the truth, but he also includes other metaphors, such as the "flood" of questions in paragraph 2. What kinds of metaphors does Freud use, and to what use does he put them?

3. Read the last section of *The Interpretation of Dreams*, and review what Freud says about wish fulfillment in "The Psychology of the Dream-Process." Does what he says in that section change your view or your understanding of what he says in the selection reprinted in this book? Are you any more or any less convinced that dreams are wish fulfillments?

SENTENCE OUTLINE: See p. 97 of this manual.
BIBLIOGRAPHY: See p. 134 of this manual.

CARL JUNG

The Personal and the Collective Unconscious (pp. 321–34)

Jung's work is never easy to understand, but this piece is one of his more accessible excursions into the nature of the mind. He follows Freud's lead in part by accepting his basic views of the unconscious. However, Jung's innovation concerns the investigation of the archetypal symbols that he asserts are part of the collective unconscious of every individual.

Depending on your students, you may find yourself discussing the very existence of the unconscious, especially in light of the fact that the person of common sense is not likely to be aware of any such thing. But even if your students agree that there is an unconscious, the concept of the archetype may be totally obscure to them. The dream that Jung analyzes is valuable for the fact that it presents one clear archetype—that of the divine. In *Archetypes of the Collective Unconscious* (1934) Jung begins with a note that one of the earliest references to the term *archetype* is in Philo Judaeus (fl. 10 B.C.) in his term *imago dei*, or the image of god. Among Jung's archetypes are the mother and the father, and if you are interested in pursuing this line of thought, you might collect your students' experience with these archetypes by having them define them as best they can.

The most interesting thing about this selection, however, is the thought that there may be such a thing as a collective unconscious revealed to us in terms of myth. Jung believes that we inherit the collective unconscious rather than acquire it from experience, and if that is true, we have a very interesting description of the mind. When I discuss these issues with students, I make every effort to avoid committing myself on the absolute truth of Jung's hypothesis. I prefer to maintain it as an hypothesis and to permit my students to work with the idea until it becomes evident to them one way or the other.

For me, one of the most important details Jung treats here is the question of self-knowledge. I try to direct students toward examining the ways in which a deeper knowledge of their unconscious can help them become more fully aware of themselves—to develop more self-knowledge. One way to do this is by asking students to write down their dreams, although there are always many who cannot remember them. Asking them to examine their dreams for the presence of archetypes of the most basic sort can be useful. Likewise, comparing students' dreams—looking for basic patterns that might be thought of as archetypal and thus revealing of a collective unconscious—is also interesting.

SUGGESTIONS FOR CLASS DISCUSSION

1. One useful strategy is to begin by questioning the existence of an unconscious mind and then go through the class finding examples of the unconscious at work. Dreams are among the most obvious examples, but there are also many examples in the Freudian slip department—when by

accident someone says exactly what should not be said (usually revealing an unconscious association, such as during an argument calling your friend by your father's name).

2. Although it might be difficult, one potentially interesting approach is to discuss the myths that students know that might be universal in their importance and that therefore may qualify as archetypal. Fairy tales offer a source of archetypes, but so do the popular books by Tolkien. I also think that Rambo in the eponymous movies represents an archetype, although I usually connect it to wish fulfillment as much as to archetypal patterns. Western films are another source of mythic content.

SUGGESTIONS FOR BRIEF ESSAYS

1. If you know of examples of psychic content that has been repressed and then ultimately revealed itself (Jung says "reassociated with") to the conscious mind, describe the process. Use the narrative technique that Jung favors in telling your story.
2. If you have been able to create a dream, describe the dream and the means by which you were able to create it.
3. The conscious mind can will action. The unconscious mind can "only wish," according to Freud. If you feel this is untrue, offer your reasons. If you feel it is true, explain why the mind works in that fashion: why is the unconscious unable to act?

SUGGESTIONS FOR LONGER ESSAYS

1. After researching the term *transference* in a textbook of psychology—or in the literature of psychoanalysis—explain the current thinking on this phenomenon. In what circumstances does transference occur? When is it healthy? Is it ever unhealthy?
2. Argue against Jung's position. How would you demonstrate that his hypothesis of the collective unconscious is unproven? Examine the weaknesses in his argument, and offer a counterstatement.
3. Assuming that Jung's view of the collective unconscious is demonstrable, how could an individual actually have such an unconscious? Must the individual be born with it as something resembling a genetic inheritance? If not, how could it be communicated to the individual without passing over the "threshold" of the conscious?
4. Examine a collection of children's literature. What archetypal images appear in the material that we might interpret as central to a child's psychic development? Do you think children are aware of the archetypal content of that literature? Were you as a child given the opportunity to absorb a wide range of children's literature? What do you think you absorbed from that literature? What could the cultural function of children's literature be for any culture?

SENTENCE OUTLINE: See p. 98 of this manual.
BIBLIOGRAPHY: See p. 138 of this manual.

KAREN HORNEY

The Distrust Between the Sexes (pp. 337–51)

This is a very clear and effective essay; therefore, you should have relatively little work to do in clarifying the ideas. What you probably will want to do in class is to examine its basic premises—for instance, the question of whether your students perceive hostility between the sexes at all. That is the first discussion question after the essay itself, and it may be the only one you will need for an hour's worth of debate. You might try to steer the discussion in order to include different kinds of hostility that might pertain to different age groups. There may be one kind of hostility perceived for people in the age group of your students' parents and another in your students' age group. This is a useful area of inquiry.

One important idea that must be discussed, of course, is that Karen Horney is trying to cite psychological issues and not just sociological issues. She constantly describes childhood events in order to establish the etiology of disorders that cause hostility. An important point you may wish to discuss at length is whether or not she postulates the hostility between the sexes as a form of disorder caused by childhood frustrations, mature envy, and forms of distrust, or whether she feels that hostility between the sexes should be considered a normal condition. Is it a product of two "kinds" of mind?

For class discussion, this essay is useful for helping students to clarify their thoughts on the issues, since it is likely that all of them will have plenty of personal experiences to share in class. Most of the writing assignments as well, both in the text and below, leave room for personal experience to illustrate a point or points. Beginning with a concrete narrated experience is naturally a good way for a student to start dealing with such a suggestive series of insights into the human mind.

Finally, the relationship between the sexes has political overtones no matter how much you may want to keep them out of the discussion. It may be wise to confront them directly, perhaps suggesting that some of the political issues are rooted in psychology as Karen Horney has described. This discussion may lead to the question of whether there is a separate psychology—or ought to be—for women and for men. The idea that Freud may be describing a masculine psychology and Horney a feminine psychology should not be ignored or avoided. That idea could lead to the discussion of whether there is a male mind and a female mind—a conclusion that might be an extreme reaction to the essay, but one that will seem reasonable to some people.

SUGGESTIONS FOR CLASS DISCUSSION

1. This essay comes from a book called *Feminine Psychology*. Do you feel there is a feminine psychology that is separate from psychology in general?
2. At one point Horney states that passion is rare because "we are loath to put all our eggs in one basket" (para. 6). Is this true from your own experience? How do people you know feel about this issue?
3. To what extent are sexual anxieties at the root of any distrust between men and women?

SUGGESTIONS FOR BRIEF ESSAYS

1. In her second paragraph Horney says, "The relationship between men and women is quite similar to that between children and parents, in that we prefer to focus on the positive aspects of these relationships." Is this an appropriate analogy? Is it true that people generally want to be positive in their discussion of the relationships she describes? To what extent is it difficult for us to be negative?
2. The image of the Madonna, the Virgin Mother, is cited as one that men are comfortable with when they think of women. Is this true? To what extent do you see evidence to support this contention? What other images do men have of women? Establish in what way the images men hold of women may affect their behavior toward them.
3. Some people, as Horney implies, may have absolutely no inkling that there is any hostility between the sexes. What might that mean? Under what circumstances might people be unaware of hostility? What conditions might prevail? Establish a scenario, drawn from your own or someone else's experience, in which a person might be unaware that there is hostility between the sexes.

SUGGESTIONS FOR LONGER ESSAYS

1. How clear an archetype, in Jung's sense of the word, is the Madonna figure as Horney describes it (paras. 13–14)? Jung had a view that the mother archetype is one of the most powerful we know. Horney establishes the power of the mother as an abstract idea in this essay. If the mother is an archetype, how would you describe it? You may wish to examine Jung's essay on the mother archetype in *Archetypes and the Collective Unconscious*, in Volume 9 of *Collected Works*. Is Horney substantially in agreement with Jung, or does her view stand in contradistinction to his?

2. Write your own essay on the subject of "The Distrust Between the Sexes." Establish the important psychological differences between the sexes, and, with reference to examples as much as possible, describe what you feel is important about these differences.

3. Do you agree with Horney when she says that "man's fear of woman is deeply rooted in sex" (para. 13)? Interview women especially to see if they agree with this idea. Then interview some men to determine if their views coincide. Are they dramatically different or just mildly different? In your essay begin by clarifying Horney's views as much as possible. Present the views of those you have interviewed; then present your own views, based on your reflections on the material you have gathered and on your own experience.

SENTENCE OUTLINE: See p. 99 of this manual.

BIBLIOGRAPHY: See p. 137 of this manual.

HOWARD GARDNER

A Rounded Version: The Theory of Multiple Intelligences (pp. 353–72)

Coauthored by Joseph Walters

A great deal of interest has been generated by the implications of the thinking of Howard Gardner for education. The efforts of Project Zero have proved useful for many schools in the Boston region, but a great many other schools have been influenced by his views. Gardner talks regularly with people in education about how their schools can reflect his findings. But perhaps more surprisingly, Gardner has been spending a great deal of time talking with CEOs about the findings and their implications for hiring and promotion.

It is certainly nothing new to observe that some of the brightest students at major universities and colleges are often dismal in their professional performances after school. In the university I attended, the tradition had always been to maintain a "gentlemanly C average," in part in recognition of that observation. What is new is Gardner's suggestion that there are identifiable intelligences that are of great importance that are not recognized as such by the schools. They are clearly recognized as important in life, however. For example, the bodily-kinesthetic is one of the intelligences that surgery and professional sports depend on. The interpersonal intelligence is central to getting along in business and life.

What is controversial about all this is whether we accept Gardner's distinctions as true intelligence rather than, say, talent. All the areas that Gardner describes have been known for eons as talents or "gifts." To label these as intelligence and to rank them with the supposedly measurable intelligence of Binet is what makes Gardner's idea interesting. Of course, many people will react negatively to this idea. It will not represent for them a discussion of intelligence. But many people will welcome it warmly because they see the traditional discussions of intelligence as too restrictive. Further, in the interests of diversity, which are central to many people's concepts of education today, the theories are especially welcome. People good at one or another of the intelligences are encouraged rather than discouraged in school if they feel their special gifts are as important as the special gifts of others. Those who excel in the logical-mathematical model have been traditionally valued highly, while those who excel in other forms of intelligence have been valued less highly. Gardner wishes to alter this balance. You and your students should have an interesting time discussing the merits of the argument.

Right now I am not sure where I stand on this argument. Gardner has an enormous operation in Project Zero, and it is based on his thinking. I am skeptical about discoveries that center on renaming things we long have been aware of. I point out that the Greeks were aware of the distinctions that Gardner proposes and incorporated them into their education system. I am aware, also, that these distinctions were present in my own basic schooling. I was provided instruction in music, movement, interpersonal relations, nature, and even, at times, intrapersonal issues. So my view is that all these things are good, but I am not as convinced as Gardner that they represent intelligence as such. By the same token, I do not think standard IQ tests tell the whole story, either. This is an interesting controversy well worth exploring with students.

SUGGESTIONS FOR CLASS DISCUSSION

1. One good line of questioning concerns what your students take to represent intelligence in people they know. How do they measure intelligence in their friends? How do they measure it in themselves?

2. Another good line of questioning takes into account whether the forms of intelligence Gardner describes are intelligence or talent. Then the question arises as to what the difference between the two, if any, might be. Is it possible that talent is just a word we use to describe intelligence?

3. The relationship between cultures and problem solving is another issue that is likely to be stimulating in class. For example, certain cultures value chess very highly; others value basketweaving. If the skills necessary to perform well in these areas are intelligences, then what is their value in relation to each culture? Is culture, then, important to a discussion of intelligence?

SUGGESTIONS FOR BRIEF ESSAYS

1. If culture is important to evaluating a specific intelligence, are we then to assume that intelligence is relative rather than absolute in the individual? Examine Gardner's biographical sketches to see which of the intelligences described seems to flourish best in which cultures. How limited is our culture in its evaluation of intelligence?

2. In paragraph 14 Gardner describes the "identifiable core operation or set of operations" necessary to identify a specific intelligence. Select one of the intelligences he describes, and establish its operations in such a way as to qualify it clearly as an intelligence.

3. If some kinds of intelligence are culturally linked and of special importance in some cultures but not others, is there one form of intelligence that is totally cross-cultural and that is of great importance in all cultures? Which one is it, and why? Which of its characteristics and values make it cross-cultural?

SUGGESTIONS FOR LONGER ESSAYS

1. Examine Gardner's original discussion of multiple intelligences in his landmark book *Frames of Mind*. What for you is the most controversial aspect of his theory? Does he develop it in *Frames of Mind* in a new way that expands your understanding? Does he make it possible for you to evaluate his argument?

2. In paragraphs 19 and 20 Gardner argues in support of the idea that "musical ability" is a specific form of intelligence. How would someone skeptical of Gardner's views argue this point? What evidence have you that would tell you that musical ability is a form of intelligence distinct from other forms? Use personal experience as well as the experience of others, such as Wolfgang Amadeus Mozart or Yehudi Menuhin.

3. Using the Internet or another research source, find as much as you can about the localized areas in the brain, such as Broca's area, which control specific abilities. From what you can tell based on your research, how reliable are Gardner's views concerning the relationship of local areas of brain development and the special intelligences he has described?

SENTENCE OUTLINE: See p. 100 of this manual.
BIBLIOGRAPHY: See p. 135 of this manual.

NATURE

The five essays in Part Five inquire into the secrets of nature. The question of what we can know, and how we can know it, interests Francis Bacon, whose approach to thinking is credited with beginning work in the scientific method in England. Bacon's scientific method is illustrated in the work of Charles Darwin, who depended on direct personal investigation in order to draw his conclusions concerning evolution, conclusions that even today may prove daunting to many of your students. The chapter that I've included from Darwin's *Origin of Species* forms the backbone of his theory of evolution, and I believe it is more controversial today than it was twenty years ago. In his stimulating essay, Gould argues that the anthropocentric way in which we often view nature creates philosophical problems for us that may be unwarranted. Michio Kaku alludes to the limits of our intellect (as do Maimonides and Plato) and then goes on to discuss the superstring theory, one of the most extraordinary potential solutions to the difficulties inherent in reconciling the theory of relativity with the quantum theory. Richard Dawkins, drawing on modern research in DNA, postulates the origin of our species in Africa, and to that end he proposes a single progenitor he calls "African Eve." This is an exciting time in the study of nature, whether in biology or physics. In their range and complexity of ideas, these essays will provide considerable stimulation for your students.

FRANCIS BACON

The Four Idols (pp. 379–94)

Bacon is a favorite of mine; I always enjoy teaching this selection. I try to give my students a bit of background concerning the Elizabethan court and how individuals made their fortunes—often by being granted some exclusive right or monopoly by the crown and then exercising enormous power for as long as they could hold on to it. Fortunes were made quickly and lost quickly. Son of a distinguished man, Nicholas Bacon, lord keeper of the great seal, and related to the powerful Sir William Cecil, Lord Burghley, Francis Bacon had close connections with Elizabeth's government. I don't usually describe the details of his rise through his influence with Robert Devereux, Earl of Essex, followed by his willingness to help prosecute Essex on behalf of the government for treason. Some biographers paint him blackly for that deed, but I generally avoid mentioning it unless a student has happened to read up on Bacon.

Rather, I emphasize the fact that he lived in such turbulent times that succeeding almost meant looking first to Machiavelli's advice. Bacon rose in King James's court, becoming Lord High Chancellor in 1617 probably through the influence of George Villiers, the infamous Duke of Buckingham. But Buckingham was not as strong or as true a friend as Bacon thought, and when Bacon's enemies began to attack in November 1620, after the publication of his *Novum Organum* had swelled Bacon's reputation among some, Buckingham did not intervene. If anything, he profited from Bacon's downfall by taking over some of his choicest London property. Eventually, Buckingham helped him by lifting a ban virtually exiling him from London; meanwhile, Bacon had found contentment in his own writing. He said that his real career began in 1620, after his disgrace.

"The Four Idols" is especially important to teach to first-year college students because it includes so much they need to know. Most are innocent of the knowledge Bacon imparts. They find that they can immediately relate to each of the idols. I usually ask students to cite instances of the idols in action, and they rarely have trouble doing so. Sometimes we can actually spot them in action in the classroom, and there are even times when a student will—weeks later—catch me up in using one. I have not asked students to collect examples in the newspapers or the magazines, but such a project might be useful and might even produce a good subject for writing.

Naturally, I spend a good deal of time going over each idol to define it clearly. Bacon makes them so clear that I need hardly do it again. Still, a few moments confirming that the idols are understood will pay good rewards.

I am particularly interested in Bacon's rhetorical strategies—a paragraph for defining the idol and then several for developing its characteristics and analyzing its qualities. Enumeration is a powerful rhetorical tool, and because Bacon represents the clearest example in the book, I like to emphasize it here properly.

SUGGESTIONS FOR CLASS DISCUSSION

1. Ask students where they have last encountered one of the idols. This can be prefaced by asking whether the idols are still at work. The answer is obviously yes, but some people may want to talk about it.
2. It is important to discuss the ways in which the idols interfere with the study of natural phenomena. If possible, see whether your students know examples of discoveries that might not have been made if a given idol of thought had persisted.
3. Ask students which of the idols they feel is most likely to restrict scientific inquiry into the nature of nature.
4. Questions about Bacon's rhetorical structures will pay off well. Because this is a translation from Latin, style isn't usually an issue, but I do consider clarity and how structure contributes to it a sound topic for discussion. I ask students what they feel they can learn from examining Bacon's structure.
5. Point out the summary paragraphs so that students can get a good idea how to use them in their own work.

SUGGESTIONS FOR BRIEF ESSAYS

1. Define the word *idols* in the sense that Bacon seems to use it. Is the word *idol* a good term to use for the idea that lies behind it?
2. Compare the importance of one idol with that of another. Is it possible to determine which is more likely to prevent the acquisition of true knowledge?
3. Which of the idols are the results of social intercourse, and which are the results of individual reflection? Would one be more likely to be free of the tyranny of the idols if one were restricted in society? Is it possible that a hermit would be completely free of the idols? Or would one become more free the more one socialized?

SUGGESTIONS FOR LONGER ESSAYS

1. Bacon tells us that the idols are not innate but that they march plainly into our minds. How is it, then, that they are so universal? If they are not innate, they are certainly persistent. Explore how people acquire these four idols, using personal experience where possible. Have any new ways of learning these idols arisen since Bacon's time?
2. What circumstances relating to tribe, cave, marketplace, and theater make them useful as categorical titles for the idols? Invent a fifth idol whose name relates to our society as well as these four relate to Bacon's.
3. If you know of an inquiry into nature that is restricted because of adherence to one or more of the idols, describe it and establish the manner in which this inquiry has been hampered.

SENTENCE OUTLINE: See p. 101 of this manual.

BIBLIOGRAPHY: See p. 130 of this manual.

CHARLES DARWIN

Natural Selection (pp. 397–412)

I have found that many science majors graduate college without ever reading Darwin, as if higher education were treating him as a literary rather than a scientific figure. That may be reasonable in some ways, particularly because he is indeed rather literate. But I also have found that virtually everyone I have heard denounce the theory of evolution has not read Darwin either. I have met no one who denounces the theory and who has also both read Darwin and done extensive researches into evolutionary biology. I encourage my students to read Darwin with as receptive a mind as possible, looking for the details that build his argument and establish his views. This passage is an excellent model for the kinds of research students might conduct in their own college careers. It postulates careful questions, marshals a good deal of evidence—gathered from many sources—and poses a conclusion. I try to point out to my students that this is a useful model for a project that demands research and evidence gathering.

There is a definite controversy at this time over the theory of evolution itself. Steady rejection of the theory has occurred since 1859, and I point this out to interested students. Frankly, however, I am not interested enough in the controversy to encourage my students to discuss it. So far, I have had no students who have demanded equal time for the creationist viewpoint. Should your students raise the issue, I would simply ask them to present the evidence for the other side. But I would insist that these students read Darwin carefully.

SUGGESTIONS FOR CLASS DISCUSSION

1. Because I am interested in Darwin's evidence gathering, I call my students' attention to the kinds and quantity of evidence in this chapter. I ask them whether they feel convinced by the nature of the evidence and whether they feel more evidence of a different kind might be needed.
2. Ask about the persuasive quality of the passage. I remind students that this is only part of one chapter in a fairly large book but also that it is one of the pivotal moments of the entire argument in favor of evolution because it describes the mechanism of evolution. If they are not convinced of the possibility of natural selection, then they cannot be convinced of the theory.
3. I like to ask my students whether there is anything offensive or repulsive about the theory of evolution. Do they feel it is demeaning for human beings to be a part of an evolutionary process?
4. Social Darwinism is also an exciting subject to discuss. I generally quote John D. Rockefeller, who defended his ruthlessness in building Standard Oil by saying that the way one breeds an American Beauty Rose is to pluck all the small roses from the stem, leaving one. It is the survival of the fittest, naturally, but in this case John D. Rockefeller, not nature, was making the choices.

SUGGESTIONS FOR BRIEF ESSAYS

1. Define the phrase *the survival of the fittest* (the title of this chapter in a later edition of *On the Origin of Species by Natural Selection*). Look for ways in which its implications can be fully understood. Look, also, for examples by which it can be illustrated.
2. Compare the breeding of animals with natural selection. Which is more directed? Which is more dominated by chance? Which is more efficient? Which is more important?
3. How does cloning affect Darwin's views? Is cloning likely to undo the beneficial work of natural selection?
4. How does human social policy affect the survival of the fittest? Are modern medicine and modern social welfare agencies causing humans to be less fit? (You might keep in mind that all such human agencies actually help make us less animal-like and more human. But it is fun to watch students make this discovery on their own.)

SUGGESTIONS FOR LONGER ESSAYS

1. If you find any of Darwin's conclusions hard to accept, offer an analysis of his argument and examples. Based on your analysis take a clear position and defend it. You may wish to reject the concept of natural selection or to accept only a part of it. Try to give examples—even if only "imaginary" ones—and structure your argument by using careful definitions and by considering opposing views.
2. Analyze Darwin's writing for instances of yielding to or avoiding any or all of Bacon's four idols. Which of the idols are likely to be most threatening to the acceptance of Darwin's thinking? To which is he likely to be most susceptible? You might consider the extent to which Darwin, who definitely read Bacon, profited from his reading.
3. Readers in Darwin's age resented several implications of his theory. One is the wastefulness of nature, permitting myriads of useless variants to die to produce one that survives. Another is the savage portrait of nature implied in the battle for survival. That chance, rather than a thoughtful plan, governs evolution is, of course, still a sensitive point. Finally, the inclusion of humans in the evolutionary scheme was particularly offensive. Using the technique of enumeration, treat each of these points from the point of view of a person contemporary with Darwin. How much do these points still affect our age? Have our views changed?
4. Analyze Darwin's rhetorical strategies in this essay. Consider his structure and organization, his use of the common topics, and his attitude toward his audience. Add style and tone—keeping in mind that Darwin was anxious to convince his audience of his views but cautious not to overstep himself and incur the wrath of those who were naturally disposed against them.

SENTENCE OUTLINE: See p. 102 of this manual.
BIBLIOGRAPHY: See p. 133 of this manual.

STEPHEN JAY GOULD

Nonmoral Nature (pp. 415–29)

This essay is especially interesting for its examination of the way in which the language we use to describe something affects the way we value it or the way we understand it. The anthropocentric views of the nineteenth century are by no means limited to that century. We hold such views and use such language in our own time, and so have people in other times. By thinking of the world of nature in human ethical terms, we introduce the Idols of the Tribe, as Bacon tells us. (You can link Bacon's essay with Gould's on that point.) We see nature through human eyes, and it has caused immense distortions. It is worthwhile to examine the ethical consequences of thinking of nature in an anthropocentric fashion and to consider whether human beings are the measure of all things, including the ichneumon.

The power of metaphor can be revealed briefly and brilliantly by reading and discussing with your class the poems "The Lamb" and "The Tyger" from Blake's *Songs of Innocence and Experience* (below). They demonstrate how people in the nineteenth century thought about nature, and they show, too, the essence of the argument that Gould counters. It is totally human to think of the lamb as not only vulnerable but also "good" and the tiger as powerful and "evil" (although that is not Blake's point). Blake's effort is to help us see these contradictions as important aspects of God in nature. Your students may be able to understand the essay better when they have considered these poems:

The Lamb (1789)

Little Lamb, who made thee
Dost thou know who made thee
Gave thee life & bid thee feed,
By the stream & o'er the mead;

Gave thee clothing of delight,
Softest clothing wooly bright;
Gave thee such a tender voice,
Making all the vales rejoice!
    Little Lamb who made thee
    Dost thou know who made thee

    Little Lamb I'll tell thee,
    Little Lamb I'll tell thee!
He is called by thy name,
For he calls himself a Lamb:
He is meek & he is mild,
He became a little child:
I a child & thou a lamb,
We are called by his name.
    Little Lamb God bless thee.
    Little Lamb God bless thee.

The Tyger (1790–1792; published 1794)

Tyger Tyger burning bright,
In the forests of the night;
What immortal hand or eye,
Could frame thy fearful symmetry?

In what distant deeps or skies
Burnt the fire of thine eyes!
On what wings dare he aspire?
What the hand, dare seize the fire?

And what shoulder, & what art,
Could twist the sinews of thy heart?
And when thy heart began to beat,
What dread hand? & what dread feet?

What the hammer? what the chain?
In what furnace was thy brain?
What the anvil? what dread grasp,
Dare its deadly terrors clasp?

When the stars threw down their spears
And water'd heaven with their tears
Did he smile his work to see?
Did he who made the Lamb make thee?

Tyger Tyger burning bright,
In the forests of the night:
What immortal hand or eye,
Dare frame thy fearful symmetry?

    Here Blake is worrying over some of the same issues that Gould addresses. Using Blake is simply a way of making the dichotomy between victim and predator in nature clearer while raising the issue of using moral terms to help interpret nature. It is difficult for some people to avoid using them, and examining Blake helps us see why.

The controversial nature of Gould's essay may be a problem. I am interested in theological issues (I teach Milton and Joyce), but you may not be. On the other hand, you may have students who are passionate about the creationist views of science. I have no insights on how to work with them other than to suggest you permit them to interpret Gould in the way they feel is most intellectually satisfying.

This essay is especially good to read in conjunction with Darwin or Bacon, but I can also see good reasons to include Machiavelli, since one could interpret the struggle of the ichneumon in political as well as ethical terms.

SUGGESTIONS FOR CLASS DISCUSSION

1. What reasons might we have for appreciating the efficiency and skill of the ichneumons?
2. How does reading this essay affect your view of nature?
3. Does the pattern of parasitic infestation of the ichneumon's host suggest a larger plan for the world of nature? For the universe?
4. Gould spends paragraphs 4 to 7 describing the ichneumons. Why are they such a problem for theologians?
5. What ethical issues do you see reflected in nature? What are the ethical issues in nature for Gould? How different are they from the ones you see?

SUGGESTIONS FOR BRIEF ESSAYS

1. Explain why it is necessary or unnecessary to think in terms of the problem of evil in the world of nature. What makes the term *evil* appropriate to human nature? If you feel that evil is present in human nature but not in the world of nature apart from humankind, how does that view help us position ourselves in the natural world? Does it disconnect us from the world of nature?
2. In paragraph 2, Gould quotes Buckland, who decided that carnivores reduce the pain in the world by their skillful, quick kills. Defend his view with examples from other kinds of predation, or explain, using examples, why Buckland is wrong.
3. Gould points to the Rev. William Kirby's views of mother love in defending the ichneumon (paras. 19–21). Establish clearly Kirby's views, and then examine them in detail and decide whether they are defensible.

SUGGESTIONS FOR LONGER ESSAYS

1. If you have read Francis Bacon's essay "The Four Idols," analyze the nineteenth-century view of the problem of evil in nature in terms of the Idols of the Tribe. Explain how completely or incompletely nineteenth-century thinking reflects the Idol. What would Bacon have recommended as a cure for the distortion that resulted? Are there examples of other idols at work anywhere in Gould's essay, either in the works to which he refers or in his own work?
2. In paragraph 22, Gould comments, "Evolution could be read as God's chosen method of peopling our planet, and ethical messages might still populate nature," referring to observations made by St. George Mivart. Write an essay that explains what Mivart means, and then go on to establish your own view on the subject. Is it possible that evolution and ethics may have a place together in our attitude toward nature? Is Mivart correct?
3. In paragraph 28, Gould says, "The answer to the ancient dilemma of why such cruelty (in our terms) exists in nature can only be that there isn't any answer—and that the framing of the question 'in our terms' is thoroughly inappropriate in a natural world neither made for us nor ruled by us. It just plain happens." Are you satisfied with the thought that there is no answer to the question? How would traditional concepts of God relate to this view? If the view is acceptable, how would it affect human behavior? How would we have to regard ourselves in relation to the rest of creation?
4. Read something else of Gould's—an essay from a recent issue of *Natural History* magazine or an essay from one of his books. How would you characterize his views on nature? Is there a

consistency of attitude, or do you find that his thinking covers widely different positions? Compare the two works carefully for their ethical and scientific views.

SENTENCE OUTLINE: See p. 103 of this manual.
BIBLIOGRAPHY: See p. 136 of this manual.

MICHIO KAKU

The Theory of the Universe? (pp. 431–47)

The title of the essay points to the fact that it is still questionable as to whether the superstring theory is the "true" explanation of the complexities of the universe. One of the challenges to the student—and to us, as well—is the fact that the ideas Kaku tries to explain are best explained in mathematics rather than in words.

In an early section of *Hyperspace* Kaku gives a useful formula that will help your students understand how mathematics can express ideas we cannot conceive. If you use the Pythagorean theorem and take a cube describing it as having a side a, another side b, and side c, then to calculate the length of a line that runs diagonally from any corner to any other corner, you use the formula $a^2 + b^2 + c^2 = d^2$. Should you wish to postulate more dimensions to the cube one need only add more terms to the Pythagorean theorem: $\ldots d^2 + e^2 + f^2$, etc. In "Mathematicians and Mystics" Kaku explains some of the subtleties of this formula by establishing that only ten dimensions are needed to explain any of the phenomena that are postulated by particle physics.

However, this theory is difficult for everyone to understand. Despite Kaku's explanation, it still remains to ask what vibrates to produce the perceived details of the universe. For example, he says that a specific vibration produces a specific particle. But we are given no indication what the superstring that vibrates really is or why it should vibrate at different frequencies. It is useful to work with students to see whether they can contribute to the discussion. Some of your students will know something about superstring theory from their experiences in their physics classes, and some will know about it from reading science fiction. It would be useful to encourage them to talk and ask their own questions. Likewise, it will help to permit students to vent their honest confusion about the theory, reminding them that this is difficult material and that the explanations are only partial at this time.

Kaku's *Hyperspace* is a best-seller, and it is also a marvelous book. "The Theory of the Universe?" is not from that book, but it relates to it because all the theories in the selection are discussed in more detail in *Hyperspace*. You probably cannot take time to read *Hyperspace*, but if you read the first chapters—"Worlds Beyond Space and Time" and "Mathematicians and Mystics"—you will have a useful grounding that will help you work with the ideas that Kaku develops.

Of course, it is also useful to connect this essay with earlier essays in the Mind and Nature parts. For example, it delights me that Plato's and Bacon's essays so helpfully set the stage for Kaku's efforts in trying to help us understand a world of more than four dimensions. The same is true for Maimonides, who shows us certain limitations to understandings that are, by implication, similar to those Kaku discusses.

SUGGESTIONS FOR CLASS DISCUSSION

1. Beginning with the problems that Kaku's theories present to everyone is a good way to start. What is crazy about the theories, and why is craziness a positive value? It is also important to ask why common sense is of reduced value in describing modern physics.
2. How can "tiny strings of energy" (para. 33) be subatomic particles? Examine the discussion beginning with paragraph 32.
3. Ask your students to discuss what they feel they know about the concept of a ten-dimensional hyperspace.

SUGGESTIONS FOR BRIEF ESSAYS

1. Explain this theory in language simple enough for your grandmother to understand.
2. How does the Parable of the Gemstone (paras. 65 ff.) clarify the problems involved in trying to explain a multidimensional universe to people who live in a universe that has one less dimension than is needed to perceive "reality"?
3. What are some of the implications of postulating a multidimensional universe? What are some of the opportunities it offers for imagining our world in novel ways?

SUGGESTIONS FOR LONGER ESSAYS

1. In the last section of his essay, Michio Kaku uses the subheading "We Are Not Smart Enough" (para. 74). What does he seem to mean by this? Why are we not smart enough to understand the complexities of the theory that ought to explain the universe to us? How does his view correlate with Moses Maimonides's contentions that there are limits to the human understanding?
2. Check back issues of newspapers and journals for information on the superconducting super collider (SSC). What precisely would this machine be able to accomplish, were it to be constructed? Should it be constructed? What has happened to the project to prevent its completion? Do you feel it will one day be constructed?
3. Research the Big Bang theory on the Internet or in your library. What is it? How valid do you think the theory is? And what has it got to do with Michio Kaku's superstring theory? Explain the relationship among these theories.

SENTENCE OUTLINE: See p. 104 of this manual.

BIBLIOGRAPHY: See p. 138 of this manual.

RICHARD DAWKINS

All Africa and Her Progenies (pp. 449–69)

Richard Dawkins is interesting in part because his own work has not led to the Nobel Prize or to conspicuous success at the highest levels of microbiology. He is quite aware that he will not become a Watson or Crick, and as a result he has decided to do what he does best—explain important developments in science to the general public. His endowed professorship is not unique. One other person holds a professorship in the public understanding of science, but that person interprets the professorship as warranting a study of how the public has understood science. Dawkins attempts to provide clear understanding to the public. The result of all this is that Dawkins relies on the work of other theorists and scientists to help him clarify his own thought and develop his own ideas. That is what happened in his treatment of the genetic level of evolution in *The Selfish Gene* when he applied theories of ethology to genes, asking how they behaved individually, how they behaved in groups, and how they interacted.

It should also be mentioned that the awards Dawkins has won are considerable and would make virtually any scientist pleased. Among his awards are the Royal Society of Literature Award in 1987, the Silver Medal of the Zoological Society of London (1989), the Royal Society Michael Faraday Award for the Furtherance of Understanding in Science (1990), and the Nakayama Prize for Human Science (1994).

In *River Out of Eden* Dawkins brings his argument to bear against those moderns who attempt to defend various superstitions as intellectually legitimate on the basis of their currency in specific cultural communities. He calls them cultural relativists, but he also carefully distinguishes them from those who hold that one cannot evaluate a culture purely from the standpoint of another culture. His efforts are really aimed at the antiscientific community and especially at the community that refuses to accept Darwinian explanations for natural development. You may have students who hold strongly to an anti-Darwinist view. If so, I am not at all sure how to advise you. I have not faced that in my own classes, but if I did, I would ask such students to argue with both Darwin and Dawkins on as scientific a basis as they could. If you have useful experiences with students who have trouble reading these selections, I would be grateful if you would communicate with me through the English Department at the University of Connecticut.

SUGGESTIONS FOR CLASS DISCUSSION

1. Probably the most useful way to begin discussion is to find out how comfortable your students are with this essay's basic ideas relating to evolution. Give your students a chance to air their views by asking them directly what makes them most uncomfortable with the theories in the essay. If they seem comfortable, ask them about the larger community in which they live: Are there people in it who are uncomfortable with these theories? Why?

2. In his final paragraphs, Dawkins points out that it is more likely that most recent ancestor—what he calls the "focal ancestor"—was an Adam rather than an Eve (para. 44–46). Do you agree with him? What difference does it make? You may uncover a feminist or antifeminist issue here, and if you do, it is interesting to follow student arguments on either side of the question.

3. In paragraphs 40 to 42 Dawkins claims there must be one female common ancestor of all modern humans. Why is this so? Does it seem reasonable to you that it should be so?

4. If you have read Darwin with your students, you might ask them how they see Dawkins as developing from Darwinian thought. Why, in other words, do people point to Dawkins as an ultra-Darwinist?

SUGGESTIONS FOR BRIEF ESSAYS

1. Dawkins admits that even if there is no specific African Eve from which humans descended—that is, if it turns out that our ancestress was on another continent—all life almost certainly descends from original life forms in Africa. Would it make much of a difference if African Eve turned out to be Asian Eve or European Eve? How would it affect our understanding of our origins?

2. Explain the theory of parsimony as developed by Dawkins beginning in paragraph 33. What does *parsimony* mean in this context, and why is it important to the efforts to find relationships among the 135 women whose mitochondria the Berkeley group sampled?

3. Why do we inherit our mitochondria from our mother only? Dawkins provides a brief answer (para. 28), but supplement his answer by researching what we know about mitochondria.

SUGGESTIONS FOR LONGER ESSAYS

1. Dawkins makes reference to the structure of DNA (para. 16). Read James D. Watson's *The Double Helix: A Personal Account of the Discovery of the Structure of DNA* (1968) for the story of Watson's and Francis Crick's pioneer work. Also read some of the current essays in *Scientific American* and other journals to acquaint yourself with current theory about DNA. In light of that reading, how valid do you think Dawkins's theories about an African Eve are?

2. In paragraph 28 Dawkins asserts that Lynn Margulis's theory of descent from bacteria is "incomparably more inspiring, exciting and uplifting than the story of the Garden of Eden. It has the additional advantage of being almost certainly true." Argue the case in favor of or against this assertion. Consult Genesis in the Bible for the story of the Garden of Eden. If you have read John Milton's *Paradise Lost*, you may bring it into the discussion.

3. Examine the "molecular clock theory" developed in paragraphs 21 to 25. How reliable do you think it is for giving us information about the development of changes in DNA? To deal with this question, you will have to conduct some research into cytochrome *c* and what is known about the mutation rate of individual genetic "letters." This theory is important to the modern understanding of mutation and natural selection.

SENTENCE OUTLINE: See p. 105 of this manual.

BIBLIOGRAPHY: See p. 133 of this manual.

PART SIX

CULTURE

The five essays in this section are all approachable, including Clifford Geertz's discussion of three important cultures and his methodology of symbolic analysis. Herodotus is one of the most readable of ancient writers, and his discussion of Egypt—religious, erotic, and exotic—is as interesting to the modern imagination as it was to ancient Athens. Cabeza de Vaca's description of his exploits with American Indians in the 1520s holds particular interest today because such encounters were rarely documented with such detail and with such care. Ruth Benedict and Margaret Mead are still among the most readable of all the great investigators of culture in the first half of the twentieth century. Their accounts offer interesting connections with other essays in this book. Geertz is one of the most celebrated of modern essayists on culture, and his essay is designed to bring all such investigations into question. All these essays work well in the classroom.

HERODOTUS

Observations on Egypt (pp. 477–95)

Herodotus's *History* is a most engaging historical document. The excerpt included in this section is extremely readable and filled with curious details. Your students will have little difficulty in following what he says, although one of the challenges for them will be sensing the ways in which he regards a foreign culture. Greek culture at the time he wrote was at or near its zenith. The Parthenon had been built on the Acropolis by the time Herodotus's *History* was being read in Athens, which was at that time the most powerful of the Greek city-states. In other words, the Greeks were at that time a very proud people, and it would have been "normal" for them to regard people from other cultures as barbarians, a term Herodotus uses. The origin of *barbarian* comes from *barbar* which was a sound that Greeks associated with all those who did not speak Greek. Interestingly, when Herodotus uses the term, it is in reference to the incident of the Dodonan doves, the women who were transported to Libya and Dodona.

Another important quality of Herodotus that students should observe is his effort to make his observations as objective and accurate as possible. He is a man who has traveled widely and seen much of the world. Strange sights are almost common to him. He makes every effort to compare what he has heard about and seen with what his audience would take as common knowledge. We could wish, on the other hand, that he did not take the Greek experience so much for granted, since there is much, such as the content of the Samothracian Mysteries, that we would be delighted to know about. Herodotus seems to have been an initiate himself into at least some of the mysteries because he refers to them as if he shares the experience with those who know about them.

Herodotus's emphasis on religion is important. Remembering that the Greeks had defeated the Persians at Salamis in 480 B.C. only a few years after Herodotus was born, we must realize that the great buildings on the Acropolis, which celebrated not only Athena but also earlier gods, meant a great deal to the culture. Divination—being able to determine whether one's action was in line with the gods' will—was thought to be extremely important. Herodotus spends a great deal of time talking about it, and in this brief excerpt it takes on great significance.

One of the interesting things you can do with this selection is compare it with the other writers in this part of the book. Herodotus is a historian, but he is also a student of different cultures. Like all students of culture he has his biases and his limitations. Students should pay attention to the ways in which they reveal themselves.

SUGGESTIONS FOR CLASS DISCUSSION

1. One interesting line of thought to follow is the nature of religion as it is described in the passage. Ask students to collect as many details as possible that point to what religious observance seems to entail.
2. Another interesting line of discussion is the attitudes toward sex that are uncovered by Herodotus in his observations. First, there are the sexual practices that Herodotus describes, and then there are the reactions he offers to them. This can follow the range from women copulating with goats to embalmers copulating with corpses.
3. You might ask what your students would like to know about the Egyptians that Herodotus does not discuss and then ask why he does not think those things are worth discussing.

SUGGESTIONS FOR BRIEF ESSAYS

1. What do Herodotus's references to sexual practices tell you about the sexual norms of the Greeks in the fifth century B.C.? What do they tell you about the sexual behavior of the Egyptians? Does Herodotus regard the Egyptians as unusually active in sexual matters? What seems to underlie his interest and concern?
2. What does it mean for an animal to be sacred? Herodotus talks about several sacred animals, but he does not explain why they are sacred or what privileges they have because they are sacred. How do you interpret these passages?
3. What is the strangest behavior described in this passage, and what does it tell you about Herodotus's true attitude toward the Egyptians?

SUGGESTIONS FOR LONGER ESSAYS

1. How accurate is Herodotus's description of embalming techniques in Egypt? Find descriptions of Egyptian embalming from modern sources, and decide how much the modern understanding parallels Herodotus.
2. Read other sections of the *History*, and write an essay that attempts to describe Herodotus's personality and intellectual qualities.
3. Collect the contradictions and apparent contradictions in Herodotus's account of the customs of the Egyptians. What do the contradictions tell you about Herodotus's respect for the Egyptians? What do they tell you about the Egyptians?

SENTENCE OUTLINE: See p. 107 of this manual.

BIBLIOGRAPHY: See p. 136 of this manual.

ÁLVAR NÚÑEZ CABEZA DE VACA

From *La Relación* (pp. 497–508)

A number of translations are available of this document, which was originally published in 1542 and 1555. For some, the Cyclone Covey translation (1961, 1983) reprinted by the University of New Mexico Press is preferred, but I have chosen the Fanny Bandelier translation (1904) because it is much more readable. The Covey translation does not match up exactly chapter for chapter with the Bandelier translation, in part because Covey alters the chapter breaks and moves certain segments for narrative convenience. Covey used Bandelier and Buckingham Smith (1851) in preparing his version. Another reason I do not use Covey is that he constantly breaks into the text with bracketed commentary that I find distracting and annoying. The book itself was suggested to me by Mike Hennessey, who has used *A World of Ideas* in his courses. I am grateful to him.

If you have students with access to the Internet, you might recommend that they look up Cabeza de Vaca at http://www.English.swt.edu/CSS. Southwest Texas State University has a remarkable site with a large collection of scholarly papers online that expand our knowledge of Cabeza de Vaca and that also offer fascinating information.

Cabeza de Vaca is unquestionably a remarkable individual. His own personality shines through the entirety of *La Relación*, and it is valuable to ask your students to read the entire book—which is very short and easy to read. The Bandelier version was reprinted in 1972 by the Imprint Society in Barre, Massachusetts, and may not be widely available. But the Covey translation is easy to find. One of the questions that should be addressed is the extent to which Cabeza de Vaca's experiences with the Indians changed his world view. Of course, it is all but impossible to answer such a question because we have only this document to go on. But it is still worth thinking about because it is plain that his regard for the Indians is complex, and he is often filled with admiration. But it is also true that he went through a great deal of difficulty early in the journey. This excerpt is from his last year of wandering. During the first year, he had to endure the capture and death of many of his companions. Dysentery carried off a good many of them right away, and it carried off some of the Indians as well. He explains that the Indians were determined to kill all the Europeans because they blamed them for the illness that had killed so many. But at the end, the Indians decided that the survivors had suffered as they had and that they were not to blame for the disease that had ravaged the community. Consequently, they let Cabeza de Vaca and his companions live and eventually leave.

SUGGESTIONS FOR CLASS DISCUSSION

1. First, concentrate on Cabeza de Vaca's attitude toward the Indians. Does he admire them? Is he fearful of them? Does he exhibit the amount of curiosity that we as moderns think is appropriate when meeting entirely new cultures?
2. You might ask whether it seems that Cabeza de Vaca has "gone native" in these chapters. This is a claim that has sometimes been made of him. It would be interesting to ask students to define the term and evaluate it.
3. Another question is why the Indians were cured so readily by Cabeza de Vaca and his companions. Without further research, your students cannot answer the question, but some may have a background that will help shed some light on the phenomenon.

SUGGESTIONS FOR BRIEF ESSAYS

1. What are the most interesting customs of the Indians? Which surprise you the most? Describe a typical day in an Indian encampment.
2. What does Cabeza de Vaca fail to tell you that you would like to know about the behavior of the Avavares? Does he seem to be blind to certain kinds of activities, or do you think that those activities simply did not go on while he was with them?
3. What is it about Cabeza de Vaca that makes him such a survivor? What personal qualities does he have that help him endure living under such harsh conditions?

SUGGESTIONS FOR LONGER ESSAYS

1. Compare Cabeza de Vaca with Herodotus in terms of their capacity to make observations about the communities in which they find themselves. Which of them is a more careful observer? Which is more thoroughly involved in the community? Do you feel any reason to trust the reportage of one more than the other? Is there anything in Cabeza de Vaca's report that you are skeptical of?
2. What is the difference in the treatment of men and women among the Indians? Cabeza de Vaca makes a number of observations about the special treatment women get. What are they? What special roles do the women take on? How concerned is Cabeza de Vaca about the way women are treated? In one chapter not included here, Cabeza de Vaca says, "The women toil incessantly." Does that seem to be the case as he describes life among the Avavares?
3. Cabeza de Vaca comments on the military habits of the Indians. What does he have to say, and how much regard does he have for their military skills? Does Cabeza de Vaca invoke in you a measure of respect for the Indian warriors? What is his view of war among the Indians? What is

yours? What is your view of a people who are constantly at war with all their neighbors almost all the time?

4. Use Cabeza de Vaca as a model for writing about a group of people different from yourself. If possible, use a group of people with whom you have spent time, such as during a period of living abroad, a period spent with a group you no longer belong to, or a time when you went to a different school with different cultural codes. Try to cover as many of the same subjects as Cabeza de Vaca, and make your description as authoritative and complete a record of the examination of a different culture as possible.

SENTENCE OUTLINE: See p. 109 of this manual.

BIBLIOGRAPHY: See p. 132 of this manual.

RUTH BENEDICT
The Pueblos of New Mexico (pp. 511–26)

The advantage of this passage from *Patterns of Culture* is that Ruth Benedict describes the Pueblo culture she studied. Her description is concrete, detailed, and specific. The passage that precedes the present excerpt (which is Chapter 4) discusses the religious ceremonies of Zuñi, emphasizing the careful preparations and the details of every aspect of garment, language, and performance. Religious ceremonies constitute the center of the culture's attention, and when the current passage begins, Benedict shifts her attention to more social issues, such as the question of courtship and marriage.

A comparison of your students' cultural attitudes toward courtship and marriage is a good starting place for discussing the essay. The fact that the marriage relationship is a personal or individual decision renders it less important than the social religious ceremonies, the performance of which would affect all Zuñi. Students are usually aware that their marriage choices are somehow more social than individual, and they may begin making comparisons. You may point to the history of dramatic comedies, which usually involve the placing of impediments between young people and their desire to marry. These impediments are ordinarily parents. One way of exploring these distinctions might be to examine the differences in family structure—matrilineal versus patrilineal distinctions, for instance. Or you might want to begin discussing differences in attitudes toward possessions and material goods. The older concept of wife as property may still be apparent in general behavior toward marriage.

Another interesting line of discussion concerns the existence in your students' experience of multiple cultures, much in the manner of the Pueblo experience. Just as the Pueblo have the Apache nearby behaving in very different ways, your students may be aware of multiple cultures and their differences of behavior and expectations. Such a discussion might be touchy for some students, but for others it may well be very illuminating. For one thing, it will begin the process of examining exactly what culture is in the immediate lives of your students. They need not go to New Guinea to experience an exotic culture. They might meet one right at home.

You may wish to read the entire chapter "The Pueblos of New Mexico" in order to help place this excerpt into perspective. A complete reading will help you integrate discussions of ceremony as a form of Apollonian activity with the vision quest as a form of Dionysian activity. You also may wish to link this passage with Nietzsche's "Apollonianism and Dionysianism," a selection that will be even more accessible in light of Benedict's use of the terminology. Nietzsche has consistently provided my students with excellent opportunities for writing and reaction, and I think you will have good results with him in connection with this essay.

SUGGESTIONS FOR CLASS DISCUSSION

1. What are some plausible definitions of a culture now that you have read about Zuñi and their neighbors?

2. What seems to be the structure of family society for Zuñi?
3. What kinds of supernatural powers seem to be derived from the vision quest?
4. Why do the Pueblos not pursue the vision quest?
5. Why is the vision quest limited to men?

SUGGESTIONS FOR BRIEF ESSAYS

1. Benedict says, "Influences that are powerful against [Zuñi] tradition are uncongenial and minimized in their institutions" (para. 14). Is that true in our culture? Examine our culture for evidence that traditions are preserved (or that they are altered) with ease or with difficulty. Can a culture that loses its traditions continue to be a culture?
2. Benedict talks about the way in which surrounding cultures differ from the Pueblo in many basic ways. She uses the Apollonian and Dionysian distinction as one sign of their differences. Do you see similar distinctions in your own environment? Are there multiple cultural groups in your environment as there were in the environment of Zuñi? Are the groups totally separate, as in the case of the Pueblo? Are they totally distinct? What are the points of intersection? Are they similar to those you see in cultures around you?
3. One of Benedict's views is that one cannot understand the culture of the Pueblo Indians without understanding the ways in which nearby Indians behave. She tells us about the behavior of the Mojave and the Apache as well as other groups. Does her description of other groups help us better understand the Zuñi?

SUGGESTIONS FOR LONGER ESSAYS

1. Consult some descriptions of the historical lives of North American Indians, and ask whether they support Benedict's view that "the American Indians as a whole, and including those of Mexico, were passionately Dionysian. They valued all violent experience, all means by which human beings may break through the usual sensory routine, and to all such experiences they attributed the highest value" (para. 15).
2. What groups in your immediate culture can be described as Dionysian given Benedict's general description? Describe their behavior in the same concrete and specific terms that Benedict uses. Can they be said to represent a culture distinct from yours?
3. Decide whether the structure of your family is matrilineal or patrilineal. Describe its structure, and inquire about the structure of your friends' families. What are the assumptions that our culture normally makes about the structure of the family? What traditions shape our cultural attitude toward the family? Can you see them at work in your own family?

SENTENCE OUTLINE: See p. 110 of this manual..

BIBLIOGRAPHY: See p. 131 of this manual.

MARGARET MEAD

Women, Sex, and Sin (pp. 529–41)

Your students will probably not know that Margaret Mead was a popular columnist and media maven. Indeed, many of her critics seemed to find fault with her largely because of her popular success. However, her work is still a pleasure to read, and her major books on the South Seas are authoritative and fascinating. The usual charges that she disdained those she studied—sometimes pushing toward a charge of racism—have been made, but they seem unwarranted. Photographs of the period, showing her in local costume, living the local life, imply that she was willing to be one with the people. Most of her critics have not had such experiences.

"Women, Sex, and Sin" is Chapter 3 of *New Lives for Old* (1966). If you can find the book, you might want to read the first chapter, "Arrival in Peri," which records most of her astonishment at the changes she encountered on her return to the island after many years. She met people she had known when they were very young, and she was able to compare their behavior before and after the change that took place in their culture. The quotations in the introduction to the piece come from this opening chapter. Generally, *New Lives for Old* is a valuable and readable book.

At root, Mead's basic purpose in writing anthropological studies is to reassure us that the differences between cultures are not necessitated by biology or even by specific geographic circumstances. Instead, she felt, they were due to the habits and traditions that cultures maintained as part of their history. In essence, people absorb the history of their culture and behave as they do because the traditions become inbuilt. For that reason, it is useful to ask students to compare the way they think about women, sex, and sin with the information Mead provides here. Mead insists that there is nothing written in stone about how people must behave, and her distinctions between female or male gender behavior suggest that she is aware of our expectations and wishes to play off against them.

SUGGESTIONS FOR CLASS DISCUSSION

1. What were the usual offenses women committed in the Old Way?
2. What are the new offenses committed by women in the New Way? For whom are such acts offensive?
3. Why did the men seem to wish to change the old cultural ways?
4. What kind of power do women have in the Manus culture? Has the shift from the Old Way to the New Way lessened their power?
5. What is the relationship between sex and love in Manus culture?

SUGGESTIONS FOR BRIEF ESSAYS

1. Mead describes the sense of relief that the Manus have about the possibility of a man and woman sitting simply and talking peacefully instead of engaging in sex. What seems to be the source of that relief? Are there occasions in your own culture when similar behavior is welcome?
2. In describing the Old Way, Mead tells us that "at no point was there a chance to develop any gentleness associated with sex behavior in marriage itself" (para. 6). Have you known cultural groups in your own area for whom the same may be true? Explain the behavior you have heard about or witnessed, and decide whether it is a cultural expression or an aberration.
3. In paragraphs 8 and 9 Mead describes the sudden changes implied by the New Way. She also explains that women had no choice: the New Way was imposed on them by the men who had returned from working in Australian households. Is it possible that the Manus women, if given a choice, would have rejected the New Way?

SUGGESTIONS FOR LONGER ESSAYS

1. Read some or all of one of Margaret Mead's studies of the South Pacific. Decide whether her methods permitted her to see the natives as they really were or whether her methods made it impossible to go beyond the prejudices and distortion that are built into her own culture. Does her work imply that she considers her own culture superior to the cultures she studies?
2. Some of the taboos that Mead describes may seem odd to you: in the Old Way a husband could not mention his wife's name or talk to her mother. Their communication was extremely limited, and direct conversation produced a sense of shame. Children were betrothed when very young and could not protest; fathers constantly flared up in anger at daughters. What similar taboos are present in your culture?
3. In paragraph 15 Mead says, "So women and sex remain associated with sin; where once they were associated with the punitive anger of ghosts, now they are associated with the jealous

anger of men and women." Compare the Manus culture in its attitude toward women, sex, and sin with the attitude of your own culture. If you see the possibility of several cultural attitudes in your own experience and observation, be sure to include them. What are the important points of similarity? Of difference?

SENTENCE OUTLINE: See p. 111 of this manual.
BIBLIOGRAPHY: See p. 142 of this manual.

CLIFFORD GEERTZ

"From the Native's Point of View": On the Nature of Anthropological Understanding (pp. 543–62)

Geertz is difficult for most students. This essay will work well, however, if you have your students read either Benedict or Mead before they come to this discussion. Some of the crucial ideas, especially regarding the role of the ethnographer in relation to the culture, are raised in those essays. Cabeza de Vaca's essay is probably one of the most useful to read with Geertz, but most of the essays in this section will work well with Geertz and will act as a good preparation.

Most students are fascinated by the questions underlying cultural anthropology. The most important involves curiosity about how other people live and act. Geertz takes that curiosity as a given, and generally he is right to do so. Students will disagree about the question of distance or closeness in relation to observing cultures. Fortunately, this is an important issue to many students, and you should be able to get a good deal of mileage out of raising it. This also may lead to the natural question of how it would feel to have an anthropologist studying your classroom or your students' dormitories. One of the issues that lies deep in the heart of anthropology concerns the fact that Europeans are always the anthropologists. In a sense, it is part of the privilege that European wealth has made possible. If you find this issue raised in the course of discussion, you may want to examine Geertz with a special concern. He "appropriated" three cultures and may even rank as a conspicuous consumer. His attitude, however, may be healthy enough to make it difficult to make overly simple judgments about the question of appropriation of culture.

One of the pleasures of this essay is that its emphasis on "symbolic forms" offers a real opportunity to help your students begin an examination of their own culture. Their music is a natural for examination, since MTV and music videos are symbolic forms that speak explicitly to the young. The thought that they might be part of a subculture may appeal to them enough to permit them to study themselves. That, then, represents a fascinating problem in addition to those raised by Geertz: When is the ethnographer also the informant? What special problems are then raised by the ethnographer-subject?

SUGGESTIONS FOR CLASS DISCUSSION

1. Geertz seems to write off the value of the informant to help the ethnographer understand a culture. Do you agree with him or not?
2. Does what Geertz say about Malinowski invalidate Malinowski's work (para. 1–2)?
3. What symbolic forms does Geertz deal with in Morocco? Does his study expand your understanding of the culture?
4. Geertz suggests in paragraph 2 that some anthropologists claim a "unique form of psychological closeness" with the cultures they study. Does Geertz do so without being aware of it? Do other anthropologists you have read do so?
5. Why does Geertz tell us about the destitute Javanese peasants discussing "questions of freedom of the will" (para. 10)?

SUGGESTIONS FOR BRIEF ESSAYS

1. Under what conditions can the ethnographer expect to do useful work in studying other cultures? Do you feel confident that anthropologists can do their job and provide us with useful information?

2. Geertz discusses etiquette in terms of "proper ordering" (para. 13). Explain how etiquette works in your culture. What are its forms, and how important is etiquette in shaping or defining your culture?

3. In his discussion of the Balinese, Geertz points out that they "have at least a half-dozen major sorts of labels, ascriptive, fixed, and absolute, which one person can apply to another" (para. 17). How many different labels can commonly be used to describe, define, or fix an individual in your culture? What is the effect of using such labels?

SUGGESTIONS FOR LONGER ESSAYS

1. Bali is a society in which all behavior is stylized. Everything that is personal and special to the individual is buried in ritual behavior, dress, and performance. People play roles assigned to them and treat themselves as if they were actors in life's drama. If you have observed people doing the same in your own culture, describe the circumstances and the results of such behavior. See paragraphs 15 to 20 of Geertz's essay.

2. To what extent do people in your culture play roles assigned to them or roles they assume on their own? Consider the roles of star student, problem child, tough guy, innocent, naughty boy, hipster, and any other roles you can observe. How willingly do people play these roles, and how effective are they in defining individuals—even if only temporarily?

3. Geertz is careful to use the native language in describing the symbolic forms that he observes defining the individual. What special uses of language do you see and hear about you that serve to define the individual in special ways? Review Geertz's descriptions of language, and then make a list of special words you hear used in the next several days. Consider how they contribute to the symbolic forms that define your culture.

SENTENCE OUTLINE: See p. 112 of this manual.

BIBLIOGRAPHY: See p. 136 of this manual.

FAITH

The seven selections in Part Seven span centuries, cultures, and religions, but they all ask two fundamental questions: How should the faithful behave? and What should the faithful believe? The answers to such questions contribute to a definition of faith. Another thing these seven passages share is a sense of awareness of the presence of God. Many of them, for example, present a dialogue between the individual and God. God, of course, does most of the talking. The Buddha's emphasis on enlightenment is easily translatable in the lives of most students. The Buddha offers a point of view that is quite different from the philosophical position that most students have reached in their own lives. The "Sermon on the Mount," in St. Matthew, centers on the blessings of faith and belief in Jesus. The *Bhagavad Gītā* presents a dialogue between Lord Krishna and Arjuna. Lord Krishna explains how one lives a life of service to God and thus becomes one with God. "The Believer," Surah 40 from the Koran, discusses primarily the fate of those who do not believe—those who are the unfaithful. However, it balances the picture by showing us the rewards of the faithful. St. Teresa's remarkable account of her visions of Jesus and angels are among the most interesting mystical experiences recorded in the seventeenth century. Her faith was so powerful that it overwhelmed the suspicious Inquisition. Nietzsche explores psychological states that develop from Greek religious practice and offers an interesting look at the powers that express themselves in faith. Finally, Martin Buber, one of the century's most important Jewish thinkers, discusses Buddhism and other faiths in the process of exploring the relationship between the individual and God, the relationship he says always remains an I-Thou relationship.

SIDDHĀRTHA GAUTAMA, THE BUDDHA

Meditation: The Path to Enlightenment (pp. 569–87)

You may wish to consult the text from which this excerpt comes, *Buddhist Scriptures*, published by Penguin Books in 1959. It is widely available. Following the excerpt in this text is information on zazen, an aspect of Zen that might be familiar to some students. The popularity of Zen in America is probably not what it was twenty years ago, but I still find that certain students are aware of its tenets and even practice meditation on their own.

I'd like to suggest that you make use here of the connection to Plato. You may want to assign one of the comparative writing suggestions below. My point is that there is a unanimity between these two great philosophical traditions in their distrust of the senses and in their confidence that self-discipline is a way of expressing one's faith.

Obviously, it is an uphill struggle, but a worthwhile one, to talk to undergraduates about self-discipline. For one thing, the perspective is fresh, and deep down most students feel that self-discipline is a good thing—especially for others. Good discussions can develop from considering this issue, and you can easily relate the entire question of faith to the question of self-discipline.

Emptying one's mind, as the poet Gary Snyder once said, is something that most people do badly. He included himself. If you have access to his poetry, you might select some of his haiku or nature poetry and discuss it from the point of view of its meditative content and its attitude toward sensory experience. He admits, however, that there is little valuable Zen poetry written by Zen practitioners.

One of the advantages in discussing this selection with your students is that you can show how three strands of religious thought tend to merge and how the East has influenced Western thought in this sphere. The best discussions will probably develop ideas from what students say is implied by the spiritual. The

Buddha denies the validity of material experience so vehemently that a lively discussion of the dispute between the material and the spiritual would be appropriate in any class working with this selection.

SUGGESTIONS FOR CLASS DISCUSSION

1. Why is there such a dispute between the material and the spiritual in this discussion of meditation?
2. Why is self-discipline so central to the Buddha's instructions?
3. What is meant by "Becoming" in paragraph 26?
4. What does the Buddha mean by "The Practice of Introversion" (para. 4)?
5. What is the relationship between self-discipline and one's faith in God?
6. What does the Buddha have faith in?

SUGGESTIONS FOR BRIEF ESSAYS

1. Compare the imagery of bondage as used by the Buddha and as used by Plato in "The Allegory of the Cave." In what ways are they similar, and in what ways are they distinct? Are the general aims of each essay relatively similar or quite different?
2. In paragraphs 13 and 14, the Buddha considers the problems of trying to please one's friends. Do you agree with him that "worldly" friends make great demands on you? Establish what you think the Buddha means by this statement. Rely on your personal experience to illustrate your points.
3. Does the lack of self-discipline in people you know cause them any of the suffering that the Buddha describes? Why is self-discipline difficult to achieve? In general, does our culture encourage or hamper the achievement of self discipline?
4. What is the Buddha's attitude toward family? Consult paragraphs 40 to 42. To what extent do you agree with him, and to what extent do you disagree? Establish first, as clearly as possible, what you feel his position is. Then consider it in light of your own values and beliefs.

SUGGESTIONS FOR LONGER ESSAYS

1. The Buddha recommends mindfulness in paragraph 29, suggesting that we not sleep our lives away but remain awake as much of the night as possible. What is mindfulness? What are its advantages? Describe your own efforts, in a specific period of time (as brief as an hour, or perhaps as long as several hours), to maintain the highest level of mindfulness that you can. How did you do it? What are the difficulties you faced? What are the benefits of such concentration?
2. If you were not a religious person, describe how the Buddha's suggestions would encourage you to live a life that had a rich spiritual dimension. Explain how the discipline of meditation would produce spiritual understanding and increase one's spiritual awareness. If possible, describe some of your own experiences in practicing the discipline that the Buddha recommends.
3. Explain why the suggestions of the Buddha would help improve daily life in the United States. What are the virtues of discipline for the social structure of the nation? How would the experience of everyday life change? Try to be as specific as possible by taking an ordinary day in a person's life and showing, hour by hour, how it might be improved if everyone adopted the practices recommended in this selection.

SENTENCE OUTLINE: See p. 114 of this manual.

BIBLIOGRAPHY: See p. 145 of this manual.

ST. MATTHEW

The Sermon on the Mount (pp. 589–99)

The question of faith is very much at the center of this selection, although it is clear only from the general context of the entire gospel. The Lord's Prayer implies a specific faith, although given the text itself, there is nothing to say that it needs to be defined in specific religious terms. It is not specifically Catholic or Protestant. The question of how relevant it is to Judaism as it is practiced today is something else, of course. One of the questions I ask at the end of the text is potentially explosive—whether the Lord's Prayer is part of a larger pattern of patriarchy as it is understood today ("Suggestions for Writing," question 4, text p. 598). A feminist perspective naturally decries patriarchy, and it may be possible to stimulate your students to considerable discussion by raising the question after they read this. I have no advice for your own position on this matter: I am sure it is clear to you. But you may find it delicate to conduct the discussion unless you are willing to have a hands-off policy and let your students develop the argument. It almost certainly will prove as interesting to you as to them.

I think that one of the great advantages of this selection for us is that the text needs examination and interpretation. For example, the "eye for an eye" text (5:38) is used frequently by people today in matters concerning criminal justice. They use it in the sense that seems implied by Exodus, but they may find it very interesting to contemplate how their thinking would change if they paid close attention to the way in which Jesus develops the idea, suggesting that raw revenge is no longer appropriate. This is a highly complex issue, connected with talon law and its growth and development. To an important extent, Jesus is signaling an end to that kind of "justice," but as we all know, many cultures still hold to it fiercely. You should be able to get a good deal out of a discussion that centers on vengeance and the law.

Another source of useful discussion is following up on the question of what exactly Jesus recommends as appropriate behavior. You might ask whether Jesus thought that his recommendations concerned only the disciples or whether a reader could legitimately claim it is designed to inform all people who have faith in Jesus. Then you might pursue the question of whether your students think it is possible to behave as Jesus recommends. "Beware of false prophets" (7:15) is easy enough for most people to pay attention to, but what about "Take no thought for your life" (6:25)? How appropriate is that directive for the modern student? And what does it really mean? Again, this is one of the statements that need close textual analysis.

Of course, one of the most interesting lines of discussion can arise from a simple comparison with the passage from the Buddha. You might ask whether there is any reason to refer more to the Lord Buddha than to the Lord Jesus—and then ask what that means.

SUGGESTIONS FOR CLASS DISCUSSION

1. Ask students what they think is meant by "Judge not, that ye be not judged" (7:1) and whether it is pertinent to their lives today.
2. How does this passage from Matthew promote faith in Jesus?
3. Why is the Lord's Prayer thought to be so important? Is it the only prayer a Christian would need?
4. Is the Lord's Prayer compatible with modern feminist thought?

SUGGESTIONS FOR BRIEF ESSAYS

1. The term *righteous* or *righteousness* is used frequently in this selection. What does it seem to mean in this context? What does it mean to you? Do you feel it is possible to live life righteously?
2. Do you think it is true that no one can serve two masters? "Ye cannot serve God and mammon" (6:24). Why is it difficult to serve God and mammon? Do you find it personally a problem, or do you feel it may become a problem in the future?

3. Give an example of casting pearls before swine (7:6). What is the point of Jesus' admonition, and what have you learned about the problem? What are the dangers of taking the expression too literally, too strictly, or too personally?

SUGGESTIONS FOR LONGER ESSAYS

1. One of the persistent commentaries on this selection is that it represents the beginning of liberalism as it has come to be understood in the West. By that is meant that this passage places great emphasis on the individual and individual responsibility. Up to this time it was thought best to follow whatever people thought was the accepted view of things. It was not up to individuals to interpret the law or to try to be different from the mass of people. This document, however, asks that individuals run counter to the main current of some societies. Do you feel that the Sermon on the Mount establishes the necessity for personal moral responsibility? Do you feel it makes the individual an appropriate critic of the limits of a venal society?

2. What connections do you see between Jesus' teachings and those of Plato and the Buddha? What are the moral issues that all seem to be concerned about? What are their ultimate hopes and goals for the individual?

3. Examine the discussion of loving one's enemies in Chapter 5, verses 38 to 48. Where do you stand on the instructions that Jesus imparts? Why does Jesus insist on forgiveness? What is the virtue of forgiveness? Why is forgiveness difficult? Why is it essential to the kind of faith that Jesus demands?

SENTENCE OUTLINE: See p. 115 of this manual.

BIBLIOGRAPHY: See p. 142 of this manual.

THE BHAGAVAD GĪTĀ
Meditation and Knowledge (pp. 601–14)

The *Bhagavad Gītā* is a difficult text in part because the culture of the Hindu religion is quite foreign to most of us. Consequently, if you have a student in your group who has firsthand experience with the Hindu religion, it will help if you ask her or him to amplify the information I have been able to provide in the text. My focus is essentially on the text of Chapters 6 and 7, and I have tried to provide enough background information so that a thoughtful reader can begin to understand the main purpose of the chapters. Obviously, the more you can bring to bear on the matter, the better. You may be quite knowledgeable about the *Bhagavad Gītā*, in which case you will be able to amplify the text on your own account. If you are not familiar with it, you may wish to look at one or two generally available books. One is Sachindra K. Majumdar's *The Bhagavad Gītā: A Scripture for the Future* (Asian Humanities Press, 1991). Majumdar translates the text somewhat differently from Edgerton (whose 1944 translation depends on an earlier translation by Sir Edwin Arnold, *The Song Celestial*, 1885). Majumdar is most interested in commenting on the text, although he usually restates it in simpler terms. For example, of Chapter 7, verse 3, he says, essentially, that many people strive after God but only a rare person ever gets there. Such a restatement is handy only for very complex verses. His approach to the text is typical of the versions you are likely to find nearby. One widely available text is S. Radhakrishnan's *The Bhagavad Gītā*, published by Harper & Row (1948, 1973). Again, this text offers extensive commentary between the verses, and it offers, as well, the original Sanskrit. W. D. P. Hill's translation, *The Bhagavadgītā*, published by Oxford in 1928 and still available, includes annotations of the traditional sort, with an extended introduction that tries to explain the "doctrine" of the *Bhagavad Gītā*. Edgerton's translation, possibly available in your library, also has useful commentary but in separate chapters after the text.

Some general information may help in communicating this text to your students. First, the beliefs in these chapters are based on the view that the body and the soul compose every individual. The soul is inactive but of great importance. It has contemplative powers. The body, including one's thoughts and mental activity, is changeable. God is not present in individual body-soul combinations, but as Lord Krishna says, they are in God. According to Edgerton, "By filling his being with love of God and doing all acts as a service to God, man attains union with Him; that is, salvation." The knowledge that is demanded of Arjuna in Chapter 7 is the knowledge of God, the Lord Krishna. The two ways by which one achieves salvation are Sāmkhya and Yoga. Sāmkhya means achieving perfect knowledge by withdrawing from the world and becoming a religious hermit. Yoga means performing the proper duties that will imply benefiting mankind, treating others as one wishes to be treated, and all good actions. Majumdar says that one approaches God "through work, devotion, wisdom, and contemplation" (p. 140 of Majumdar). All these points are clearly present in the selection in the text.

SUGGESTIONS FOR CLASS DISCUSSION

1. I think one of the most workable ways into the text is through the question of discipline. The term is used often in the text, and it is worth seeing what your students understand by it. Lord Krishna emphasizes the control of the senses because the senses lead to desire and desire leads away from the contemplation of the Lord.

2. Another interesting topic of discussion concerns the "thought-organ," or mind and its necessary training. The concept of training the mind may be novel to some of your students. I had one irate student once declare to me that I would never change her mind. I had to remind her that the state of Connecticut was paying me to change her mind by improving it. The role of the "thought-organ" in resisting discipline is quite interesting in the text, and your students will have a great deal to say about it based on their own experience.

3. The seventh chapter is called "Discipline of Theoretical and Practical Knowledge." While the chapter itself does not define the distinction, it permits your students to explore the idea in their own way. The difference between the two forms of knowledge is worth contemplating, and it is worth examining the text to see which form of knowledge seems to get the most attention.

SUGGESTIONS FOR BRIEF ESSAYS

1. Why is there such an emphasis on discipline in the *Bhagavad Gītā*? Why does discipline seem so important to most religions? To what extent is discipline important to you?

2. In Chapter 7, verses 11 to 13, Lord Krishna talks of three states of being—goodness, passion, and darkness. These states are variously translated as harmonious, passionate, and slothful; serene, active, dull; purity, energy, and darkness. They are called the three gunas of nature. Explain what these three states of nature are and which, if any, of them is to be preferred. If you wish, use your own experience to develop your understanding of each. What does Lord Krishna mean when he says, "I am not in them; they are in Me"?

3. What does it mean to worship Lord Krishna? In Chapter 7, verse 16, Lord Krishna says "Four-fold are those that worship me"? What are those who worship him? Why are there four divisions? What is their significance?

SUGGESTIONS FOR LONGER ESSAYS

1. One of the constant practices of the translators of the *Bhagavad Gītā* is the extended commentary on the text. This is composed of reprinting a verse and then explaining the meaning of the verse. Take a section from either chapter—choose from three to seven verses on the same subject—and write your own commentary on the text. Rely on personal experience, on observation, and on your understanding of what the text means. Consider that you are explaining the text to someone who has trouble understanding it.

2. Why is it so difficult to discipline the "thought-organ"? Make an effort to discipline your thought-organ using the suggestions Lord Krishna supplies. Record your experiences and describe the efforts you go through. What are the problems that you face in your attempt?

3. Research the term *Nirvana*, which means "enlightenment." It appears in Chapter 6, verse 15, in a section that recommends a temperate way of life. In the recommendations of the Buddha, the

middle way is the way of temperate life; in the recommendations of Aristotle, the way is the way of the golden mean. Here Lord Krishna recommends temperate behavior—not too much and not too little of anything. Why is this the way to enlightenment? Why do so many religions recommend temperate behavior? What are the advantages of temperate behavior? What are its disadvantages?

4.   Connect the issues raised in the question directly above with the concerns of Nietzsche in his "Apollonianism and Dionysianism." Where do the *Bhagavad Gītā* and "Apollonianism and Dionysianism" come into conflict? Which seems to you to be a more desirable description of the world of faith as it ought to be?

SENTENCE OUTLINE: See p. 116 of this manual.

BIBLIOGRAPHY: See p. 131 of this manual.

THE PROPHET MUHAMMAD

From *the Koran* (pp. 617–26)

One of the interesting things about this surah—called "The Believer"—is that it concentrates on the fate of those who do not have faith in Allah. Those who do have faith are rewarded by paradise in the hereafter and with peace of mind in the present. But those who do not have faith are dealt with very harshly. The extent to which you wish to deal with this is up to you, of course, but I have tried to be as neutral as possible in presenting the text and in devising questions that I think will stimulate discussion among heterogenous groups of students.

Incidentally, I chose this translation not because it is especially more faithful to the original or because it is cited by commentators, but because it is approachable by modern students in English. The individual verses are lost, but only those who wish to comment on the text for the purpose of communicating with other distant commentators would need the exact verses. My expedient of numbering paragraphs is nothing but an expedient and is designed to help in making reference to the text.

If you are fortunate enough to have Muslim students, you might ask them to offer their views on the Koran and on the surah selected for the book. Commenting on the Koran may be difficult for your Muslim students, however. If they are reluctant to comment on the text, you might point out to them that there is a great tradition of commentary and that they may find themselves a place in that tradition. You might recommend Helmut Gätje's *The Qur'an and Its Exegesis: Selected Texts with Classical and Modern Muslim Interpretations* (University of California Press, 1976). Unfortunately, Gätje does not comment on this surah, but he does give a range of possible commentaries that will help Muslim students recognize the ways in which they may discuss the text profitably.

Much of the traditional interpretation is conducted on the level of the philologist, dealing with technical issues of language, including grammar and etymology. Your students cannot participate in this level of interpretation unless they know classical Arabic, and even then it would be difficult. My suggestion is that you aim to clarify the nature of faith as expressed in the text, reminding your students that the faithful are the believers—those who recognize Allah as God.

The way in which you handle the relationship of Allah with Yahweh and Jesus is again up to you. Styles in ecumenism are such that some commentators feel that God is God no matter what the name. You might ask your students whether the tone of this surah would support such a view. Muhammad saw Jesus as an apostle or prophet, much like himself. He saw Moses in the same fashion. He never claimed to be God, and he saw Islam as a religion with the most recent and most reliable revelations, replacing other religions.

Among the central questions you might concentrate on is that of how this surah defines faith, how it describes faith, and how it rewards faith. These are crucial concerns throughout the Koran.

SUGGESTIONS FOR CLASS DISCUSSION

1. What is the nature of the faith described in this surah?
2. After reading this surah why would one wish to become one of the faithful?
3. What are the rewards of the faithful? What forms of afterlife does the surah propose?
4. The surah talks about the signs of God. What would a modern person regard as the appropriate signs of God?

SUGGESTIONS FOR BRIEF ESSAYS

1. In paragraph 11 we read: "God will judge with fairness, but the idols to which they pray besides Him can judge nothing." Relying on the entire surah, how fair do you feel God's judgments will be? Which passages imply fairness? What does fairness consist of? Remember that this surah is known as "The Believer" as well as "The Forgiving One." Is God a forgiving God in this surah?
2. Examine paragraphs 36 to 48. They describe God and God's works. In modern terms, how would you rewrite this section to explain to one who does not believe in God exactly what God has done for humanity.
3. One of the questions that will be asked at judgment day is, "Where are the gods whom you have served besides God?" (para. 47). How would a modern person answer this question? What are the gods that we as moderns are likely to serve instead of God? Is this question a fair question in a religious sense?

SUGGESTIONS FOR LONGER ESSAYS

1. Describe the situation in paragraphs 4 through 8 and decide whether the way in which unbelievers are dealt with is fair according to the principles expressed in this surah. Do you feel that justice in a general sense is served in this section? What is the nature of justice in relation to those who believe and those who do not believe? Is justice as important as faith in this surah?
2. What does Pharaoh try to do in this surah? Why does he turn against Moses? Why does he order Haman about as he does? What modern figures could you compare with Pharaoh? How would a modern Pharaoh behave if faced with a religious prophet who threatened the status quo? See the passages beginning with paragraph 13.
3. How do the beliefs stated in this surah compare with the religious beliefs you are familiar with? How does the God presented in this surah compare with the God that you are familiar with? How would modern young people respond if it were demonstrated conclusively to them that the God of the Koran was the God to which they would have to answer at death? What would change? If you were convinced beyond a doubt and therefore became a believer, how would you change?
4. Compare the God of the Koran with the God of Matthew, with Lord Krishna of the *Bhagavad Gītā*, and with the concept of godliness in the writings of the Buddha. What have all these religious tracts on faith in common? How do they diverge in their thinking? Is it possible to defend the view that all these figures refer to the same God and simply use different names?

SENTENCE OUTLINE: See p. 118 of this manual.

BIBLIOGRAPHY: See p. 139 of this manual.

ST. TERESA OF AVILA

The Raptures of St. Teresa (pp. 629–39)

St. Teresa is a fascinating person. I say that partly because it is certainly true, but partly because in her writings she manages to express a substantial sense of her personality. She speaks very directly and with fervor. Richard Ellmann once said that he thought William Butler Yeats's poems seemed as if they were all written for an emergency. To an extent, I think the same can be said for the writings of Teresa. She brings an intensity and seriousness of purpose to all her writings—similar to some of the mystical writings of Yeats.

Teresa's *Life* is generally available in libraries and perhaps in some large bookstores. You may wish to recommend it to some of your students, especially those who find this passage intriguing. *The Interior Castle* is widely available in two translations and is worth reading in preparation to discuss her work. Both these books are mystical in nature, and both center on the meditative, prayerful life. Fortunately, both are well translated and quite direct in their language.

One marvelous quality of the selection in this book is its pertinence to the next piece, Nietzsche's discussion of the Apollonian and the Dionysian. It may be unfair to compare Teresa with the Dionysian, but it is not unfair to point to the ecstatic qualities that she shares with the Dionysian world view as Nietzsche describes it. There is a strong rational streak to Teresa's writing. She is aware that people think it odd that she has visions: she thinks it odd herself. She is capable of being logical and controlled in her thinking, but she also values her visions for what they are. She constantly complains that no one who has not had them could possibly understand them. And she wishes the visions on those who remain critical and unbelieving.

Another wonderful connection is with the *Bhagavad Gītā* because it places the human figure in direct contact with the divine. The important differences are that the dialogue with Lord Krishna in the *Bhagavad Gītā* is quite one-sided and is intensely verbal. Teresa's experiences are intensely nonverbal. They center on sensory experience—touch, sight, and sound. However, in both cases, the humanity of the two divine spirits is central to the experience. Teresa's language centers on sensory memory and does not shrink from the significance of the experience.

The modern Freudian will see in the selection repressed sexuality. The arrow will be interpreted as phallic, and the pain and groans will be perceived as sexual in nature. The experience seems to be a clearly sexual union. This may seem a bit strange to many of your students. However, you may remind them of the religious orgies Herodotus alludes to and mention to them that the carvings on Hindu temples are often frankly sexual. In other words, the sexual experience is a common religious metaphor for communion with the divine. The intensely frank approach to the beauty of the heavenly bodies she sees may seem contradictory to some students, especially those who inherit a puritanical view of religion. But in the chapter preceding this excerpt in her *Life* Teresa, speaking directly to her confessor, says, "I will only say that, if there were nothing else in Heaven to delight the eyes but the extreme beauty of the glorified bodies there, that alone would be the greatest bliss. A most especial bliss, then, will it be to us when we see the Humanity of Jesus Christ. . . . Although this vision is imaginary, I never saw it, or any other vision, with the eyes of the body, but only with the eyes of the soul." St. Teresa is claimed by the Counter-Reformation as a powerful figure, and her fleshly testimony counters the sensory muffling of the Protestant Reformation. Recognizing the sexual nature of her visions is unavoidable, but one ought also to remind readers that Teresa was a virgin despite her powerful emotional understanding.

You may wish to read portions of Richard Crashaw's poem on St. Teresa, "The Flaming Heart," available in Volume 1 of the *Norton Anthology of English Literature*. He wrote two poems about Teresa while he was in Rome. He read the *Life* and was moved by it. He may also have seen Bernini's drawings for his famous sculpture of the ecstasy of St. Teresa in Santa Maria della Vittoria in Rome. It was unveiled shortly after Crashaw died, but he could have seen it in Bernini's workshop.

SUGGESTIONS FOR CLASS DISCUSSION

1. I think one of the most interesting ways to open class discussion may be with an exploration of your students' attitudes toward the kind of visions Teresa describes. Some students will be absolutely rock-hard skeptical, while others will be more open to the possibility of responding to the visions as genuine psychic events.
2. Most students who credit the visions will insist that they are psychological events that have nothing to do with genuine religion. Yet it should be pointed out to them that in most religions visions are a staple ingredient. If your students believe the visions are merely psychological, ask

them how they know this to be true. What is their evidence? If you are interested, you might even press them to explain how they know the visions were not "real" encounters with angels.

3. You will certainly get students anxious to talk about encounters with aliens. If so, I suggest you let them discuss the subject. However, I recommend that you also point out that in an age like ours, dominated with science and technology, such visions seem widespread, whereas in Teresa's age, dominated by religion, visitations with angels were the "norm." You then might ask whether the dominating ideas of the age might affect people's "visions."

SUGGESTIONS FOR BRIEF ESSAYS

1. Teresa says there is nothing we can do about visions. We cannot call them up or banish them. Is she correct? Judging from your experience and what you know about people who have had visions, is it true that the individual has no control over them?

2. Teresa talks a great deal about her experiences, but she records very little of the words of the figures in her visions. Judging from what she does say, what do you suppose is imparted by the figures she sees? What do they wish her to do? What do they tell her that is important? What does she learn about divinity and the meaning of faith?

3. What is the value of Teresa's revelation about her visions for the modern reader? Why would this be a useful book for modern people to know about? How can moderns make use of the ideas she presents us?

4. Is Teresa writing primarily for women? Should she be regarded as a feminist heroine, a feminist role-model, or a feminist liberator? Do you find that her description of her experiences is liberating and empowering? What makes Teresa a strong and interesting figure?

SUGGESTIONS FOR LONGER ESSAYS

1. Some commentators have suggested that Teresa's writing is rudimentary and not very skillful. Others have suggested that she is a gifted stylist and that she is writing for a dual audience—her male confessors and her female sister nuns. Take a stand on this issue. Analyze her writing in such a way as to settle the question.

2. Would the experiences of St. Teresa tend to reinforce a person's religious faith, or would they tend to undermine them? Does the answer to this question depend on whether that person were born in the sixteenth century or in this century? That is, does the general spirit of the age condition the effect of reading about Teresa's experiences? Or is it true that the era has nothing whatever to do with the question of faith?

3. Read more selections from Teresa's *The Book of Her Life* (which is sometimes translated as *The Life of Teresa of Jesus* or *The Autobiography of St. Teresa*). Be sure not to mix her up with another Carmelite, the modern St. Thérèse of Lisieux. What, for you, are the most moving aspects of her religious life? How would you evaluate the nature of her faith? Is she bothered by doubts? Does she harbor ill feelings toward others? Is her life primarily a moral life, or is it a life centered on contemplation? What is her idea of perfection, and how does it compare with that of Krishna or Buddha?

SENTENCE OUTLINE: See p. 119 of this manual.

BIBLIOGRAPHY: See p. 147 of this manual.

FRIEDRICH NIETZSCHE

Apollonianism and Dionysianism (pp. 641–59)

I have found this a difficult essay to teach because the students usually find the substance of what Nietzsche says rather obscure. In some instances I have had to take charge in explaining what is going on in the essay. But in some classes I have also discovered that I really have to explain very little and just clarify what the two principal terms mean—and then the essay falls right into place. Your experience may prove different. Let's face it, it will prove different, but it's hard to tell how in advance. The point I want to make is that you should be prepared to go over the main distinctions between Apollonianism and Dionysianism very carefully.

Once you've done that there are some good lines of discussion to follow. I find the fact that some of the passage is very hard to understand—and therefore Dionysian in character—terrific, and I try to make good use of that point. Then I explore how each of us can see the traits Nietzsche describes at work within ourselves. That makes talking about this passage a lot easier than it might otherwise be.

Nietzsche was particularly moved by Wagner's *Ring of the Nibelung* (finished in 1874) because he found that it invoked his passions as well as his rational faculties. The *Ring* is itself a tragedy, although not based on a Greek model, on the subject of the death of the old gods. Remember that Nietzsche was the one who announced that "God is dead." Wagner's vision of a secular succession in the heroic fearlessness of Siegfried deeply moved him and led him to consider the nature of the human psyche by beginning with music—the concept of harmony and orderliness as expressed by the god Apollo. The darker forces of disorder and passion were, naturally, right at hand and easy enough to represent in the guise of Dionysus. This is an elegant and enduring distinction that makes sense to most students.

SUGGESTIONS FOR CLASS DISCUSSION

1. One point most students want to talk about is the extent to which these distinctions are visible in college students. By this point in the course, most will have witnessed or at least heard about the collegiate beer bacchanals that devastate many campuses. Talking about the Apollonian and Dionysian in their peers is generally a good way to begin clarifying the distinction.

2. Another interesting line of discussion concerns the style of religious observances. Some are very Apollonian, and others are very Dionysian. Ask students to describe experiences with either form of worship, either personal or observed.

3. An appeal to each individual to spot the duality of behavior in himself or herself is also effective. Most of us will sense such a duality within ourselves. You may be surprised at some of the examples you will hear in this kind of discussion.

4. A discussion of mob behavior and peer pressure will be of some use here too. But you may find that the Dionysian is more relevant to certain forms of mob behavior than it is to others. Moreover, peer pressure is distinct from the Dionysian impulse.

SUGGESTIONS FOR BRIEF ESSAYS

1. Nietzsche calls Apollo and Dionysus "art-sponsoring deities" (para. 1). What are art-sponsoring deities, and how do these two gods rate such a definition? What is the relationship between art and the faith of religious practitioners? What arts might be sponsored by the deities mentioned in this part of the book?

2. What other forms of behavior do you find operating in the human mind distinct from the two Nietzsche identifies?

3. What antecedent conditions bring out the Apollonian or Dionysian in you?

SUGGESTIONS FOR LONGER ESSAYS

1. Establish what Nietzsche means by "the original oneness of nature" in paragraph 8. With what does he contrast it? Is it possible to understand how Nietzsche values this original oneness? Should we value it? What problems does it pose for us? What promise does it hold? Consult paragraph 14 as well as paragraph 8 in answering these questions.

2. Read a Greek tragedy such as Euripides' *Iphigenia in Aulis*, Aeschylus' *Agamemnon*, or Sophocles' *Oedipus Rex*. Analyze it carefully for its Apollonian and Dionysian qualities. How effective is their union? Is it apparent? How relevant are Nietzsche's observations for this analysis? Are there things you would want to point out to him if you could?

3. To what extent are the forces of Apollo and Dionysus in conflict in the average psyche? Is Nietzsche's analogy of a duality between the sexes effective? Is his concept of their periodic

reconciliations reasonable? Examine the duality with an eye to demonstrating exactly how these two forces conflict and how they agree.

4. How do Apollo and Dionysus express themselves in modern religions? Concentrate on a specific form of religious expression, and describe it in enough detail that we see how it is indebted to one of these two polarities of expression.

SENTENCE OUTLINE: See p. 120 of this manual.

BIBLIOGRAPHY: See p. 143 of this manual.

MARTIN BUBER

From *I and Thou* (pp. 661–74)

Martin Buber is among the most important modern Jewish thinkers and is distinguished by the fact that his influence on Protestant theologians has been considerable. Unfortunately, this fact along with Buber's relative inattention to the literature of the laws of Judaism has led some Jewish theologians to disregard him "for not being Jewish enough." By the same token, he has a great many advocates among Jewish philosophers and remains important for all modern religious thinkers.

More important for our purposes is his reputation for being difficult. The selection I have presented here, I am happy to say, is much clearer than some of the rest of the book. The first of the three sections is extremely poetic and sometimes very difficult for literal-minded students to pin down. The selection in the text is from the third part of the book, which explores the individual's relationship with God. One thing he says in the opening pages is, "Men have addressed their eternal You by many names. When they sang of what they had thus named, they still meant You: the first myths were hymns of praise. Then the names entered into the It-language; men felt impelled more and more to think of and to talk about their eternal You as an It. But all names of God remain hallowed—because they have been used not only to speak *of* God but also to speak *to* him" (p. 123 of Buber). Buber reveals a certain ecumenism that stays with him throughout his work.

One of the interesting aspects of the selection is that it implies a complex attitude toward faith, one that seems to move through psychology. The question of I and Thou is on one level a matter of human psychology, but on the level that Buber has in mind, it is on the level of religion. The point is that Thou is the Thou referred to when one thinks of or addresses God. Moreover, Buber assumes that one will address God. The dialogue between people and God is meant to be ongoing and continuous. Buber's attitude toward the need God may have for humanity must be understood in relation to his overview of the I-Thou relationship: God does not consider humanity an It any more than humanity can assume God is an It.

One need not read the opening section of *I and Thou* to make sense of the passage in the text. However, I do recommend that you ask your students to read the introduction to the piece carefully because I try to set up the main ideas in a fashion that is clear enough to guide them into the subtleties that Buber works with. I think this is an interesting piece for students to read because it is not dogmatic and it does not duplicate the views of other writers in this section. If anything, it offers a remarkable contrast—although it is by no means in opposition to the ideas presented in other passages.

You may want to read this piece in relation to other selections in this section, such as the Buddha or St. Teresa. Any of them will work well, and each will open up different avenues of discussion.

In my view, your first efforts ought to be directed to establishing what Buber says in each of the two parts of the selection. Then move on to the more demanding issues of what the implications of his ideas might be.

SUGGESTIONS FOR CLASS DISCUSSION

1. Discuss the concept of an equal relationship implied by the term *I-Thou*. Examine it for the significance of the empathy that each person in that dialogue would have.
2. Ask whether the idea of dependence is significant for many of your students. Some antiaddiction organizations, such as Alcoholics Anonymous, explore this idea with interesting results. If you have a student who has had experience with such organizations, you might explore the question openly.
3. Discuss the implications for faith in Buber's suggestion that God is somehow dependent on humanity or in his thought that dependence works both ways. What would mark the dialogue between God and humanity if he were right?
4. Compare Buber's concept of God with that of St. Matthew or the *Bhagavad Gītā*. How important is the concept of dialogue with God in any of the other writers? What does Buber leave out in his discussion that the others emphasize?

SUGGESTIONS FOR BRIEF ESSAYS

1. Of what value is the individual as an "actual person" (para. 24) in Buber's view? Would this selection qualify as "liberal" in the sense that it validates the individual and emphasizes the worth of the individual?
2. When Buber speaks of the Buddha, he makes reference to the Buddha's concept of perfection. See paragraph 26 and thereafter. What are we to understand by the concept of perfection in that context, and how much weight does Buber place on it? How seriously is he concerned with perfection?
3. What aspects of Buber's teaching do you have most difficulty with? Explain your views and why you have problems with the ideas he presents. Be as specific as possible, but also rely on your own experience and your understanding of the concepts that make Buber's ideas problematic.
4. What does the concept of redemption seem to mean in Buber's thinking? See paragraph 29. How do you understand it? How does Buber's thinking help us achieve redemption?

SUGGESTIONS FOR LONGER ESSAYS

1. Examine Buber's theory that individuals actualize themselves in relation to other individuals. What evidence do you have from your own experience that would bolster this view? How does dialogue with others achieve the actualization that Buber values so highly? Have you evidence that the individual does not need the interaction with others in order to achieve actualization?
2. Buber tells us that the goal for the Buddha was "the annulment of suffering" (para. 28). How are we to understand this idea? Explain what it means in Buber's context, and then go on to question Buber's own views about suffering. What concern does he seem to have with the idea of suffering? Does the selection you read from the Buddha support Buber's interpretation of his attitude toward suffering? What would you like to see Buber address in relation to suffering?
3. Examine the selection from the Koran in comparison with Buber's work. Would the term *believer* be applicable to Buber? Would those who follow Buber be rightly called believers? How different is the faith implied by the positions held in each selection? Comment on the nature of the dialogue that God has with Muhammad, who is often referred to as *You* in the text. Would Muhammad be likely to agree with Buber's attitude toward the nature of God?

SENTENCE OUTLINE: See p. 121 of this manual.
BIBLIOGRAPHY: See p. 132 of this manual.

PART EIGHT

POETICS

The five selections in Part Eight discuss poetry and interpretation. Aristotle discusses the elements of tragedy in a form that emphasizes the concept of mimesis. His analysis underlies much, if not all, of what we do in contemporary commentary on texts. Alexander Pope, a neoclassicist, makes concrete suggestions for ways in which critics might achieve more and behave better. His advice is still useful. William Wordsworth, a romantic poet, justifies his practice in his and Coleridge's *Lyrical Ballads*. He essentially defines poetry in English for his time. Virginia Woolf's essay is a bit more relaxing and offers a change of pace. She is chatty, personal, and approachable. Susan Sontag's famous essay, while challenging, says something that students don't mind hearing. And it gives us a chance to get a little workout in the mines of criticism. As far as introducing students to good thinking, these essays are quite useful.

ARISTOTLE

Tragedy and the Emotions of Pity and Fear (pp. 681–96)

The *Poetics* is so fundamental to the history of criticism that it needs to be discussed and understood by every student. Yet it is also obvious that the document is very subtle and will be understood imperfectly by all of us. I think that is something of a given, and we ought not be discouraged by the natural limitations of young people in the face of this excerpt. I've tried to choose a segment that is intelligible and complete in itself, but as you know, there is much omitted, and you may wish to consult a complete text and introduce some of your own favorite concepts.

For example, I don't have time to explore the concept of mimesis adequately in the introduction, but it's important. You may wish to do so on your own. I am interested in the current views of Derrida and De Man regarding the deconstructivist attitude toward language, as derived from an analysis of Saussure—namely, that language is necessary to create aspects of what it treats. As Robert Scholes puts it, they tend to deny any objective world that seems to exist without language. Scholes's discussion in *Textual Power* (Yale University Press, 1985, chaps. 5 and 6, "The Text and the World" and "Reference and Difference") is worth taking a look at.

Nonetheless, even if you are not interested in these issues, the concept of mimesis is important at least to introduce to your students. The concepts of peripety and recognition should also be mentioned early in your discussions so that students will have a chance to use them in relationship to their examination of literature.

I like to rely on what is at hand when using this essay, so I often either suggest that students observe a television drama closely for the use of peripety and recognition or ask them to recall such moments in recently observed television dramas. I am interested in having them see that the people who write for television have also been careful readers of Aristotle—something obvious to us but not to our students.

The question of whether tragedy needs a noble character for its principles to work in our time is always interesting, and it is natural to combine this with a discussion of *Death of a Salesman*, even if your students have not read or seen it. This gives us a chance to talk about the way the assumptions of a given society will shape that society's attitude toward its literature. We are not aristocratic in our outlook, and therefore the concepts that Aristotle expresses have to be understood in a somewhat different way from that in which he intended them.

I also make good use of the categorical approach to discussion in this essay. I think that students can learn a good deal from practicing this approach, since it offers two important things—a built-in structure and a forcible clarification of thought. The categorical approach is not self-evident to beginning writers, but my approach in using it as a method of organization has been encouraging (at least to me) because I see that students can catch on to it quickly. Of course, along with the categorical approach goes the technique of definition—always a useful exercise for beginning writers.

SUGGESTIONS FOR CLASS DISCUSSION

1. What does Aristotle reveal about his society in this passage? What does he reveal about the importance of art and drama to the society?
2. Aristotle places great emphasis on probability and necessity (paras. 21–22). Why are these important considerations in drama?
3. Do you feel this is a finished essay for a general public? Or is it, as some have speculated, a lecture for an academic audience?
4. In paragraph 18 Aristotle says that a poet is still a poet even if he describes events that actually happened. What does he mean by this?

SUGGESTIONS FOR BRIEF ESSAYS

1. Do you agree with what Aristotle says in paragraph 13: "Beauty depends on size and order; hence neither can a very tiny creature turn out to be beautiful (since our perception of it grows blurred as it approaches the period of imperceptibility) nor an excessively huge one (for then it cannot all be perceived at once and so its unity and wholeness are lost)."
2. One of the key statements Aristotle makes in his discussion is in paragraph 12: "Tragedy is an imitation of an action which is complete and whole and has some magnitude." Examine this statement in detail, clarifying each key term and explaining it as if to a person who has not read the essay. The key terms that need definition are "imitation of an action," "complete," "whole," and "magnitude." Do you agree with the statement? Do you see that the principles of the statement are applied by those who write tragic dramas?
3. In paragraph 15 Aristotle says that "an element whose addition or subtraction [from a drama] makes no perceptible extra difference is not really a part of the whole." What does he mean by this, and is he correct? Can you think of moments in dramas you have seen or read that could have been omitted without losing the sense of the drama? Are any of them dispensable entirely? How does Aristotle's view qualify his sense of what the whole is?

SUGGESTIONS FOR LONGER ESSAYS

1. Judging by what Aristotle says of historians and poets, is it possible to write poetically about history? What exactly would that mean in Aristotelian terms? Consider any history plays you may have read, such as *Julius Caesar*. What is it that makes them poetical? What must the poet do in order not to remain simply an historian? What is the poet's obligation to the truth of events? Aristotle comments on Homer's *Odyssey*. If you have read it, consider it as an historical epic. Is Homer primarily an historian, or is he primarily a poet?
2. Consider the two forms of plot that Aristotle mentions, simple and complex, in paragraph 21. Establish your definition of each, and find an example from literature of each plot. Which do you feel is more successful as a work of literature? Do you think its success is due to its simple or complex plot? Which would Aristotle have preferred?
3. In paragraph 24 Aristotle mentions three key elements of tragedy—peripety, recognition, and pathos. He never gets the chance to develop pathos but describes it as actions related to pain, wounding, death, and "all that sort of thing." *Pathos* generally refers to our emotional responses, our reaction to the pain of others. Write an essay that continues the discussion, establishing the nature of pathos, how it functions, and what forms it takes in any literature of your choice. What is its importance? Why is it so significant that it comes third in Aristotle's categories?

SENTENCE OUTLINE: See p. 123 of this manual.
BIBLIOGRAPHY: See p. 129 of this manual.

ALEXANDER POPE

From *An Essay on Criticism* (pp. 699–712)

The selection omits only the last stanza of Book II. I mention that because I try to avoid extensive ellipses or unnatural breaks in these selections primarily because such cuts annoy me and usually do disservice to the piece itself. As it is, Book II stands alone very well and offers some good insights into poetry. The interesting thing about this selection is that it is poetry talking about poetry. Other selections in the book are set up in verse, such as the *Bhagavad Gītā*, but because it is in translation, the sense of the poetic is lost. I regard the version included in this book as essentially prose set up to look like poetry. But with Pope, the form is definitely poetry.

You might spend a little time talking about your students' reaction to the *Essay on Criticism* as poetry. One of its virtues is its couplet rhyme. With the current mood toward poetry—I'm thinking of poetry slams and rap artists—rhyme and rhythm define poetry in the minds of most people who do not study it. Pope's rhyme is strong, and his rhythm is steady.

One thing that would help your students would be to explain the basic form of iambic pentameter and have some of the lines read out loud with a special effort to find the iambic stresses. This will help students grasp the concept of the "numbers" that Pope talks about.

I strongly recommend that you give your students plenty of opportunity to talk about the general message Pope offers regarding criticism. One of his injunctions, against evaluating the part rather than the whole, will be pertinent to our own practices regarding the evaluation of our students' essays. If some students raise the issue of nit-picking in corrections, you might remind them that the grade or comments you offer reflect the paper's overall success, while the detailed criticism gives students a chance to improve and learn the basics.

While commenting on the critics and their criticism, you might try to move your students toward considering what Pope recommends regarding good practices in poetry. He offers us a model in his own work. Pope would recommend rhymed iambic pentameter couplets, which are very supple in his hands, but couplets are especially useful for poems that have a message or a didactic purpose, such as *An Essay on Criticism*. Pope recommends a very direct language, and a close examination of lines 105 to 136 would be useful for discussing writing of any kind.

SUGGESTIONS FOR CLASS DISCUSSION

1. You might begin with considering one of Aristotle's concerns—the relation of form to sense. Aristotle is less concerned with form than sense and points out that in poetry you can't have one without the other. However, it is worthwhile to look at the pleasures that your students derive from the form of their favorite couplets and the messages those couplets contain. Discuss the way in which the couplets add pleasure to the message of the poem.
2. The opening stanza treats the subject of pride, but it also treats the subject of knowing oneself. Discuss the role of pride in criticism. Discuss also the couplet in lines 13 and 14.
3. Some students feel they have problems with any poetry. Ask them if they find this poetry gives them problems, and if it does, explore what they are and why your students have problems.

SUGGESTIONS FOR BRIEF ESSAYS

1. In line 115, Pope discusses "true Expression." What is true expression, and why does it do what Pope says it does?
2. Pope says in line 165 that in poetry, "The sound must seem an Echo to the sense." Is this important advice for a poet? Which lines in this poem best carry out Pope's advice?
3. Is the advice to "Avoid Extremes" (l. 184) generally good for people to follow? Pope suggests that advice for critics, but is it applicable in general? Why would Pope give this advice, and why would anyone feel it is generally useful for people?

SUGGESTIONS FOR LONGER ESSAYS

1. In line 215 Pope refers to "Quality," by which he means aristocracy. The next ten lines talk about the fact that some poems would be ignored by a critic if the critic thought they were written by someone ordinary, like Pope himself. But if the critic thought they were written by a lord or lady, then they would suddenly be "exalted stanzas." Is there a sense in which a similar pattern of behavior works in modern criticism? If so, describe it, and comment on its nature. You may consider film criticism or pop music criticism for this project.

2. Offer your own advice to critics. If possible, use a metrical line of ten syllables, and if you wish, use rhyme.

3. Write your own "Essay on Poetry." You need not use rhyme and meter, but discuss the main issues of poetry and how they should be managed. Discuss the question of conceit (use of metaphor and simile), language, "numbers" (rhythm and metrical effects), and the thought that the poem maintains. What are your recommendations concerning each of these? If possible, include samples that illustrate your point.

SENTENCE OUTLINE: See p. 125 of this manual.

BIBLIOGRAPHY: See p. 144 of this manual.

WILLIAM WORDSWORTH

From the preface to *Lyrical Ballads* (pp. 715–28)

Lyrical Ballads was published anonymously by an essentially unknown (in London) press in Bristol, not far from the place where Dorothy and William Wordsworth took their walks. Consequently, it received relatively little notice from the established critics of the day. Those who did notice it hardly knew what to make of it. Consequently, the Preface, which was made possible by the fact that the first edition sold out in two years, takes great pains to explain what the volume tried to do. This selection from the Preface is careful to take the main points and omits primarily some pages discussing individual poets and their work in contrast with what Wordsworth was doing. Wordsworth gives very little by way of specific reference to his own poems or to those of Coleridge. For that reason, it is a useful general document focusing primarily on the practice of poetry as Wordsworth understood it at the dawn of the romantic period.

Defining romanticism has always been a challenge. An interest in the role of feeling in verse, concern for the common person, a growing sense of democracy, response to the supernatural, and an uncluttered style that avoids extensive reference to Roman or Greek learning are some of its hallmarks. Wordsworth points out that the lowness of the subject matter—in contrast with Aristotle's concerns for the aristocracy in Greek drama—may surprise his readers, and then he goes on to defend his choices on the grounds that ordinary people deeply feel their experiences. The term *ballad* is used loosely by Wordsworth. The poems in *Lyrical Ballads* are often monologues spoken to the reader, and they are also often narrative, in the sense that ballads tell a story. Few of the poems could be considered authentic ballads.

One useful procedure in class would be to photocopy one or two poems from *Lyrical Ballads* and have them read in class. A few poems from *Lyrical Ballads* appear in the *Norton Anthology of English Literature*, Volume 2. "Lines Written in Early Spring" and "We are Seven" are especially useful for such a purpose. Hear what your students have to say about the nature of the language and the feelings expressed in the poems.

SUGGESTIONS FOR CLASS DISCUSSION

1. One interesting way to begin is to ask your students how Wordsworth might have responded to rap poetry. Rap poetry is urban, rather than rustic, but it could be said to satisfy some of Wordsworth's requirements for poetry with a purpose. You may get an interesting discussion

that either praises rap or criticizes it as doggerel (although your students are not likely to know this term).

2. If you give your students copies of poems from *Lyrical Ballads*, another interesting point of discussion could involve a comparison with Pope's poetic style. You may also want to compare Pope's advice concerning poetry with Wordsworth's. The distinctions may not seem as extreme as the differences in style.

3. It is worth developing a study of the role of poetry in the life of your students. Most of what they experience as poetry is in song lyrics, some of which outwardly fit the description of the poems in *Lyrical Ballads*, in that they tell a story of the common person in a language that is simple and direct.

SUGGESTIONS FOR BRIEF ESSAYS

1. Explain what Wordsworth means when he says, "Another circumstance must be mentioned which distinguishes these Poems from the popular Poetry of the day; it is this, that the feeling therein developed gives importance to the action and situation, and not the action and situation to the feeling" (para. 3). You may wish to refer to one of Wordsworth's poems to develop this essay.

2. Offer a critical discussion of the poem Wordsworth quotes from Thomas Gray. If possible, keep in mind the injunctions that Alexander Pope offers the critic of poetry. Examine the poem for its subject, its use of devices such as metaphor, its language, and its "numbers" or metrical qualities. Is it a successful poem in your estimation?

3. Which is preferable to you—poetry that rhymes or poetry that does not rhyme? Defend your view with reference to the work of Wordsworth and if possible to the examples found in *Lyrical Ballads*.

SUGGESTIONS FOR LONGER ESSAYS

1. Would today's country and western song lyrics be comparable to Wordsworth's "humble and rustic" life (para. 1)? Are those lyrics poetry in the sense that Wordsworth describes? Do they seem to arise from a "spontaneous overflow of powerful feelings" (para. 15)? Would Wordsworth approve of them? What might he have said on listening to them? Choose a number of country and western lyrics and refer to them specifically in constructing your essay.

2. Who among the poets you respect would Wordsworth especially like? What would he find admirable in your poet's work? What do you find admirable in the work? Do you have any sense that your poet may have been an admirer of Wordsworth? Would your poet agree with most of Wordsworth's claims, such as poetry being the "spontaneous overflow of powerful feelings" (para. 15)?

3. Wordsworth talks about his age's craving for "extraordinary incident" in literature (para. 4). What does your age crave for in literature? What do contemporary readers want to find in literature? If possible, restrict yourself to poetry in dealing with this issue. Is contemporary literature weakened by a craving for the sensational in literature? If so, why? What are the problems that Wordsworth reacted to? Do you find yourself in agreement with him?

SENTENCE OUTLINE: See p. 126 of this manual.

BIBLIOGRAPHY: See p. 148 of this manual.

VIRGINIA WOOLF

A Letter to a Young Poet (pp. 731–49)

Because it is a letter, this selection is not especially difficult for students to respond to, although because it is about poetry, it may seem at first somewhat intimidating. My introduction is intended to clarify the progression of the primary ideas in the essay and should act as a reasonable guide to what Woolf is doing. The poems Woolf cites are not especially exciting, and the fact that most students simply cannot respond warmly to them is actually to their advantage, since Woolf does not respond to them either. As she says, after her analysis in paragraph 9: "Poetry, though still breathing—witness these little books— is drawing her breath in short, sharp gasps."

One of your first strategies in class might be to examine what Woolf recommends, mainly a move away from the self-reflexive poetry that she seems to see about her, and a move toward including life at large—other people, other things, other experiences. She uses Shakespeare as a model, and in many ways her advice is ironically opposite to what she does in her best novels, which are inner-directed and which use stream of consciousness. Yet she sees in her novels the strategies that were used by earlier narrative and dramatic poets. Creating character, a topic she refers to frequently, is of great importance to her in her ideas about what the poet ought to be doing.

One useful approach, once the general message of the essay has been opened up for discussion, is to photocopy three samples from contemporary poetry. I hesitate to suggest anything specific for obvious reasons, but I like to take samples from recent student poetry publications because they are close to the students in my class and because they are therefore more like what they might themselves produce were they to write poetry. This is, after all, what Woolf does when she goes to the slim volumes in front of her: they represent the kind of achievement her poet aspires to. Discussing these samples in light of Woolf's concerns can be enlightening. You might even ask your students to bring in samples and use them for your discussion.

The writing assignments here include letters and poems. I find them both useful. Many students are interested in writing poems, and I often get some good and interesting work. But I also like to have students write commentaries on what they did as they composed their poems or what their processes and final reactions were. It makes them conscious of the act of writing and thereby connects their poetry to Woolf's essay.

Properly handled, this essay and the writing assignments can be a happy way to end a discussion of the poetic impulse.

SUGGESTIONS FOR CLASS DISCUSSION

1. What is the effect on the general reader of referring to such a large number of important older poets, such as Crabbe, Shelley, and Tennyson? Should Woolf refrain from such references?
2. Choose a single passage in the letter that you think is most feelingly written. What kinds of emotions does it seem to express? How well written is the passage? What are its best moments?
3. Woolf imagines an adversary whom she names Peabody. Why does she do this? Is it an effective rhetorical technique?
4. Woolf seems to have received a letter from this poet because she was a famous writer. What evidence in her letter reveals that she is a famous writer? If you did not know something about her achievement, would you have known she was one of the best regarded writers of her generation?
5. Do Woolf and her correspondent seem to feel that poetry is important? Why? Do you?

SUGGESTIONS FOR BRIEF ESSAYS

1. In paragraphs 13 and 14 Virginia Woolf implores the young poet not to publish until he is thirty. Is this generally good advice? If so, why? If not, why not? If you were an aspiring writer, would you be able to follow her advice on this count?
2. In paragraph 14 Woolf condemns the effect of fame on the writer. She points out that Shakespeare and Donne, to name only two, were writers who did not care about fame. That point is, of course, debatable, but the message is clear. Fame is a kind of blight on the soul of the writer. Is this true? You may wish to refer to the effects of fame on other kinds of artists in order to respond to this point.
3. What does Woolf mean by the comment she makes in paragraph 10: "Clearly therefore you have it in you to deal with a vast variety of subjects; it is only a temporary necessity that has

shut you up in one room, alone, by yourself"? Explain what she means and what her advice, if taken, might achieve for the poet.

SUGGESTIONS FOR LONGER ESSAYS

1. Find someone with whom to work. Write a letter to your colleague requesting advice about one of the arts that interests you most. Have your colleague do the same for you. Then, when you have received your colleague's letter and when your colleague has also received your letter, respond as fully as possible. Both of you should hand in all your letters as your assignment.

2. Compare Virginia Woolf's letter with that of Martin Luther King, Jr. Consider their respective audiences and the demands made on a letter when it is addressed to more than one person, as King's is, or when it is addressed to only one, while also being aware that an audience, such as a class of college students, may one day read it, as is the case with Woolf's letter. Compare the qualities of the writing, the effort each puts into the act of persuading the intended audience, the levels of allusion, and the expectations of the advice being taken. You need not decide which is the better letter: they are too different in intention to be evaluated in that fashion. Rather, attempt to qualify their nature and establish their respective achievement as letters.

3. Write a letter to Virginia Woolf asking her advice on writing poetry. Try to imagine that you are addressing her in much the same way this young poet addressed her, but do not worry about trying to recreate his letter. Rather, include your own interests and concerns about the state of poetry today and your position as an aspiring poet.

SENTENCE OUTLINE: See p. 127 of this manual.

BIBLIOGRAPHY: See p. 148 of this manual.

SUSAN SONTAG

Against Interpretation (pp. 751–67)

This is a stimulating essay, particularly for those of your students who are studying English or art history. The question of interpretation in both those fields differs, but the fields are coming closer together. Most students like the idea of an essay that attacks interpretation if only because the act of interpretation is so difficult that it is naturally unpopular. But there is also that group of students and teachers who feel that interpretation is a destructive act in that it ruins one's responses to works of art. My feeling is that it definitely changes one's responses but rarely ruins them. The impression of their being ruined results from the resistance to having ideas and feelings changed in the course of interpretation.

On the one hand, the essay should appeal to students who resist critical analysis and interpretation. On the other hand, it appeals to us who practice such interpretation professionally if only because it is important for us continually to examine the premises of our profession. Sontag's argument is carefully couched, and her conclusions may not be those that you would reach. Personally, I find her ideas useful, and they reinforce some of my own theories (see *The Humanities Through the Arts*, F. David Martin and Lee A. Jacobus, McGraw-Hill, 1997; and *Humanities: The Evolution of Values*, Lee A. Jacobus, McGraw-Hill, 1986). But one thing I argue is that Sontag seems to rely too heavily on a dichotomous attitude toward the arts. She dichotomizes form and content while saying, as we mostly do, that they are not separable. But that also applies to interpretation and description (which I see as part of her "erotics of art"—perhaps more aptly termed a loving description). If form and content cannot be separated, then it seems to me that interpretation and description, hermeneutic and erotics, cannot be separated, and yet she seems to want to do that very thing.

One of the best ways to get some of these points across is to bring some examples into class and begin their study. For example, I use some slides. One I really like is Paul Delaroche's *Execution of Lady Jane Gray* from the National Gallery, London. It is rich with content, but it also has some interesting formal

74

aspects. Delaroche is the man who said, in 1839 after seeing the first formal demonstration of Daguerre's photographic process, that now painting is dead. He was wrong, but it is interesting, when looking at his work (which is itself photographic), to see why he said that. The pop art examples always arouse interest, particularly Andy Warhol's Campbell's soup cans and Jasper Johns's sculpture of two ale cans. But you can do this just as well by using examples from literature. I sometimes contrast two poems—one whose content is readily apparent, the other whose form is readily apparent. For the first, Shakespeare's Sonnet 73, "That time of year thou mays't in me behold," is useful because it needs a bit of interpretation to clarify what is being said. Then I like to use E. E. Cummings's "1(a" from *95 Poems* because it is, like a shaped poem, clarified only through an understanding of its form. It is a visual form, however, and not a literary one, so I also like to use Dylan Thomas's "Do not go gentle into that good night" because it is a villanelle, and its formal qualities are less visually obvious.

So while this is a difficult essay for average students, it is more in the mainstream of the interest of the average instructor, and therefore it is a stimulating essay to use with your students. Naturally, you will want to refer to both Plato and Aristotle and maybe even to Freud and Marx.

One very important delight of this essay is the fact that Susan Sontag refers to a number of important thinkers whose essays your students either may have already read or can read. I find it very rewarding at the end of the book to see how many students respond to the fact that they now know something about the major thinkers who often appear in contemporary writings.

SUGGESTIONS FOR CLASS DISCUSSION

1. Is it true that "interpretation takes the sensory experience of the work of art for granted" (para. 39)?
2. In which poems do you find the sensory experience most intense? Why?
3. Do you feel that Susan Sontag's definition of interpretation is accurate? Does interpretation come between you and the work of art? Must it?
4. Discuss the idea that interpretation is sometimes good and sometimes bad, depending on the age or the era.

SUGGESTIONS FOR BRIEF ESSAYS

1. Offer your own definition of *interpretation*.
2. Sontag says in paragraph 39 that "ours is a culture based on excess on overproduction; the result is a steady loss of sharpness in our sensory experience." To what extent is this true? Use your experience in the arts, music, painting, literature, drama, or any other artistic media to examine the validity of this statement.
3. Sontag says that some art is "a flight from interpretation" (para. 27). What works of art do you know that are especially resistant to interpretation? Do you think they are that way intentionally, or is it just an odd quirk?

SUGGESTIONS FOR LONGER ESSAYS

1. Is it true that real art has the capacity to make us nervous? Refer to a work of art that you can defend as being "real art," and examine it for its capacity to make us nervous. What does it mean for a work of art to make people nervous? If you need to refer to a secondary source, consider the effect of Marcel Duchamp's *Nude Descending a Staircase*, which was the cause of a sensation and scandal at the 1913 Armory Show of modern art in New York City. You might also refer to Pablo Picasso's *Guernica*, which was shown at the International Exposition in Paris in 1937, and ask the same questions of it.
2. In a way, Sontag's request that we create an erotics of art implies that we pay close attention to the facts of art. However, Nietzsche says, as she tells us, that there are no facts, only interpretations. This is a far-ranging philosophical statement because it implies that we know things only in terms of our interpretation of them. Some important linguists agree with Nietzsche and say that we know things only through the language we use to interpret them with. How is it possible

to reconcile the two views? Write an essay that explores these issues. Define the kind of facts that pertain to the arts, and examine the extent to which they are perceived in terms of an interpretive approach or an interpretive attitude. Does interpretation color the facts? Would it be possible for a human being not to use interpretation? Would it be possible to have the kind of erotics of art that Sontag desires?

SENTENCE OUTLINE: See p. 128 of this manual.

BIBLIOGRAPHY: See p. 146 of this manual.

SENTENCE OUTLINES

The following sentence outlines are arranged
in the order in which the selections appear in the text.

LAO-TZU

Thoughts from the *Tao-te Ching* (pp. 17–31)

Verse 3: The Master leads not by seeking power and control but by refraining from action and letting events unfold on their own.

17: The Master rules quietly, drawing no attention to himself; when he accomplishes something, the people believe that they themselves accomplished it.

18: When there is disorder and evil, order and goodness appear.

19: If you refrain from imposing artificial categories, good will appear naturally; let all things take their own course.

26: The Master should be steady, serenely content within herself.

29: The world is sacred and cannot be improved; there is a proper time for all things. Recognizing this, the Master remains still and does not try to control events.

30: The wise ruler does not use force; doing so only produces a counterforce. Understanding that the universe is beyond his control, he submits to the Tao and lives content within himself.

31: Peace is the greatest good. The decent man resorts to violence only as a last resort, and he does so with great sorrow and with compassion for his enemies.

37: If the powerful could center themselves in the Tao, all would be transformed, and people would be content and free from desire.

38: By not acting, the Master leaves nothing undone; by acting, ordinary men leave much undone. Loss of the Tao can lead to empty ritual and chaos; therefore, the Master concerns herself with profound truths rather than illusion.

46: In harmony with the Tao, a country lives in peace rather than preparing for war. We should put aside the illusion of fear, put aside preparations to defend ourselves against enemies.

53: When the affluent prosper and the poor suffer, balance is lost. To achieve balance, stay centered within the Tao.

57: When the leader stops trying to control, the world governs itself. The more control you impose, the less order there will be.

58: In governing a country, tolerance is preferable to repression. Attempts to force the people to change will fail. Thus the Master does not try to impose his will.

59: The best leader is moderate: open-minded, tolerant, flexible.

60: The leader should govern as unobtrusively as possible. Evil will lose its power if the leader follows the Tao.

61: The greater a nation's power, the more humble it should be. A great nation acknowledges its faults and corrects them; it tends to its own affairs and does not meddle in the affairs of others.

65: The ancient Masters taught the people to not-know, for when the people understand that they do not know, they find their own way. If you wish to govern, live a simple life so that you can lead people to rediscover their own true nature.

66: Governing the people requires humility. Even though the Master is over the people, no one feels mastered by her.

67: Those who think deeply will see that my teaching is wise. I teach simplicity, patience, and compassion.

75: When government is unobtrusive, the people thrive.

80: If a country is governed wisely, the people will be content with what they have and where they live.

NICCOLÒ MACHIAVELLI

The Qualities of the Prince (pp. 33–49)

Paragraphs 1–6: A prince's sole concern and profession must be war, its institutions, and its discipline. An unarmed man is unsafe and despised among armed men. Even in peacetime a prince must keep his body and his mind in shape for war, studying terrain, strategy, and the history of successful commanders.

7–8: To hold his position, a prince must be realistic rather than idealistic; he must learn how not to be good. He should avoid the reputation of vice, except for those vices he needs to hold his state.

9–11: The prince who displays generosity (except in looting and sacking with his soldiers) will lose his wealth and the regard of his subjects. He is wiser to maintain the resources he needs to defend against enemies and be thought a miser than to become poor or known for rapacity.

12–18: A little judicious cruelty shows more compassion than excessive mercy, which permits disorder. A prince must be cautious but decisive and is safer being feared than loved. He should take lives when necessary, but he should never earn his subjects' hatred by taking their property or women, even during war.

19–22: Shrewd manipulation of men's minds is more essential than keeping promises. Men fight with laws, while beasts fight with force; but since laws often fail, a prince must be a fox to recognize traps and a lion to frighten the wolves.

23–25: The prince need not be virtuous but only *seem* to be: he should appear merciful, faithful, and full of integrity, kindness, and religion, while in fact doing whatever is necessary to hold power. He must avoid seeming changeable, frivolous, effeminate, cowardly, or irresolute.

26–28: Danger to a prince can be external (from foreign powers) or internal (from subjects conspiring against him). Good troops and friends will prevail over external threats; satisfying the people and avoiding their hatred will protect him from assassination and overthrow.

JEAN-JACQUES ROUSSEAU
The Origin of Civil Society (pp. 51–71)

Paragraphs 1–2:   What is the basis of government? This inquiry examines human beings as they are and laws as they might be and considers justice and utility as inseparable. Being a citizen and voter is enough qualification and reason to investigate the nature of public affairs.

3–7:   Man is born free, and everywhere he is in chains. The social order—and its constraints—arise from conventions and not from nature. In a family, self-preservation binds children to their father; if the bond lasts after they become self-sufficient, then the family exists by choice and convention. So too with government, where both ruler and people cede their freedom only so far as it benefits them.

8–14:   Some commentators, such as Grotius, take slavery as proof that political power is never exercised in the interest of the governed. In illogically deriving right from fact, they are in effect denying membership in the human race to most of humanity. Force, not nature, makes slaves.

15–18:   Those who take power cannot hold it forever unless they cast might as right, and obedience as duty. This is logical gibberish, however, for might is physical, not moral, and right would be invalid if it vanished whenever might changes hands. No man is under an obligation to obey any but the legitimate power of the state—legitimacy being conferred by agreement among the people.

19–23:   The argument that a people can subject themselves to a king as a slave does to a master is false—the slave surrenders his liberty for his subsistence, whereas the kind subsists off the people. To be legitimate, a government must not impose more hardship than it prevents, and it must be accepted freely by each new generation.

24–30:   The argument that a slave agrees to yield his liberty in exchange for his life implies that one man has the right to kill another in war. Wars, however, are between states, not individuals. We are justified in killing our enemies only while they fight as soldiers against us—that is, only when we cannot enslave them. Thus the alleged right to enslave is based on the alleged right to kill, and vice versa, proving that slavery has no validity.

31–43:   Conquest may turn individuals into slaves or masters, but kingship must be conferred by the people. A group comes to function as a people by virtue of a social contract enlisting the community's strength on behalf of each individual, while preserving individual freedom. Any abridgment of individual freedom cancels the contract.

44–47:   The body politic—the entity created by and comprising the individual parties to the social contract—cannot bind itself to any agreement that would violate that contract. Any attack on one of its members is an attack on the whole body, and vice versa.

48–51:   The body politic need not give a guarantee to its members, as it exists at their will and for their benefit. An individual member's private and public interests may diverge, however. The body politic is therefore entitled to compel members' compliance with the general will.

52–54:   The passage from the state of nature to the civil state substitutes justice for instinct in individual behavior, creates a moral basis for action, and gives reason priority over desire.

55–61:   With regard to property, physical strength and the right of the first-comer are replaced by the rights of ownership under the social contract. Individuals cede their property to the state, and the state legitimates their claim to it. A person's title to land is based on the land being unoccupied and on the owner taking only as much as he needs and will use.

62:   Far from destroying natural equality, the social contract substitutes for it a moral and legal equality that compensates for people's physical and intellectual differences.

THOMAS JEFFERSON

The Declaration of Independence (pp. 73–80)

Paragraphs 1–2:   When a people rejects past ties in favor of equal sovereignty, they should explain their reasons. Because all men are created equal and form governments to protect their rights, they are entitled to cast off any government that abridges their equality and rights and to replace it with a better one. Thus the thirteen United States of America cast off the king of Great Britain.

3–29:   The king has in diverse ways prevented his legislature from representing and acting in the interests of the states and has harassed and oppressed their citizens.

30–31:   The American people's petitions to the king and his subjects in Britain have been ignored, proving him unfit to be the ruler of a free people and necessitating a separation.

32:   The representatives of the United States of America therefore declare the colonies free and independent, with all the rights and powers of states, and pledge their mutual support.

HANNAH ARENDT

Ideology and Terror:
A Novel Form of Government (pp. 83–101)

Paragraph 1: Totalitarian governments use more extreme methods of domination than do other types of oppressive government.

2–4: It is possible to trace the rise of totalitarianism to events in recent history and to explain it as a form of government that borrows methods from other systems of oppression. But such explanations cannot account for the uniqueness of totalitarianism, its difference from all governmental systems that have existed throughout history.

5–6: Another way to understand totalitarianism is to say that it destroys the distinction between lawful and lawless government. Yet totalitarianism does claim to obey fundamental laws of nature and history. These laws, it asserts, have higher legitimacy than legal codes designed by human society.

7–8: Totalitarianism claims to apply the laws of nature and history directly to humanity as a whole without concern for the behavior of individuals. In so doing, totalitarianism rejects the legal consensus shared by civilized nations and separates the fulfillment of the law from any actions or choices made by individuals. Instead, totalitarianism claims to make humanity as a whole the "embodiment of the law."

9: This notion that humanity embodies the law is contrary to the more widely accepted belief that human laws are based on an eternal presence, such as nature or God, that is separate from and beyond man.

10–12: Totalitarian systems, such as those of the Nazis or the Bolsheviks, rest on the idea that history and nature move inevitably forward, regardless of human efforts—an idea drawn from the theories of Marx and Darwin. All laws thus become "laws of movement." Law is not a framework of stability in which human actions or motions can occur but the expression of motion itself—the inevitable processes of history or nature.

13–14: Totalitarian governments translate the "laws of movement" into political reality by the use of total terror. The main goal of terror is to enable the force of history or nature to move swiftly through humanity unhindered by the actions of individual people.

15–18: Terror thus eliminates the individual for the sake of the group, making all men "One Man." In constitutional governments, law promotes both individual freedom and a sense of community; in totalitarianism, the "law" of terror crushes individuality and makes freedom impossible.

19: Terror is a means of accelerating the forces of history or nature. By eliminating individual actions, terror allows historical or natural forces to move more quickly toward their inevitable end.

20–21: In free societies, laws set limits to actions, telling people what they should *not* do rather than what they should. Likewise, in totalitarian societies, terror—which replaces law—serves to limit individual action but not to guide or inspire it.

22–24: In its ideal form, totalitarian government does not need a means of inspiring action because its goal is to eliminate the capacity of men to act as individuals. But in practice, such governments must prepare people for whatever roles they will play in the process of nature or history. For this purpose, totalitarian governments adopt ideologies.

25–28: Ideologies are *-isms* (such as racism) used to explain everything on the basis of a single principle. Ideologies pretend to be scientific in approach. They also claim to explain the whole movement and meaning of history—past, present, and future—according to the logic of a single idea.

29–31: The idea in an ideology (such as race in racism) is the basis from which all conclusions are drawn. Events happen according to the logic developed from this one idea. The greatest danger of ideological thinking is that it causes people to exchange their capacity to think freely for the "strait jacket of logic." This logic is a force almost as violent as the force of an outside power.

32–34: Racism and communism are the two major ideologies used by totalitarian governments in the twentieth century. There are three totalitarian elements common to all ideological thinking: (1) such thinking claims to explain past events and present conditions and to predict the future; (2) it ignores the lessons of ordinary experience, insisting on a "truer reality" behind all perceptible things; and (3) it draws all conclusions from a single accepted premise, following a consistency that exists nowhere in reality.

35: Hitler and Stalin used this type of stringent logical consistency to transform their respective ideologies (racism and communism) into totalitarian movements.

FREDERICK DOUGLASS

From *Narrative of the Life of Frederick Douglass, an American Slave* (pp. 107–21)

Paragraphs 1–2:   My new mistress was a kind woman who had never owned slaves before. But the "dehumanizing effects of slavery" caught up with her and changed her quickly from warm and decent to harsh and unjust.

3:   Mrs. Auld started to teach me to spell, but her husband made her stop because it was illegal to teach a slave to read. Mr. Auld's explanation that learning would make a slave "unfit . . . to be a slave" made me understand that learning to read was a crucial first step toward gaining my freedom.

4:   In general, city slaveholders (such as the Aulds) treated their slaves far better than plantation slaveholders; but Mrs. Hamilton, who lived on our street, whipped her slaves mercilessly and also grossly underfed them.

5–8:   While I lived with the Aulds, I taught myself to read and write. Though my mistress was initially helpful, she soon refused to let me see the newspaper to make sure I couldn't educate myself in any way. Still, I learned to read by befriending hungry white boys; I traded them bread for reading lessons.

9–10:   When I was twelve I came across *The Columbian Orator*, a book including dialogues and speeches denouncing slavery as morally wrong and arguing for emancipation. The book gave me the language for ideas I had been previously unable to articulate, but it also gave me cause to hate my enslavers more and more. My master had been right: learning to read made me discontented, even tormented, for now I understood my oppressed condition but remained powerless to do anything about it.

11–12:   I began to hear about "abolition" and learned from the newspaper what it meant; I also learned from two dockworkers that slaves could run away to the North, where they would be free. I resolved to do so when the chance arose and, in the meantime, to teach myself to write. I did this by copying the letters I saw carpenters write at the shipyard and then telling boys who could write that I could do it too; to prove me false, they would write more than I could, so I learned the letters they wrote. I copied from Master Thomas's copybooks as well.

13–17:   When my old master died, his estate had to be divided between his children; as part of the "property," I had to return to the plantation. People and animals alike were grouped together, examined in the same callous way, assigned a particular value, and divided between Andrew and Lucretia. We were all terrified of being sent with Master Andrew, whose cruelty I witnessed firsthand when he savagely beat my little brother in front of me. In the end, I was sent back to Baltimore and the Aulds, who were as glad to see me as I was them.

18–19:   My grandmother's fate vividly illustrates the barbaric oppression of slavery and the monstrous cruelty of slaveholders. When Lucretia and Andrew both died, my grandmother, who had served my old master from his birth to his death and supplied his plantation with four generations of slaves, was left by his heirs to fend for herself in a hut in the woods where she could not possibly take care of herself alone in her ailing condition.

HENRY DAVID THOREAU

Civil Disobedience (pp. 123–48)

Paragraphs 1–2: "That government is best which governs least." Governments, like armies, are a means for the people to express their will, but also may be used by a few against the people's interests. Governments do not act, but facilitate (or impede) action by individuals and groups.

3–6: We need not immediately abolish government but should improve it. Governments rule by majority, not by justice, and thus may improperly overrule individual conscience, turning men into tools of the government. Those who follow their consciences and resist the government are treated as enemies by it.

7–15: The present American government, which supports slavery, forces men of conscience into resistance. Those who fail to oppose wrongdoing with action, but simply voice or vote their convictions, are leaving justice to chance. A real man refuses allegiance on any level to a government that pursues immoral policies.

16–19: We should not be deterred from rebelling against unjust laws, or persuaded to wait for a majority vote to change them, by our fear of causing more harm than good. A just government would prevent such harm; in its absence, we should concern ourselves with living justly and not with reforming the government.

20–24: Those in Massachusetts who believe in abolishing slavery should withdraw their support from the state, refusing to pay taxes and going willingly to prison. Money prevents the man who has it from living in accord with his convictions; anyone who needs the government's protection is reluctant to disobey its rules.

25–37: I myself, having little property, have declined to pay various taxes and was once imprisoned overnight. In jail I saw the barriers between me and my neighbors and particularly between me and the state. My perspective on my town became that of a foreign traveler, which lasted even after someone paid my tax and I was released.

38–43: Unlike natural forces, a government of men warrants resistance. Those who pay much attention to the government, however, or work within it, are paying homage to a static manifestation of human values rather than to those values themselves. The ideal government would be just to all men and would treat every individual with respect.

MARTIN LUTHER KING, JR.

Letter from Birmingham Jail (pp. 151–71)

Paragraphs 1–4: While here in jail I read your statement calling my activities "unwise and untimely" and indicating bias against "outsiders coming in." I came here at the request of our Southern Christian Leadership Conference affiliate in Birmingham. More basically, I came to carry the gospel of freedom. Injustice is here, and injustice anywhere is a threat to justice everywhere.

5–9: You deplore the demonstrations here but not the conditions that caused them. Any nonviolent campaign has four basic steps—collecting facts, negotiation, self-purification, and direct action. Our fact collecting has shown the depth and breadth of racial injustice in Birmingham. We negotiated and won promises that have been broken. We prepared for action with self-purification—a series of workshops on nonviolence. Then we planned our action.

10–11: You call for negotiations; so do we. The purpose of direct action is to dramatize the issue so that it can no longer be ignored. We are here to create the constructive, nonviolent tension necessary for growth.

12–14: You ask, Why not give the new city administration time to act? No administration here will act unless prodded: freedom will not be offered voluntarily by the oppressor but must be demanded by the oppressed. *Wait* has almost always meant *never*, and given the lynchings, beatings, poverty, cruelty, and degradation we suffer, we cannot afford to wait.

15–22: You deplore our willingness to break laws. Though we urge people to obey just laws, we have a moral responsibility to disobey any law that conflicts with the law of God. Segregation is not only politically, economically, and socially unsound, it is morally wrong and sinful. Our civil disobedience shows respect for law and is part of the great Christian and American traditions.

23–24: I have almost concluded that white moderates, not rabid segregationists, are our greatest stumbling block—those who value order over justice, prefer reducing tension to achieving peace, agree with our goals but reproach our methods, and believe they can set a timetable for our freedom. I had hoped you would understand that tension must be released to be alleviated and that injustice must be exposed to be cured.

25–29: You accuse us of precipitating violence by our nonviolent actions. As the federal courts have affirmed, it is wrong to urge anyone to give up his constitutional rights because seeking them may precipitate violence. Nor will time inevitably bring redress; progress requires work. You speak of our activities in Birmingham as extreme; yet I stand between the opposing forces of passivity and hatred, espousing the nonviolent middle course.

30–36: The American Negro has become aware of his birthright of freedom and is not willing to remain oppressed. Try to understand his yearning rather than squelch it. If I am an extremist, so were Jesus, Paul, Martin Luther, Lincoln, Jefferson, and others. I had hoped the white moderate would recognize the need for creative extremists, responding to the cry of the oppressed race as a few white brothers have. Instead, some white church leaders have opposed us outright, while too many others choose caution over courage.

37–41: The early church was powerful, when Christians acted energetically in defense of their beliefs. Today it is often weak, passive, and ineffectual, a bulwark of the status quo. Yet some noble souls have broken loose and joined our struggle for freedom. I hope the church as a whole will meet this challenge. But whether it does or not, we will reach our goal because freedom is the goal and heritage of America.

42–44: You commend the Birmingham police for keeping "order" and "preventing violence," when their dogs attacked unarmed demonstrators, and the policemen are habitually cruel and inhumane to Negroes under their control. Their public display of nonviolence in defense of segregation uses a moral means to achieve an immoral end. I wish you had commended courage and discipline of the demonstrators, who one day will be regarded as heroes.

45–47: I hope circumstances will soon make it possible for us to meet, not over civil rights but as fellow clergymen and Christian brothers.

SIMONE DE BEAUVOIR
From *The Second Sex* (pp. 173–86)

Paragraph 1:   The destiny of women has always been controlled by men. Whatever success women have achieved in worldly affairs has been achieved in terms defined by men.

2:   Historically, when granted social status, women have been denied legal rights. And when they enjoyed rights equal to those of men, they have been excluded from meaningful participation in society.

3:   Caught in this opposition between concrete social customs and theoretical legal rights, women have achieved greatness only in rare circumstances where gender did not matter—for example, as sovereigns or as saints.

4:   Because of their subservient position, women in general play no more than a negative or indirect role in political life. True control of the world has always been in the hands of men.

5:   Women generally exist on the margins of history. Those who achieve heroic status are oddities, better known for their unusual fates than for the importance of their actions.

6:   Women have managed to assert themselves with considerable success in the domain of culture. But however great their collective role in this domain, the contributions of individual women have been less significant. Again, it is the marginal situation of women in the world that prevents them from attaining genius.

7–8:   The fact that a few women have achieved greatness does not counterbalance or excuse the subjection of women as a whole. Today many women demand rights and opportunities equal to those of men. But true equality between the sexes, despite some gains, still does not exist.

9:   Marriage places greater burdens on women than on men, making it more difficult for wives than for husbands to reconcile their domestic roles with their roles as workers.

10:   This difficulty is seen in the lives of French peasant women, who are burdened with heavy domestic duties as well as field work.

11–12:   Businesswomen and female employers occupy a privileged position legally and socially; they have relatively few difficulties combining household and domestic duties. Women workers and professionals, on the other hand, face great difficulties.

13:   Women who seek independence through work have fewer opportunities than do their male counterparts.

14:   While more possibilities are now open for women, society still regards marriage as the highest calling. Because girls are taught to view marriage as a means of social and economic advancement, they often are less prepared to succeed professionally than their brothers are.

15:   For many female employees, work is a drudgery with few compensating rewards. Society holds out marriage as an escape from this drudgery, but women today, having achieved self-awareness, are loath to accept domestic subjection. Women laborers are thus caught between the drudgery of unfulfilling work and the largely illusory hope of escape through marriage.

16:   Women today still exist in a state of subjugation to men.

ADAM SMITH

Of the Principle of the Commercial or Mercantile System (pp. 193–206)

Paragraph 1:   Money (or gold and silver) is commonly thought to be the measure of a man's wealth.

2:   The wealth of a country is also thought to depend on its supply of money (or gold and silver).

3:   Locke says that gold and silver are the most substantial part of a nation's wealth because they are portable and unlikely to be consumed.

4:   Others say that a nation's wealth could be measured by its abundance of consumable goods if it did not have to maintain fleets and armies abroad, which must be supported by money.

5:   Because of the widespread belief that money is the measure of wealth, European nations have long tried to prohibit gold and silver from leaving their boundaries.

6:   When nations became commercial, merchants found it inconvenient to trade without gold and silver and therefore argued against prohibition on exporting these metals.

7:   Merchants argued that using gold and silver to purchase foreign goods might increase, rather than decrease, the nation's supply of these metals.

8:   They also argued that while nations could not entirely stop the export of gold and silver, they could retain these metals by controlling the balance of trade. By exporting more goods than it imports, a nation is owed a balance by other nations, a balance that must be paid in gold and silver.

9:   While the merchants' arguments had some merit, they were also partly fallacious.

10:   Nevertheless, the arguments convinced those in power, and prohibitions against exporting gold and silver were eased. Thus, governments turned from the fruitless task of controlling the export of gold and silver to the more difficult and equally fruitless task of controlling the balance of trade.

11:   But, in fact, without any control from the government, freedom of trade will naturally supply all the gold and silver that a country can purchase or use.

12:   The supply of every commodity in every country naturally regulates itself based on the demand for that commodity. This process of regulation works most efficiently with gold and silver because they are easily transported from place to place.

13:   When the supply of gold and silver exceeds the demand, no effort by the government can prevent the export of these metals. Likewise, when the demand exceeds the supply, the government cannot prevent the import of gold and silver.

14:   Because gold and silver are easily transported, their value fluctuates less than does the value of other commodities.

15:   If there is a shortage of gold and silver in a country that can afford to purchase these metals, the shortage can be addressed by various means, including the use of paper money.

16:   Scarcity of money is a common complaint, but this complaint stems not from any real shortage of gold and silver but from merchants' buying on credit and then being unable to borrow sufficient amounts to pay their debts.

17:   Money (or gold and silver) makes up a small part of a nation's wealth; the bulk of that wealth consists of what can be purchased with money.

18:   While money is the established instrument of commerce, it is ultimately desirable not for its own sake but rather for what it can purchase. The goods that money can purchase serve many ends, but money serves no end other than to purchase goods.

KARL MARX

The Communist Manifesto (pp. 209–34)

Paragraphs 1–6:   The specter of communism haunts Europe, whose powers have allied to oppose it. Every opposition party, advanced or reactionary, is labeled communistic. Therefore, Communists of various nationalities have gathered to publish their views and goals.

7–11:   The history of society is a history of class struggles. In our own epoch, society is more and more splitting into two great hostile classes: bourgeoisie and proletariat.

12–22:   The bourgeoisie sprang from burghers, became merchants, and grew into the present industrial middle class. Modern industry has established the world market, causing commerce and navigation to burgeon. Meanwhile, the bourgeoisie has swamped all other classes. It has replaced old ties and values—veiled exploitation—with the naked exploitation of treating everything as a cash transaction.

23–26:   The bourgeoisie cannot exist without constantly revolutionizing the instruments of production and thereby the relations of production, and with them the whole relations of society. In its rush to achieve, it has generated constant uncertainty and agitation. It has superseded local patterns of production of consumption with multinational industries and markets, creating new wants and dependencies among consumers.

27–30:   By improving the means of production and communication, the bourgeoisie has forced the world into its own mold. It has subjected the country to the towns and undeveloped nations to civilized ones. It has centralized population, production, and property control as well as stimulated enormous technical change.

31–34:   Although built on a feudal foundation, the bourgeoisie's development of productive forces burst the fetters of feudal property relations. In stepped free competition, with accompanying social and political adaptations. But the productive forces have grown too strong for bourgeois control and create a periodic chaos of overproduction that endangers bourgeois property and society. The bourgeoisie fights back with greater market exploitation, paving the way for worse crises and its own eventual ruin.

35–38:   The bourgeoisie has not only forged the weapons of its destruction but called into existence those who are to wield them—the proletariat. The proletariat is a class of laborers who live only as long as they find work and who find work only as long as their labor increases capital. Like all commodities, they are subject to market fluctuations. They function as appendages of machines, slaves of the bourgeois class and state, doing simple monotonous tasks.

39–46:   Old workers, children, women, small tradespeople, and those with specialized skills all sink into the proletariat. Their initial struggle with the bourgeoisie is individual and local; workers attack the instruments rather than the conditions of production, seeking to restore their feudal status. As the proletariat becomes concentrated and aware of its commonality, workers form broader geographic unions, in which lie their ultimate strength.

47–55:   The bourgeoisie, embattled on numerous fronts, needs help from the proletariat and therefore gives workers weapons against itself. Sections of the ruling class also fall or jump into the proletariat. Unlike all previous classes, the proletarians have nothing of their own to fortify; their mission is to destroy the existing system of individual property. Unlike all previous historical movements, theirs is not a minority but a majority upheaval.

56–59:   The proletarian-bourgeois struggle is national at first. It begins as a veiled civil war and then breaks out into revolution and the proletariat's violent overthrow of the bourgeoisie. The bourgeoisie is unfit to rule because it cannot even ensure its slaves' existence within their slavery but lets their situation degenerate to where it must feed them. As industry ends laborers' isolation and competition with each other, the fall of the bourgeoisie and the victory of the proletariat are inevitable.

60–93: The Communists are not separate from or opposed to other working-class parties but work on behalf of the proletariat worldwide. They favor the overthrow of the bourgeoisie and the abolition of private property, ending the dominance of capital and enriching the life of the worker. They do not aim to sweep away freedom and individuality, only the bourgeoisie and their system of buying and selling.

94–110: Bourgeois culture, laws, and institutions, like bourgeois productivity, exist only to benefit the ruling class. The exploitive bourgeois family will vanish along with wage labor when capital vanishes; the bourgeoisie has already destroyed the proletarian family. Those who criticize communism for planning to make women, like the means of production, common to all, ignore that bourgeois marriage is in reality a system of wives in common.

111–126: National divisions are already obsolescent and will vanish under the supremacy of the proletariat. Bourgeois religion and philosophy also must disappear along with the capitalist system to which they correspond.

127–134: The victorious proletariat will centralize all instruments of production in the hands of the state. Private property, inheritance, and child labor in factories will be abolished; a heavy income tax will be instituted. The state will take over property, credit, communication and transportation systems, and education. Everyone will be equally liable to labor. The distinctions between agriculture and manufacturing, between town and country, and between classes will disappear.

135–146: The Communists have established a role in relation to existing working-class parties in England, America, France, Switzerland, Poland, and Germany; but they focus chiefly on Germany because that country is on the eve of a bourgeois revolution that will be followed immediately by a proletarian revolution. The Communists everywhere support all revolutionary movements against the existing order, emphasizing the property question and the international union of workers.

JOHN KENNETH GALBRAITH

The Position of Poverty (pp. 237–49)

Paragraphs 1–3:   Alfred Marshall suggested at the turn of the century that solving the problem of poverty is the central concern for economists. In modern America, however, the poor are considered more as a reason for economists to go on working than as an urgent national issue. Economic expansion has changed poverty since Marshall's time from a majority to a minority affliction.

4–7:   People with enough income to survive are still poor if they cannot afford to eat, dress, and live at a standard the community considers decent. Though this degradation is better understood now than formerly, poverty has not been eliminated. By the Department of Health, Education, and Welfare's standards, 13.4 million American households were poor in 1959, and 24.4 million in 1972.

8–13:   Case poverty derives from an individual's inability to master his or her environment. Insular poverty exists throughout a community, creating a poor "island" within the larger society. Case poverty is easily blamed on the sufferer's deficiency and also presumably easily solved with charity. Insular poverty is more widespread, harder to explain, and most common in rural and urban slums. Though it is often characterized as geographic, no correlation in fact exists between the natural resources of an area and its residents' tendency toward poverty.

14–16:   Poverty is disproportionately high among blacks, Hispanics, and the old; heads of poor households are very often female and/or unemployed. Race, which restricts mobility and thus access to jobs, is clearly a contributing factor. So are poor educational facilities and the disintegration of family life. A general rise in income therefore will not cure insular poverty (or case poverty) because the poor cannot share it.

17–19:   As poverty shifted from a majority to a minority position, it became a less attractive issue to politicians.

20–21:   An affluent society that is also both compassionate and rational would ensure a decent standard of income for all its members. Such a policy also would prevent parents from passing on poverty to their children. When the poor were a majority, guaranteeing a minimum income to all was unrealistic. Now it is an essential first step in the attack on poverty.

22–24:   If we continue to assume the only remedy for poverty is helping people to help themselves, we miss the chance to improve the living conditions, and thus the future prospects, of poor children. Those outside the insular poverty community need to invest in high-quality schools, health services, nutrition, and recreation for children whose parents cannot provide such necessities. In addition, plentiful decent low-cost housing and mass transit, plus a safe environment and health care, would help poor people overcome the restraints imposed by their situation. Case poverty, too, might be alleviated by such remedies.

25–27:   Though we search for social explanations of the urban ghetto, partly in hopes of avoiding a huge investment in the public sector, only money is likely to solve the problem. Allowing poor people to participate in the economic life of the larger community also would increase their productivity as well as the nation's. The survival of poverty in a country as affluent as the United States is a disgrace.

ROBERT B. REICH

Why the Rich Are Getting Richer and the Poor, Poorer (pp. 251–68)

Paragraph 1:   In the United States, a worker's role in the economy determines his or her financial success: symbolic analysts (people who identify and solve problems) are succeeding, while service workers are doing badly, and routine production workers are doing worse.

2–3:   In the past, regardless of their role in the economy, most American workers shared similar fortunes, based on the health of the nation's economy as a whole. As the middle class grew and bought more of the products it produced, the national economy flourished.

4–10:   But as new technology permits quick, efficient, and inexpensive transmittal of information around the world, many major American companies are using cheaper labor that is readily available in other countries. As a result, not only are there fewer jobs in the United States in both heavy industries (such as manufacturing) and light industries (such as data processing and computer programming), but the wages and benefits for those that still exist are declining. This pattern is occurring not just in the United States but all over the world.

11–15:   While production workers in developing countries benefit by getting more and better jobs, workers in advanced economies suffer. Unions and collective bargaining agreements that used to protect these workers are no longer effective, in part because of the decline in the traditional unionized industries.

16–18:   Lower- and middle-management production jobs are also disappearing. Foreign companies are doing *some* production here using American workers, but technology is making many of these workers obsolete.

19:   The decline in routine jobs has hurt men more than women because men's jobs in manufacturing traditionally paid more than women's jobs in textiles and data processing; the gender gap in wages began to close in the early 1980s not because women were making more money but because men were making less.

20–24:   Service industry jobs are also in trouble, although less dramatically. Service workers, who earn less than production workers and have fewer (if any) benefits, now have to compete with former production workers, people who would have looked for production work were it available, and immigrants. Like production workers, service workers are also threatened by labor-saving machinery and technology.

25–26:   The fortunes of service workers will temporarily improve due to changing demographics. But the standard of living of service workers won't really improve because the people demanding their services won't have enough money to pay for them; therefore, the workers themselves will bear the brunt in the form of taxes and social security.

27:   The service workers' standard of living also depends indirectly on the standard of living of those they service; if the latter do well in world commerce, they'll have more money to spend on service workers.

28–36:   The outlook for America's symbolic analysts, on the other hand, is bright, especially for those at the highest levels. Demand for their ideas has grown steadily as new technologies allow them to communicate their ideas clearly, rapidly, and cheaply. Symbolic analysts include anyone who works with images and ideas. Symbolic analysts not only make large sums of money but, unlike those in production and service jobs, enjoy their work.

37–41:   At midcentury when America was a national market dominated by major corporations, there were constraints on the earnings of people at the highest level. No one was supposed to make too much or too little; this way the workers had money to spend, and national economic growth continued. But by the 1990s, symbolic analysts' earnings were unlimited.

42–44: Major American corporations were vanishing by the 1990s, as were the ethics associated with them. As American corporations sold goods and services all over the world, there was no connection between the bosses and their workers, many of whom were not in this country. The purchasing power of American workers became far less relevant to a company's economic survival, and top executives are getting richer while the workers are getting poorer.

PLATO

The Allegory of the Cave (pp. 275–86)

Paragraphs 1–14: Imagine prisoners living since childhood in an underground den, chained so they cannot move or see anywhere but straight ahead. Behind them is a fire that casts shadows on the cave wall in front of the prisoners as people carry various objects past the fire. The prisoners, seeing nothing but shadows, assume the shadows are all there is to reality.

15–18: If a prisoner were released and turned toward the light, he would not immediately be able to see the objects whose shadows he formerly watched. Nor would he believe that these objects are more real than the shadows but would cling to his old idea of reality.

19–26: If the prisoner were taken out of the cave, he would be still more blinded by the sun's light. At first he would see shadows and reflections most easily, then objects, the heavens, and at last the sun, which he would reason about and deduce to be a sort of god of the visual world.

27–34: Remembering his old life in the cave, the prisoner would pity his companions and rejoice in his own good fortune. Their contests at shadow watching and prediction, with honor and glory attached to winning, now would seem not enviable but repellent. But if he were taken back to the cave and forced to rejoin the contests before his eyes got used to the dark, his fellow prisoners would pity his blindness and keep any others from leaving the cave.

35–40: The cave is the world of sight, the firelight is the sun, and the journey upward is the soul's ascent into the intellectual world. The sun is the idea of good, author of all things beautiful and right, the power on which men who would act rationally must fix. Those who reach this upper world dislike returning to the cave, where they are forced to argue about justice with people who have never seen it.

41–52: The eye can be blinded by either abrupt light or abrupt darkness, but sight cannot be put into blind eyes. Rather, the soul must turn from darkness to light to use its capacity for perception of the good. A clever rogue might have been a wise and good man if his soul had been cut off in youth from sensual pleasures that lowered its vision.

53–62: In the ideal republic, neither the uneducated nor those who never end their education will make able ministers of state. The founders of the state will compel its best minds to attain the good and then to descend again for the benefit of the state. The rulers of this state will be philosophers, enlightened and uninterested in fighting for power. The state whose rulers are most reluctant to govern is governed best.

63–65: These philosopher-rulers will take office as a stern necessity. The political arena must offer them better rewards than power and wealth, so that those rich in virtue and wisdom will be willing to hold office.

MOSES MAIMONIDES

On the Limits of Man's Intellect (pp. 289–304)

Paragraph 1:   The powers of the human mind, like those of the senses and the body, are limited.

2–3:   Some men have greater intellectual power than others, but there is a limit beyond which no human mind can penetrate. Men do not desire to know some things that lie beyond this limit; other things they do desire to know but inevitably must struggle without success to know them. Alexander Aphrodisius has identified three causes that prevent people from discovering truth. A fourth cause is habit: because they are accustomed by habit and training to think in familiar ways, people cling to false ideas.

4–6:   Just as you may weaken your eyes by overstraining them, so you may weaken your mind by overstraining it. If you accept the limitations of your intellectual power, you will achieve the highest possible degree of perfection. If you try to exceed those limitations, you will become exceedingly imperfect.

7–8:   In moderate amounts, knowledge nourishes the mind just as honey nourishes the body, but an excess of either is harmful. Many wise sayings confirm that we should not try to reach beyond the limits of human understanding.

9:   This does not mean, however, that we should close our minds to learning but only that we should not pursue knowledge beyond the boundary of human reason.

10:   It is harmful to begin study with metaphysics or other complex subjects. Rather, the young and less intelligent should start with simple forms of learning and gradually advance to higher ones.

11:   Those of limited intellectual capacity—children, women, and common people—cannot comprehend fully the truths in the Torah and must therefore be taught those truths only partially and indirectly. Those with sufficient intelligence may be led gradually to understand what they at first grasped imperfectly.

12–13:   There are five reasons why we should not begin instruction with metaphysics and should not attempt to teach the "true essence of things" to those of limited intellectual capacity.

14:   First, the subject matter of metaphysics itself is "difficult, subtle, and profound."

15:   Second, even those with great intellectual potential are at first incapable of grasping profound truths.

16–21:   Third, most men are unwilling to endure the difficult preliminary work that must precede the study of metaphysics. This work includes learning the disciplines of logic, mathematics, astronomy, and physics. Studying these disciplines raises doubts and problems that need to be resolved before we can safely begin metaphysical study. In Proverbs, Solomon points out the failings of those who wish to know final results without the work of preliminary study—a failing shared by many scholars.

22–24:   Fourth, those who wish to reach metaphysical knowledge must be of the best moral character—"calm, pure, and steadfast." The Talmud and the writings of the rabbis confirm that the highest knowledge should be entrusted only to the morally upright. Young men, being by nature rash and hot-blooded, lack the moral character for metaphysical study, as do ordinary people, children, and women.

25:   Fifth, people distracted by the ordinary cares of life are not properly suited for metaphysical study. Only a privileged few, not beginners or the common people, should undertake such study.

SIGMUND FREUD

From *The Interpretation of Dreams* (pp. 307–18)

Paragraphs 1–2: We have discovered that dreams are not aimless, senseless occurrences but "fulfillments of wishes"—the mind's way of granting our desires. This discovery raises several questions about dreams.

3: For now, though, we must focus on one particular issue—whether *all* dreams, or only some, are wish fulfillments.

4: We can show easily that many dreams fulfill wishes. If I eat salty food before bed, I can induce a dream in which I drink water to quench my thirst. This is a "dream of convenience," for it conveniently satisfies my wish for a drink without my having to wake up.

5–8: Other simple dreams (mine as well as those of colleagues, patients, and friends) are obvious wish fulfillments, suggesting that dreams satisfy various desires—for more sleep, for relief from pain, for freedom from or help with the demands of motherhood.

9: The examples cited thus far show that wish-fulfillment dreams are common and exist in various conditions. Studying the dreams of children may provide further evidence.

10: Because they are frequently pure, simple, wish fulfillments, children's dreams offer evidence that dreams in general are essentially fulfillments of wishes.

11–12: Two dreams reported by my children show how their wishes were satisfied in dreams. My son, disappointed because we were unable to visit a mountain lodge, later visited it in a dream. Similarly, my daughter's desire for some chocolate bars and her wish to establish a relationship with a young man were both fulfilled in a dream.

13–17: A friend reported that his daughter had a dream much like my son's, and two of my other children recounted wish-fulfillment dreams. Also, my daughter Anna, when only nineteen months old, called out in her sleep for strawberries, omelet, and pudding, presumably dreaming because she had gone to bed hungry. My nephew also dreamed of food at a young age, enjoying in his sleep some cherries he had wished to eat that day.

18–19: The theory that dreams are wish fulfillments is summarized in the question and answer of a simple proverb: "What do geese dream of?" "Of maize." An expression in common language also supports the theory that dreams represent fulfilled wishes.

CARL JUNG

The Personal and the Collective Unconscious (pp. 321–34)

Paragraphs 1–3:   According to Freud, the unconscious contains only those parts of the personality that are repressed by the conscious mind. I believe, however, that the unconscious also contains other psychic material.

4:   It is ordinarily assumed that all unconscious material, including dreams and fantasies, derive from our personal experiences. But observation shows that the unconscious also contains material unrelated to personal experience.

5:   The experiences of one of my patients illustrates my point. Through psychoanalysis, this woman sought to break her emotional tie with her father and to form a relationship with a man, but her feelings remained unresolved, divided between these two male figures. During treatment, she experienced what Freud calls transference. That is, she transferred the image of both her father and her lover to me (the doctor); I became the object of her conflict. Transference often provides temporary relief for the patient.

6–7:   In successful treatments, the state of transference is temporary and leads to a cure. But my patient became locked in this state, dependent on me as a sort of savior.

8:   Unable to break the deadlock, we decided to study her dreams, hoping that they would provide a solution.

9:   Dreams contain images that we produce unconsciously, and they provide an objective picture of our psychic processes.

10–11:   My patient's dreams contained two actors, herself and her doctor. The latter usually appeared as a figure of supernatural size, often extremely old, sometimes resembling her father. At the same time, this figure was woven into nature, often associated with the wind. These dreams convinced me that, in her unconscious, my patient was clinging to me as a father-lover of almost divine proportions.

12:   While the patient understood rationally the nature of her transference, her unconscious continued to cling stubbornly to the fantasy image it had created.

13:   What could be the purpose of this fantasy? Was the godlike figure in her dreams merely an image of a human person? Or did her dreams indicate an instinctual longing for a god, a longing deeper and stronger than any love for a human person?

14–15:   Such a possibility seems incongruous in a modern setting, and we must carefully test the hypothesis that this woman's dreams represent the longing for a god.

16:   The woman herself doubted this hypothesis. Gradually, she was able to separate herself from me. This occurred, I think, because of the guidance provided by her dreams, which were not merely fantasies but representations of her unconscious life that enabled her to escape her dependence.

17:   In her dreams, the woman had what amounts to a vision of God. Though a nonbeliever, she found comfort in a giant primordial father figure associate with the wind (or spirit). At this point, we can distinguish what may be called the personal unconscious. We gain deepened self-knowledge by bringing material from this layer of the unconscious into conscious awareness. Psychoanalysis facilitates this process as does dream analysis.

18:   My patient derived her primitive god image not from the personal content of her unconscious but from a deeper impersonal source shared by people of various times and from various parts of the world. The god she dreamed about is an archetype, an ancient image reactivated by unconscious patterns of thought common to all humans.

19:   The preceding discussion shows that, along with personal elements, the unconscious contains impersonal (or collective) elements. The latter exist in a deeper level of the unconscious called the *collective unconscious.*

KAREN HORNEY

The Distrust Between the Sexes (pp. 337–51)

Paragraphs 1–3: In relations between men and women, as between children and parents, we prefer to assume that love is predominant and that hostility and other disturbances are accidental and avoidable. Yet the regularity of tension between the sexes suggests common denominators.

4–8: Much of the suspiciousness between women and men is understandable and even justifiable, considering the intensity of the emotions involved. Our instinct for self-preservation restrains us from the surrender of self that accompanies passion, while we resent such restraint in the partner. Projecting our own negative feelings onto the partner, we become distrustful. Moreover, love tends to release all our secret expectations and wishes, which we focus on the partner without realizing they are doomed to disappointment.

9: Frustrations in childhood also contribute to sexual tension. When the child's strong desires are thwarted or dismissed by adults, his pent-up anger turns into fantasies of violent vengeance. The resulting anxiety carries over into adulthood as a fear of love for what it might cause us to do to the partner, and vice versa.

10–11: Suppose that a little girl is badly disappointed by her father, causing her to deny her maternal instincts and transform her instinctual wish to receive from a man into a vindictive urge to take from him by force. She might become the kind of woman who fears that men suspect her of wanting something—that is, that they guess her repressed wish. Or she might project her wish and fear that men want to exploit her. A reaction formation of excessive modesty might mask her wish, causing her not to demand or accept anything from her husband. Or repressing her aggression might drain her energy, so that she feels helpless and shifts the responsibility for her life onto her husband.

12–13: Though men's attitudes toward women are influenced by their early experiences, some attitudes can be traced historically and across cultures. The Old Testament, for example, denies and devalues women's capacity to give birth by depicting Eve as created from Adam's rib and cursed to bear children in sorrow; it also shows her as a sexual temptress who plunges man into misery. Man's fear of woman is deeply rooted in sex: nubile women are the focus of diverse cultural taboos to protect men from their dangerous magic powers. Though our culture no longer burns witches, men continue to define women in relation to themselves and to cast their differences as inferiorities.

14–15: Men venerate motherliness for it is the embodiment of the woman who fulfills all their expectations and longings. Their regard for female fecundity, however, is mingled with jealousy, inciting men to create state, religion, art, and science, and to dominate all aspects of culture. A residue of resentment has led men to glorify their genitality, while devaluing pregnancy, childbirth, and women in general.

16–17: Male cultural supremacy is a fairly recent sequel to matriarchy. At present, as women struggle to regain their equality, we should not hope for female ascendancy but for an end to the conflict, which inevitably overvalues the weaker and rationalizes the discrepancy.

18: It appears likely that men's dread of women is due to their sense of yielding power during intercourse, the psychological association between the mother and death, and the greater sexual dependency of the male on the female than vice versa.

19–20: The other reason we focus on love rather than hostility between the sexes is love's incomparable potential for happiness. Analysts can help diminish distrust by uncovering the real motives of the struggle, by working to resolve childhood conflicts, and by attempting to forestall some of those conflicts in the future.

HOWARD GARDNER

A Rounded Version: The Theory of Multiple Intelligences (pp. 353–72)

Paragraphs 1–3:   Intelligence tests given to children reliably predict their later success in school.

4–5:   Such tests work as predictors because they measure problem-solving skills typically needed for academic success. From this perspective, intelligence is a general ability that all individuals possess to varying degrees.

6–7:   While accurately predicting academic success, intelligence tests are not good indicators of professional success in later life. Our society narrowly measures intelligence by a person's ability to solve certain types of logical and linguistic problems.

8–9:   Such an approach cannot account for the extraordinary abilities of many people. This chapter offers an alternative approach—the theory of multiple intelligences (MI). We believe that intelligence consists of several different abilities and that all normal individuals possess each of these to some extent.

10–11:   MI theory expands the traditional definition of intelligence. According to this theory, an intelligence is a capacity for solving problems or creating products valued by a culture.

12–15:   Before it can be regarded as an intelligence, a problem-solving skill must be universal in the human species (that is, biological in origin) and culturally nourished. We considered evidence from several sources and established additional criteria in developing our list of intelligences.

16:   The following section describes the seven intelligences we identified.

17–20:   Violinist Yehudi Menuhin demonstrates extraordinary musical intelligence. Evidence from various sources supports the interpretation of musical ability as a separate "intelligence."

21–24:   Baseball player Babe Ruth possessed exceptional bodily-kinesthetic intelligence. Controlling complex bodily movements requires cognitive problem-solving ability as well as physical skill.

25–29:   Biologist Barbara McClintock's problem-solving ability is an example of logical-mathematical intelligence. This type of problem solving can occur rapidly and may be nonverbal. Logical-mathematical reasoning, along with language skill, is the basis for traditional IQ tests.

30–31:   Writer T. S. Eliot demonstrated exceptional linguistic intelligence. The ability to use language skillfully meets the various empirical criteria we used to identify an intelligence.

32–36:   People use spatial intelligence for tasks that require them to visualize and manipulate space—for example, navigation, map making, playing chess, drawing, painting. Research in biology and medicine verifies that spatial reasoning is a distinct intelligence. The autistic child Nadia demonstrated prodigious visual ability in her drawings.

37–44:   Helen Keller's teacher Anne Sullivan possessed unusual interpersonal intelligence. This type of intelligence, which is verified by biological evidence, allows us to develop insights into other people and to interact with them socially.

45–50:   The writer Virginia Woolf demonstrated exceptional intrapersonal intelligence—a deep understanding of her own self and an ability to use that understanding to guide her life. Again, as is the case with interpersonal intelligence, intrapersonal intelligence meets the criteria we established for defining an intelligence.

51–52:   In identifying the seven intelligences, we have used a nontraditional approach—starting with the problems people solve and then working back to the intelligences that enable them to solve those problems. Also, we have included a particular intelligence only if scientific evidence justified doing so.

53–54:   We have shown that, to some extent, each of the seven intelligences functions independently of the others. Nevertheless, any sophisticated role in society requires that we use a combination of several intelligences.

FRANCIS BACON

The Four Idols (pp. 379–94)

Paragraphs 1–7: Four classes of idols and false notions interfere with the human mind's ability to perceive the truth. The best remedy for them is inductive reasoning. Idols of the Tribe are distortions arising from the limits of human perception and understanding. Idols of the Cave arise from individual idiosyncrasies and experience. Idols of the Marketplace are caused by the imprecision of language; and Idols of the Theater result from misleading philosophies and principles.

8–16: Human understanding has several tendencies that comprise the Idols of the Tribe. We impute more order and regularity to the world than it actually contains. We ignore evidence that conflicts with our preconceptions. We base our preconceptions on those phenomena that strike us most readily, rather than on a thorough examination of our surroundings. We muddy our observations with unjustified interpretations. What we believe is colored by our wishes. We trust our senses for information that should be obtained by experiment.

17–22: The Idols of the Cave come from an individual's physical and mental constitution as well as education and experience. The most important are men's gravitation toward a favorite subject, shaping their other ideas around it; their tendency to attend too closely to either the similarities or the differences between things; their partiality to a particular age and its judgments; and their inclination to focus on the minute aspects of a thing while ignoring the large and general, or vice versa.

23–26: Most troublesome of all are the Idols of the Marketplace, misconceptions that have crept in through words and names. Words tend to oversimplify what they represent. Some words name things that do not exist or that are ill-defined; others can be interpreted in a variety of ways and lack a clear, specific meaning. Different classes of words—nouns, verbs, adjectives—contain different degrees of distortion.

27–28: Idols of the Theater are not covertly and inevitably deceptive like Idols of the Marketplace but are presented to the mind by incorrect philosophies and methods of investigating the world. The preferable method of investigation would not rely on individual intelligence and reasoning but on objective observation.

29–34: Most philosophies abstract too much from too little evidence, or vice versa. Some manipulate the facts to conform with their ideas; others interweave science and superstition. The last is most widespread and dangerous, as can be seen in certain Greek and subsequent schools that offer religious and other nonobjective explanations for natural phenomena.

35: Human understanding must be cleansed of the Idols' misconceptions; for those who would enter the kingdom of man founded on science, like the kingdom of heaven, must come as a little child.

CHARLES DARWIN

Natural Selection (pp. 397–412)

Paragraphs 1–2:   The principle of selection applies in nature as in human-controlled breeding. Man cannot create the numerous variations we see in domesticated species but can only preserve and accumulate those that occur. Given how many variations have benefited and been fostered by man, we must assume that many more occur that benefit the being in question and are fostered by the survival advantage they confer. This preservation of favorable individual differences and variations, and destruction of injurious ones, comprises natural selection, or the survival of the fittest. "Natural selection" does not refer to volition or Deity but merely to the action and result of natural laws.

3–4:   Any change in a given environment opens a niche for different species migrating in from outside or for variations in resident species, which adapt them better to their altered surroundings. Changing conditions appear to increase variability. Adaptation occurs even in a constant environment, however, for no species is ever perfectly suited to its locale.

5–7:   Man selects only those variations he can see and utilize, while Nature can act on any aspect of an organism, at any level of subtlety, and in any way that may improve the organism's ability to exploit its environment. Natural selection is constant, though we see it only when changes accumulate over time and become visible. For significant modification to occur, the initial favorable variation must be followed by others.

8–12:   Natural selection operates even on characters and structures that appear minor to us, as these may significantly affect an organism's survival advantage; and it can work in directions we cannot anticipate. Variations can affect creatures at any stage of their life and can change the relation of offspring to parent. Favorably adapted creatures do not always survive; but natural selection never perpetuates a variation that confers no advantage.

13–15:   Nature, like man, often alters males and females differently within a species. A variation may benefit a creature over others of its species. This sexual selection operates not by conferring a direct survival advantage but by increasing the individual's chances of producing offspring. Stronger males, and those more attractive to females, are more likely to pass on their characteristics to the next generation.

16–18:   Variations are perpetuated that occur in numerous members of a species rather than just one; for a single individual, however well adapted, has little chance of passing on a trait to whole succeeding generations. Even if a particular advantageous trait is not transmitted to offspring, however, a tendency to vary in that manner may gradually strengthen within the species.

19:   Because most plants and animals stay close to home, any modification tends to occur locally at first, spreading wider insofar as it confers an advantage over other nearby populations.

20–22:   A variation that does not benefit the creature directly may be perpetuated if it increases the species' chance of reproducing, as when a plant yields nectar in such a way as to attract more pollinating insects. Characteristics such as sexual dimorphism may arise in this way. At the same time as a plant species' variations make it more attractive to bees, the bee species is likely to vary so as to adapt better to its changing food source.

23:   Modern geology has banished the instant excavation of great valleys by huge waves in favor of the long-term cumulative action of ordinary visible forces. So too will natural selection banish the belief that new beings are continually created or suddenly modified.

STEPHEN JAY GOULD

Nonmoral Nature (pp. 415–29)

Paragraphs 1–2:   The most pressing problem of natural theology in the nineteenth century was as follows: if God is benevolent and creation displays his "power, wisdom and goodness," then why are we surrounded with pain, suffering, and apparently senseless cruelty in the animal world? William Buckland, considering carnivores to be at the center of this problem, concluded that being killed and eaten spared victims the greater anguish of disease, injury, decay, and starvation.

3–7:   Worse than predation, however, is slow death by parasitic ingestion, which is the modus operandi of the ichneumon fly. The ichneumons and related wasps compose perhaps hundreds of thousands of species. The female lays her eggs inside or on a caterpillar, aphid, spider, or other host, sometimes paralyzing the victim at the same time. When the egg hatches, the larva eats the still-living host slowly from the inside out, destroying the organs necessary for life to last.

8–16:   The struggle between wasps and hosts recalls human battles and tortures. Sometimes the host struggles and escapes, but the ruthless efficiency of the parasite is more impressive. The wasps use various ingenious strategies to outwit their victims; and they strike early (some parasitize an egg rather than a larva or an adult), quick (one species can deposit up to seventy-two eggs in a single second), and often (some lay their eggs in many victims or produce eggs that divide into many larvae). The wasp offspring are as efficient as their mothers, eating every edible morsel of the host and sometimes using its shell as well.

17–22:   Nineteenth-century natural theologians devised varied rationales for a benevolent God creating the ichneumon. Charles Lyell decided the wasps were God's way of keeping caterpillars from destroying too much vegetation. William Kirby focused on the mother wasp's dedication and courage and on the larva's care to preserve its victim's life as long as possible. St. George Mivart insisted that there is no ethical message in a beast's suffering and, anyway, that beasts suffer much less than "cultivated and refined human beings."

23–28:   Charles Darwin, in contrast, could not persuade himself that a beneficent God would have created the misery and cruelty he saw everywhere. Thomas Henry Huxley took this idea a step further by claiming that the moral lesson of nature for man is to do the opposite of what we see. Taking Darwin's idea in the other direction are those who contend that nature holds no messages for us: the world was not created for us, is not ruled by us, and should not be interpreted in our terms.

29:   Julian Huxley has pointed out the lack of relationship between natural selection and religion. It is thus ironic for modern creationists to accuse evolutionists of preaching an ethical doctrine against which their unscientific and discredited views deserve equal time. If nature is nonmoral, it can teach no ethical theory, either religious or antireligious.

MICHIO KAKU

The Theory of the Universe? (pp. 431–47)

Paragraphs 1–12:   As a child, I was fascinated by Albert Einstein's search for a theory that would unite all physical laws into a simple framework. This theory eluded Einstein and others. But today, some scientists claim to have found such a theory, one that explains the four fundamental forces in the universe.

13–22:   These forces are gravity, electromagnetism, the strong nuclear force, and the weak nuclear force. Our understanding of these forces has produced major changes in civilization. The next question is whether a single "super force" unites them all.

23–31:   There are currently two widely accepted theories that explain how the four forces work—the quantum theory and the general theory of relativity. The quantum theory explains the electromagnetic force as well as the strong and weak nuclear forces by describing the behavior of subatomic packets of energy called *quanta*. The general theory of relativity explains the force of gravity by describing the curvature of space-time. The problem facing scientists is to merge these two theories, which offer different—and seemingly irreconcilable—explanations of the physical world.

32–38:   Some scientists have proposed a solution—the "superstring theory, which postulates that all matter and energy can be reduced to tiny strings of energy." Superstrings vibrate in different frequencies, much like strings on a violin. These vibrations are the subatomic particles whose behavior is described by quantum theory. At the same time, the vibrating strings cause surrounding space-time to curve in a manner consistent with the general theory of relativity. Thus, superstring theory merges the two theories (quantum and relativity), providing a single explanation for all known forces in the universe.

39–49:   The most controversial aspect of the superstring theory is its prediction that the universe has multiple dimensions. We conventionally understand space as having three dimensions—height, depth, and width—but some scientists claim that our universe has a fourth dimension that we cannot visualize. From a mathematical point of view, adding this dimension allows scientists to describe a greater number of forces and to unify the laws of physics.

50–55:   According to superstring theory, the universe was initially ten-dimensional but then broke into two parts. One part is the expanding four-dimensional universe created in the Big Bang. The other part is a six-dimensional universe that collapsed into an infinitesimally tiny ball.

56–59:   Some scientists reject the superstring theory because it cannot be tested. Because the theory claims to elucidate the workings of all forces in the universe, including creation itself, testing it would require the impossible—experimentally reconstructing the instant of creation.

60–64:   It may be possible, however, to test some ideas about the instant of creation using the superconducting super collider (SSC) that is under construction. This enormous machine will generate temperatures that have not been reached since the instant of creation. Even if these experiments fail to verify the superstring theory, they may give indirect evidence to support it.

65–73:   A parable about a gemstone illustrates the difficulty of merging the quantum and relativity theories and shows why the superstring theory is so controversial.

74–81:   Supporters of the superstring theory argue that the fundamental problem is theoretical and not practical. Instead of building the SSC to verify the theory, we should work to understand the theory itself. Unfortunately, the mathematical tools currently available are inadequate for the job.

RICHARD DAWKINS
All Africa and Her Progenies (pp. 449–69)

Paragraphs 1–4: Some people contend that scientific explanations of human origins are no more "true" than those of myth or religion. But, in fact, scientific beliefs are based on verifiable evidence, whereas myths and faith are not.

5: This chapter explains an important scientific theory of human origins, the theory of African Eve.

6–8: A simple mathematical calculation shows that each person now on earth had at least a trillion trillion ancestors alive two thousand years ago. But this calculation is obviously flawed because it does not consider shared ancestry. In effect, all human beings are cousins, much more closely related than is generally recognized.

9–10: A branching tree is a common model for describing ancestry or descent. A better model is that of a "river of genes" flowing through time, constantly mixing our genetic material. In any large crowd, there are probably many people whose genes will be mingled one day in shared descendants.

11–13: A similar crowd from the distant past could be divided into two groups—those who are ancestors of everyone now alive and those who are not. Even further back, we could find a lobe-finned fish that is ancestor to us all. But we don't need to go that far to find a common ancestor.

14–15: In 1930, Sir Ronald Fisher speculated that, with some exceptions, our common ancestry dates back about 2000 years. Today, molecular biology enables us to go beyond speculation and trace our origins to a single ancestor—African Eve.

16: Just as scholars can trace the path of a biblical text that has been copied and passed down through time, so scientists should be able to trace human ancestry by examining DNA—the genetic "text" written in our bodies.

17–19: Unfortunately, sex is a major obstacle to tracing DNA. Biblical scholars face only minor copying errors in the texts they trace, but scientists must deal with the scrambling of DNA texts caused by the mixing of male and female chromosomes.

20–22: There are two cases in which sexual mixing is not a problem—African Eve (discussed later) and cross-species relationships. DNA texts taken from different species show how those species are related. We can determine, for example, how closely we are related to horses, pigs, and yeast.

23–25: The molecular clock theory suggests that we also can determine when a given species branched off on its own evolutionary pathway. This determination is possible, in part, because different genetic texts change over time at different rates and with different effects.

26: To determine how recently we can claim common ancestry with all other humans, we must study a type of DNA evidence different from that used to establish our connections with other species.

27–30: That evidence is found in mitochondria—bacterialike bodies swarming in all of our cells. Mitochondria have their own DNA, which is passed down from one generation to the next strictly through the maternal line. In other words, the DNA in mitochondria does not undergo the sexual mixing that scrambles other genetic texts in our bodies. Mitochondria thus provide an uncontaminated record of human ancestry.

31–32: Though uncontaminated, mitochondrial DNA does mutate over time, and these mutations indicate how far back our ancestors diverged in the female-only line. Mitochondrial DNA is ideal for dating common ancestry within a species.

33: A group of researchers in Berkeley, California, studied mitochondrial DNA from 135 women worldwide, using a computer to analyze how the women might be biologically related.

34–36:   Some coincidental similarities exist among DNA of different species (such as horses, pigs, and yeast). Within a single species, such as humans, the rate of coincidence among individuals is much higher. Therefore, in analyzing the DNA data the Berkeley researchers programmed their computer to find the most parsimonious family tree—the one with the fewest coincidental resemblances.

37–39:   But even the fastest computer could not analyze every possible family tree relating the 135 women, so researchers used random sampling to reduce the size of the task.

40–41:   The researchers at Berkeley concluded (1) that "the grand ancestress of all of us lived in Africa" (the so-called African, or Mitochondrial, Eve) and (2) that this Eve lived between 150 and 250 thousand years ago.

42:   The African Eve theory claims that, if we go back a few hundred thousand years, all living humans are of African descent. Even if this Eve is not African, we know from fossil evidence that our more remote ancestors, going back millions of years, are African.

43–44:   The research at Berkeley has spawned two misunderstandings. The first is that African Eve was the only woman on Earth. The correct claim is that, while she had many male and female companions, African Eve is the most recent woman from whom all modern humans are descended in the female-only line. The other misunderstanding is that African Eve is our most recent common ancestor. The correct claim is that she is our most recent common ancestor only in the purely female line; there are many other lines of descent besides this one.

45:   Actually, because males are capable of producing more children than females, our most recent common ancestor is somewhat more likely to be male than female.

46–47:   We can state six conclusions based on the preceding discussion. The story of African Eve is a small part of the much grander span of human evolution.

HERODOTUS

Observations on Egypt (pp. 477–95)

Paragraph 1:   A Greek story about the Egyptians' treatment of Heracles shows how little the Greeks understand Egyptian customs.

2:   Egyptians do not sacrifice goats; they regard these animals as holy, associating them with the god Pan.

3:   Egyptians regard the pig as unclean, fit for sacrifice only at festivals honoring the Moon and Dionysus.

4–5:   Egyptians celebrate the festival of Dionysus much as the Greeks do. Melampus, who introduced Dionysian ritual in Greece, learned it, I believe, from Egypt.

6–7:   Likewise, I believe that the names of most Greek gods originate in Egypt. But it was from the Pelasgians, not the Egyptians, that the Greeks adopted the practice of making statues of Hermes with the penis erect.

8–9:   According to priestesses at Dodona, the names of the Greek gods came indirectly from Egypt by way of the Pelasgians. It is my belief, however, that the poets Homer and Hesiod created for the Greeks their theogony.

10–13:   Explanations vary regarding the origin of oracles. Egyptians claim that priestesses taken from Thebes in Egypt became the first oracles. Some Greeks claim that oracles originated from the pronouncements of two black doves that flew from Thebes. I believe, however, that the first oracle was an Egyptian woman sold into slavery who, after learning Greek, founded a place of prophecy in Greece. This woman was called *dove* because her Egyptian speech sounded to the Greeks like the talk of birds.

14:   In any event, it is clear that methods of prophecy and many religious practices of the Greeks originated in Egypt.

15–19:   Egyptians hold six religious assemblies annually at various cities, each honoring a particular god. They travel noisily to Bubastis to honor Artemis, and once there, they celebrate with sacrifice and wine drinking. Isis is honored at Busiris, with much lamentation following the festival. At Sais, where Athena is honored, the people burn lamps through the night. The god Helios is honored at Heliopolis, the god Leto at Buto. At Papremis, the celebration for Ares includes groups of priests battling each other in a violent ritual.

20:   Egyptians were the first people to feel religious scruples, especially regarding sexuality.

21:   Egyptians consider animals sacred and appoint keepers to protect them. In some cases, killing an animal is a capital offense.

22–23:   Egyptians hold cats in especially high esteem, mummifying dead ones. Though it is protected, the cat population is reduced by the animals' self-destructive behavior and by male cats' killing of kittens in order to entice female cats to mate.

24–26:   The crocodile lives on land and water and manifests a number of unusual physical features and behaviors. Some Egyptians regard the crocodile as sacred and treat it with great respect. Others, denying its sacredness, hunt it for food.

27–30:   Egyptians regard various other animals as sacred, including the hippopotamus, the otter, and some serpents. The phoenix is a rare sacred bird that, according to the people, performs extraordinary feats, though I myself doubt the claims made about this bird.

31–32:   Near the city of Buto, I saw countless skeletons of winged serpents from Arabia that had been killed by ibis birds. For keeping these serpents out of Egypt, the ibis—a wonderfully black, cranelike bird—is much honored.

33–34: Egyptians enjoy excellent health because of their climate. They believe that food, while nourishing, is also a source of disease, and so they use emetics and purges regularly. Their diet includes bread, wine, fish, fowl, and other meats. It is their custom, at the end of a banquet, to be reminded of their mortality.

35–36: Other customs include the singing of their only chant, a song identical to one sung by the Greeks. Some Egyptian customs for greeting people are also similar to Greek customs.

37: Egyptians wear linen and wool, but their religion forbids the use of wool in temples or as a burial garment.

38–39: Egyptians associate each month and day with a particular god and believe that the day of a man's birth influences his future. They also believe that events follow recurrent patterns, and they use various means of divination.

40: Egyptian doctors specialize strictly by disease.

41–44: Egyptians mourn in the streets after the death of a well-known member of their household. The corpse is then prepared by embalmers. Three forms of embalming are available. The most perfect form requires extensive preparation of the body, followed by wrapping and enclosure in a body-shaped coffin. The middle and low forms require less elaborate preparation of the corpse.

45–46: Families retain the bodies of great or beautiful women for several days after death in order to prevent embalmers from copulating with them. The bodies of those who die in the river are regarded as more than human and thus buried with special care.

47: Egyptians generally avoid following Greek customs, but in one city, Chemmis, the people claim Egyptian ancestry for Perseus and honor him in a Greek manner.

48: Egyptians who live in the marshes have customs much the same as those who do not. However, the marsh dwellers use water lilies and papyrus as a food source.

ÁLVAR NÚÑEZ CABEZA DE VACA
From *La Relación* (pp. 497–508)

Paragraphs 1–2: Indians brought us their sick, asking Castello to cure them, which he did by praying to God. Later, we encountered other groups of Indians.

3–5: Two Susolas asked Castello to go with them to cure a wounded man. Castello feared that he would fail, so I went instead. I discovered that the wounded man had died but prayed over him anyway. Later we learned that he had revived. The grateful Indians gave us gifts of *tunas* and flint stones.

6: We lived among the Avavares for eight months, curing many of their sick.

7–8: The Indians told us of a frightful man who once wandered among them, mutilating people and causing disturbances. We explained that the man was a demon and could not harm them if they believed in Christ.

9: Although the Indians treated us well, our living conditions, like theirs, were austere.

10–11: We encountered the Maliacones and the Arbadaos. The latter were badly malnourished. Living among them, we suffered great hunger, eventually obtaining two dogs for food. Our naked skin was constantly burned by sun and wind.

12: We were also cut badly by thorns and spikes, my only comfort being to recall the greater suffering that Christ endured for me.

13: Our work for the Indians included scraping and tanning skins. The scrapings provided food, as did occasional pieces of meat.

14–16: After regaining our strength, we set out traveling and met other Indians. They were afraid of us at first but eventually treated us with great hospitality, giving us what little food they had.

17–19: The various tribes we met had similar customs. Husbands do not live with wives during pregnancy, and in childless couples, the young men may leave their wives and remarry. Mothers nurse children until the age of twelve.

20: Settling disputes in an Indian village involves physical fighting. Those who quarrel leave the village for a time but are later welcomed back.

21–24: The men are skilled warriors, protecting their families and fending off enemies. While living with the Aguenes, I witnessed a violent ambush and counterattack. The warring tribes, however, were soon reconciled.

25: The Indians stay alert and armed all night if they suspect attack.

26–27: In battle, they bravely dodge the arrows of their foes and the shots of our weapons, but they greatly fear our horses.

28: Whoever fights Indians must show no fear or desire to take their possessions, for the Indians take heart in the fear of an enemy and later seek revenge.

29: The Indians recover quickly from battle wounds and have superior eyesight, hearing, and physical stamina.

RUTH BENEDICT

The Pueblos of New Mexico (pp. 511–26)

Paragraphs 1–5: The Zuñi, or Pueblo, is a strongly socialized culture in which the individual is not important. Marriage and divorce are conducted very casually because the strongest bond in Zuñi culture is that of the matrilineal family. Whether or not they are married, women remain in the household into which they were born for life, and men return to their mother's home for all important occasions.

6–7: While this "blood-relationship group" is ceremonially the most important group in Zuñi culture, it is not the functioning economical group; a man lives with his wife's family and provides for them unless there is no male labor in his mother's house. Thus, men have double allegiance to women, both as spouses and as brothers, with the latter usually holding more social weight.

8–10: Wealth has little importance in Zuñi tribes; a family's value is determined by the sacred objects it owns and the ceremonial roles its members have undertaken. While ceremonial objects are personal property, they can be used by anyone qualified; those who own these objects "have no monopoly of their supernatural powers." Ceremonial participation is the responsibility of a group of people rather than the individual.

11–13: While the Zuñi are a ritualistic people, so were most of the other American Indian cultures. What sets the Zuñi apart from these cultures is their attitude toward existence. Borrowing Nietzsche's concepts of the Apollonian and Dionysian personalities, the Pueblos are Apollonian (measured, reserved, intellectual, and rational), while the other cultures are Dionysian (emotional and given to intoxication and excess as a means to entering a different psychological state).

14: The Pueblos see individualism and change as disruptive, even when it refines or enlarges the culture's tradition; they prefer to commit to the known rules and customs of their tradition.

15–21: Other American Indian cultures as a whole were Dionysian, valuing violent experience and anything else that broke through "the usual sensory routine." While these groups do not have a uniform culture, they do share a "practice of obtaining supernatural power in a dream or vision" through some powerful exercise of concentration. These quests took place alone and often involved self-destructive acts, such as torture or fasting, though the participants didn't see them as self-destructive because they were seeking not only a vision but also to become stronger or to succeed in a particular venture.

22–23: Since it was up to the individual to decide whether or not he had a vision and since the individual was always alone, in theory these experiences granted great freedom to the individual. But in practice, the traditions of these cultures remained largely unchallenged. In cultures where prestige was a great privilege, usually passed down through families, the vision quest was seen as disruptive; in these cases the supernatural experience might be considered insignificant.

24–27: The supernatural experience itself, however, was openly pursued by entire tribes, who used alcohol and drugs such as peyote and jimson weed in ceremonies to "obtain the blessed state which was to them supremely religious."

28–32: This practice of obtaining supernatural power from a vision prevails everywhere among North American Indians except in the Southern Pueblos, who do not value excess and who perceive disruptive experiences as something to be avoided rather than pursued. For them, elements of the Dionysian experience exist, but they have been reinterpreted and transformed so that they fit the Pueblos' Apollonian character. Pueblo men go to feared and sacred places alone at night, but they are looking for omens, not visions; fasting is required for ceremonial cleanliness rather than to create an altered psychological state; and jimson weed is used to get someone to confess to a theft, after which it is purged from his body.

MARGARET MEAD

Women, Sex, and Sin (pp. 529–41)

Paragraphs 1–2: The Manus value essentially masculine personalities such as active, demanding, and assertive natures over maternal, soft, or feminine personality traits.

3–4: Girls are betrothed at a very young age, and both young men and young women were expected to guard their reputations out of loyalty to their relatives and fear of having to pay high penalties for angering their ancestors. But young men were indulged more for their indiscretions, while young women were abused.

5–6: A girl's fiancé was supposed to evoke shame both in the girl and in her whole family; the girl was not supposed to look at or even think about him. This naturally resulted in women shrinking from their husband's touch once married, and in women being attracted to other men, men they were not required to think of with shame. Manus women had no models with which to associate the idea or practice of gentle sexual behavior in marriage.

7: It was into this background of "inhibited and chaperoned girlhood set against the ever present possibility of seduction and rape" that the Catholic mission entered. In addition to learning to read, write, and sing, Manus girls were taught feminine traits such as obedience, neatness, and discipline. But because their teachers were nuns, they still had no opportunity to learn about gentleness in marital sex.

8–9: In 1946, Manus men declared the emancipation of women by "the New Way," having learned about women choosing their own mates, public displays of affection, and men being generally kind to their wives from working among the Australians and from American films. Just as men had dictated women's behavior before, they continued to do so now, declaring that women would be spontaneous, responsive, and actively loving. Manus men also learned from the Australians to help with the child care.

10–14: Before the New Way, women were deprived of "affectionate domesticity," but they did have a public economic role that women in other societies lacked. This public role and any autonomy that went with it was lost with the introduction of the New Way. While women now had choices about their husbands, these choices did not mean that much in a society in which women did not know how to be loving and tender. Further, the New Way redefined love "as a relationship in which sex can be ignored in favor of affection," while sex was still associated with anger and "rights," an association that worked against women.

15: For all the emancipation, women and sex were still closely connected to sin; before, their attitude toward sex revolved around fear of their "ghosts," and now it revolved around fear of angering their spouses.

16–17: Intelligent, ambitious, active women lost at least as much as they gained from the New Way. Before, they could have public roles and responsibilities; now they are supposed to keep house and raise children in a modern way, yet even in child care their husbands take precedence. In the old days, there was the possibility of some tenderness among aging couples as the shame of the taboos were off; now they don't even have this.

18–19: Public opinion tends to side with the wife when she is asked to do more than her share in supporting the household, but as a woman ages it tips toward men.

20: Women are still repudiated, both as citizens and as mothers, while men are exalted.

CLIFFORD GEERTZ

"From the Native's Point of View": On the Nature of Anthropological Understanding (pp. 543–62)

Paragraph 1:   *A Diary in the Strict Sense of the Term*, a book by the well-known anthropologist Bronislaw Malinowski, shattered the myth that the field anthropologist was completely immersed in and in tune with the culture he was studying.

2:   While critics attacked Malinowski's moral character, most missed the serious question the book raised about whether or not it was really possible to understand things from a "native's point of view."

3:   This has been a central question in anthropology in recent years; the psychoanalyst Heinz Kohut's concepts of "experience-near" and "experience-distant" are useful in discussing it.

4:   An experience-near concept is one that someone (such as an informant or member of the culture being studied) might naturally use to define what he or his people see, feel, or think. An experience-distant concept is one that specialists such as scientists and ethnographers use to advance their scientific or practical aims.

5–6:   The real question is how an anthropologist should use these concepts in order to produce an interpretation of the way a people live that is not limited or defined by either the anthropologist's or the informant's perspectives or experiences. The challenge is to simultaneously remain distanced enough to be able to make meaningful connections with current anthropological concepts but to get close enough to "figure out what . . . [these people] think they are up to."

7:   Trying to immerse yourself in another culture's experience doesn't work because people use experience-near concepts almost without realizing they *are* concepts. The unself-conscious nature of these concepts makes it impossible for the ethnographer to perceive the same thing his informant perceives.

8–9:   In my studies of Javanese, Balinese, and Moroccan societies, I tried to understand how these people define themselves by analyzing the symbolic forms (words, images, institutions, behaviors) they used to represent themselves. This seems a reasonable starting point because the concept of a person is universal, existing in some form in all social groups. Still, we must set aside our Western concepts of self to understand this concept in other cultures.

10:   Despite the extreme poverty of the Javanese people in the 1950s, the poorest and least educated of these people were engaged in passionate intellectual and philosophical reflections about such things as God, reason, free will, and the nature of the self.

11:   The contrasting ideas of inside/outside and refined/vulgar form the conception of the self through which the Javanese perceived themselves and one another.

12–13:   The inside concept refers to the emotional lives of human beings, while the outside concept refers to external actions, movements, postures, and speech. Both these inward feelings and outward actions are conceived as identical across all individuals and as independent of one another. The goal is for both realms of the self to be "refined" or "put in proper order." This is achieved in the inner realm through meditation and religious discipline and in the outer realm through a strictly followed etiquette.

14:   The result is a conception of a divided self composed of "an inner world of stilled emotion and an outer world of shaped behavior" strikingly different from, but every bit as legitimate and forceful as, our own notions of the moral importance of honesty, deep feeling, and sincerity.

15:   The Balinese engage in an intricate and obsessive ritual life vastly different from that of the reflective and phenomenological Javanese.

16:   The Balinese stylize and ritualize their lives to the extent that all individual characteristics are muted; they adhere to their assigned places in the drama of Balinese life, where it is the play rather than the players that matters.

17–20: The Balinese have an elaborate system of labels and titles related to birth order, caste, kinship, gender, and profession, each of which indicates a fixed spot in the Balinese hierarchy and social structure. These labels represent people as generic types rather than as individuals with unique fates. In fact, the Balinese experience-near concept of *lek* refers to stage-fright, or the fear that what we would call "the personality . . . of the individual will break through to dissolve his standardized public identity."

21: In contrast to Java and Bali, Morocco is an informal, even wild place full of culturally diverse, "emphatic," and "rugged individuals."

22–23: The *nisba*, the terminology that defines people according to where they come from—their ethnic roots, religions, tribes, professions, and family relationships—is the symbolic means Moroccans use to "form an idea of what it is to be a person."

24–26: The *nisba* is incorporated into one's personal name and is often the main thing others know *about* a person; people are defined by the associations they have with the surrounding society rather than by their own personalities or current circumstances. Which *nisbas* are used when changes according to social context.

27–29: The Moroccan concept of selfhood "marks public identity contextually and relativistically, but yet does so in terms—tribal, territorial, linguistic, religious, familial—that grow out of the more private and settled arenas of life and have a deep and permanent resonance there." *Nisba* distinctions are deliberately adaptive; they classify men but do not type them or prescribe attitudes or behaviors, so that people retain a strong individual sense of self.

30–32: Note that my method throughout (and the method of anthropologists who have conducted similar analyses) is a "continuous dialectical" movement between the minute details (or parts) and the big picture (or whole). The movement shifts back and forth between general patterns and specific observations in such a way that each explicates and elucidates the other.

33: The capacity to really understand other peoples comes not from the experience of living their lives but from the ability to interpret their "modes of expression" or symbolic systems.

SIDDHĀRTHA GAUTAMA, THE BUDDHA

Meditation: *The Path to Enlightenment* (pp. 569–87)

Paragraph 1: The practice of secluded meditation confers many benefits on the practitioner.

2–3: The twenty-eight advantages of secluded meditation promote good health and happiness through removal of all of the causes of sorrow and discontent from the practitioner's consciousness.

4–28: The serious follower of the practice of meditation must withdraw from the world in order to eliminate distractions. The fleeting nature of human existence does not justify allowing oneself to lose sight of eternal truth through giving reign to the passions, the desire for worldly gain, and the transient friendships of this life. It is better to live alone and with few possessions. A person is born alone and must die alone; no one can share these ultimate realities. Each incarnation should be seen as a step along the way to eternal release from earthly concerns.

29–31: The first step in the practice of meditation involves distancing oneself from the assaults of the five physical senses—those insatiable connoisseurs of transient, worldly pleasures. One must constantly stand guard, through mindfulness, against their attempted intrusions. To avoid ensnaring oneself in the cultivation of likes and dislikes for the objects of the senses, do not add to or subtract from the true reality of that which the senses perceive.

32: The perceiver does not get caught up in the objects of his perception unless he adds the element of imagination to the data of the senses. To see a thing as it really is liberates one from bondage to sense objects.

33: Too much food leads to the mental and physical torpor of satiety; too little food leads to the inefficiency that comes through depletion of strength. The wise man takes care of his body only because it serves as a vehicle to get him past the sufferings of incarnation.

34: At night, one must throw off sleepiness in order to continue the practice of yoga. A person cannot afford to sleep as long as faults are still with him. Three hours of the night should be spent in the practice of yoga before giving in to the need for sleep.

35: If a practitioner of meditation is constantly mindful of his postures, his speech, and all that his body does, he cannot be taken unawares by assaults from the passions.

36: In order to attain detachment of the mind, one must find a place to live that is free of people and noise.

37: Concentration and focusing of thought through systematic meditation act as water that is cast on the smoldering fire of the desire to indulge in ruinous physical pleasures.

38–39: A holy man will find it possible to refrain from entertaining ill-will toward others because he knows that the mortal condition already entails enough suffering. He tries to avoid thinking unwholesome thoughts by practicing their opposites.

40: Incarnations make it impossible to know who one's relations are. Therefore, it is foolish to worry about your family's well-being.

41–42: Do not worry about conditions in your country because there is no place on earth that is free from all causes of suffering.

43: Never take continued life for granted; death waits in ambush even for the young and strong. It is senseless to make plans that do not take death into account.

44–48: The essential nature of reality rests on these four truths—first, that suffering is omnipresent; second, that the cause of suffering is birth or incarnation, which opens our senses to the world of suffering; third, that extinction of suffering comes through escape from it; fourth, that salvation is achieved through adherence to the path that leads to tranquility. To escape from suffering, one must turn away from the passions and from worldly activity. The attainment of dharma, or the absence of birth, comes through cultivation of morality, wisdom, and the promotion of tranquility through concentration.

ST. MATTHEW

The Sermon on the Mount (pp. 589–99)

Chapter 4. Verses 23–25:   Followed by great crowds, Jesus traveled in Galilee healing the sick.

5.1–2:   On a mountain, he taught them, saying:

5.3–12:   Great rewards await those who are poor in spirit, who mourn, who are meek, who long for righteousness, who show mercy, who are pure of heart, who make peace, and who suffer for my sake.

5.13–16:   You are the salt of the earth and the light of the world. Let your light shine as an example to others.

5.17–20:   I have come to fulfill, not to destroy, established laws and prophecies. Those who wish to enter heaven must obey the law.

5.21–26:   Avoid unjust anger, seek forgiveness from those you have wronged, and make peace with your adversaries. Failure to reconcile yourself with others will put you at risk of judgment.

5.27–30:   To look lustfully at a woman is to commit adultery with her in your heart. If one part of your body causes you to sin, rid yourself of that part rather than put your whole body at risk.

5.31–32:   Except in cases of fornication, divorce is wrong. Those who remarry after divorcing commit adultery.

5.33–37:   Those who swear oaths come to evil. Instead of swearing oaths, answer simply yes or no.

5.38–42:   Do not seek revenge. When people ask something of you, give them what they ask and more.

5.43–48:   Imitate your Father in heaven by treating all people, even your enemies, with love.

6.1–4:   Do not make a public show when you give alms; those who give alms without show will be rewarded in heaven.

6.5–15:   Pray privately and without vain repetition. Acknowledge your heavenly Father and ask for your daily needs, for forgiveness as you forgive others, and for protection from temptation.

6.16–18:   Likewise, fast privately without outward show.

6.19–23:   Do not store up your treasure on earth but in heaven. Keep your eye focused only on good.

6.24–34:   No one can serve both God and worldly riches. Therefore, do not worry about bodily needs or the future. Just as your heavenly Father cares for birds and flowers, he will care for you.

7.1–6:   Do not judge or admonish others lest the same be done to you.

7.7–12:   Ask for what you need, and your Father will give it to you.

7.13–14:   The wide path leads to destruction. Follow the narrow path, which leads to life.

7.15–20:   Shun false prophets; they are wolves disguised as sheep. Avoid the corrupt tree, which yields only bad fruit.

7.21–23:   Not all who claim to know me will enter heaven.

7.24–27:   Whoever follows these teachings will thrive; whoever does not will perish.

7.28:   The people were amazed by Jesus' teachings.

THE BHAGAVAD GĪTĀ

Meditation and Knowledge (pp. 601–14)

Chapter 6. Verses 1–4:   Krishna, the Blessed One, said: He who acts in accord with religious duty, unconcerned about what he may gain from his actions, is a man of discipline. To achieve discipline, one must renounce purpose and detach oneself from physical things and from actions.

6.5–6:   One must control the self, make it one's friend, for the uncontrolled self is an enemy.

6.7–9:   The disciplined, self-controlled man faces life with poise and equanimity. His senses are subdued; he regards all things with detachment and dispassion.

6.10–15:   A man of discipline should meditate in seclusion, in a clean place, subduing his thoughts and soul, focusing his attention. He should sit with body immobile, spirit tranquil, firm in his vow of celibacy. In this way, he achieves enlightenment and rests in me.

6.16–19:   In eating, in sleeping, and in all activities, the disciplined man strives for moderation and thus avoids suffering. He is free from longing for things outside the self; he is like the steady flame of a lamp in a windless place.

6.20–23:   Content within himself, his mind at rest, having achieved a joyful awareness that is beyond the senses, valuing nothing other than this awareness—this is the state of the disciplined man, a state that frees him from all suffering.

6.24–32:   The disciplined man must abandon all purposes and restrain his senses. Gradually, he should abandon all thought, achieving self-control. In this tranquil state, freed from passion, he achieves supreme joy and approaches spiritual perfection. The man thus disciplined sees the oneness of all things, sees all in me and me in all.

6.33–34:   Arjuna said: Because the mind is so volatile and powerful, I see little hope of restraining it.

6.35–36:   Krishna, the Blessed One, said: Though it is powerful, the mind may be disciplined by the man who practices self-control.

6.37–39:   Arjuna said: What hope is there for the man of faith who strives for discipline but fails to achieve perfection? Will he perish? Only you can answer this question for me, Krishna.

6.40–44:   Krishna, the Blessed One, said: No harm will come to the man who does right. He will be rewarded for what he has done and will later be reborn into a noble or disciplined family. There he will regain the level of discipline he had achieved in his former life and will continue striving for perfection.

6.45–47:   The man of discipline, perfected through many rebirths, will ultimately reach the highest goal. Arjuna, be a man of discipline, for such a man is superior to men of austerities, of knowledge, or of ritual actions. The man of greatest discipline is he who honors me with faith.

7.1–3:   Krishna, the Blessed One, said: I will tell you, Arjuna, how you may know me completely, and I will explain to you all theoretical and practical knowledge. Few achieve this knowledge.

7.4–7:   My lower nature has eight aspects. My higher nature is the source of all life; I am the origin and the disintegration of all the world. There is nothing higher than me.

7.8–11:   I am everything. All that exists is contained in me.

7.12–14:   From me come the three states of nature—goodness, passion, and darkness. The world is deluded and cannot see that I am eternal and beyond these states. Only those who resort to me alone perceive this deeper truth.

7.15–19:   Evil men do not resort to me. Four types of virtuous men worship me, but of the four, the man of knowledge is the best. After many reincarnations, this rare man of knowledge realizes that I, Krishna, am all.

7.20–23: Deprived of knowledge and limited by their own natures, men resort to gods other than me. So long as they worship their gods faithfully, I sanction the faith of these men. When they obtain favors from their gods, it is because I grant the favors. But the rewards of these men are limited compared to the rewards of those who worship me.

7.24–26: Fools think that I am manifest in the world. But I am veiled in illusion and not revealed to most men. The world does not understand that I am eternal and know all that is past, present, and to come.

7.27–30: At birth, all creatures are confused by a delusion of opposites arising from desire and hatred. Men of virtue are freed from this delusion and rely on me. Such men strive for freedom from old age and death, and they achieve knowledge. Those who know me have disciplined their hearts.

THE PROPHET MUHAMMAD

From *the Koran* (pp. 617–26)

Paragraphs 1–3: This book is revealed by the one true God. Only unbelievers dispute what he reveals, and they will be punished.

4–7: On the day of judgment, those who are with God will ask him to forgive and reward believers. But unbelievers will not be forgiven.

8–10: God gives his signs and his spirit to those whom he chooses. Worship God, for at the judgment day, he will triumph, and all will be rewarded or punished.

11–12: Warn unbelievers that nothing can save them. Have they not seen what God has done to punish unbelievers in the past?

13–16: We sent Moses to tell the truth to Pharaoh, Haman, and Korah, but they rejected the truth and sought to slay Moses and those who believed.

17–20: One of Pharaoh's relatives, a secret true believer, urged Pharaoh to spare Moses and warned the people about God's punishment. Pharaoh insisted on his rightness, but the true believer again warned the people, reminding them of their past lack of faith.

21–22: Pharaoh persisted in his doubt, and his actions led to destruction.

23–24: The true believer again addressed the people, urging them to follow the right path and to turn away from false gods.

25–26: Entrusting himself to God, the true believer was saved, but a scourge came on Pharaoh's people. On the day of judgment, they will be sent to the fire.

27–30: In the fire, they will argue among themselves and plead for relief from torment. But their pleas will be useless because they did not believe.

31–33: We will help those who believe and will punish the guilty. We gave guidance to the Israelites; therefore, wait patiently and trust in God.

34–38: Despite the many signs of God's power and goodness, most men continue to disbelieve.

39–40: God has created all things. There is no other god, yet men turn away from him.

41–43: Blessed be God. Pray to him, worship him, reject idols, and surrender to the "Lord of the Universe."

44–45: God created you, giving you life from infancy to old age. He is the author of all things.

46–49: Those who deny the revelations of God, will see the truth hereafter and will suffer in hell. They will be chastised for their wicked lives.

50–51: Be patient, and God's promise will be fulfilled. Muhammad, even if we do not let you glimpse in this life the punishment that awaits unbelievers, we will bring the unbelievers to justice. We have sent other apostles before you, and they gave signs through the power of God.

52–56: God gives men animals to use for food and transportation. His signs are many. Unbelievers fail to see the fate of those before them who rejected God. Boastful and proud, they scoffed at God's signs, repenting too late, only after they had seen God's might.

118

ST. TERESA OF AVILA

From *The Raptures of St. Teresa* (pp. 629–39)

Paragraph 1: We may create in imagination an image of Christ, but the kind of visions described here are not products of the imagination but revelations from the Lord.

2–3: My visions were not within my control. It was not a matter of wanting or not wanting them; they came through no effort of my own.

4: The Lord appeared to me in his glorified bodily form. Many who heard of my visions said that I was possessed by the devil. This did not trouble me, for I regarded the visions as a great favor from the Lord.

5: One of my confessors, thinking that I was deceived, ordered me to resist the visions. I obeyed reluctantly even though I continued to regard the visions as a favor from God.

6: In resisting the visions, I felt that I was rejecting the Lord. I asked him to forgive me, and he offered comfort and reassurance.

7: In one vision, the Lord transformed the wooden cross of my rosary into four precious stones. The more I tried to resist my visions, the more often they came. It was not in my power to cease thinking of the Lord, and he told me how to answer my critics.

8: Later, the Lord (his majesty) gave even clearer signs of his presence. I was overpowered with violent love and longing for him and regarded death as the only way to fulfill my longing.

9: My impulses were not simply the kind of religious feeling that can be controlled by reason. Such feelings, like those of a sobbing child, should not be allowed to boil over but must be soothed and turned into inward reflection.

10: My impulses were of a different, more powerful, kind. Rather than coming from within, they were thrust on me, like arrows driven into my entrails and heart. This indescribable wounding by God was enormously painful and distressing and, at the same time, deeply satisfying. In this state, the soul would gladly die for the love of God.

11: My distress and bliss overwhelmed me. God's love sparked in my soul a fire of unbearable longing.

12: At times, my pain abated. At other times, the impulses were so strong that they paralyzed me spiritually and physically.

13: On rare occasions, I had a vision of an angel who pierced my heart with a golden spear. This experience, which was both painful and sweet, left me aflame with love for God.

14: During my raptures, I walked about in a stupor and clung to my pain and bliss. I am grateful to the Lord for transporting my soul and sending me these ecstasies.

FRIEDRICH NIETZSCHE

Apollonianism and Dionysianism (pp. 641–59)

Paragraphs 1–2:   Art owes its continuous evolution to the Apollonian-Dionysian duality—that is, to both the rational (Apollonian) and irrational (Dionysian) characteristics of human nature.

2–3:   We experience dreams with a sense of delight and necessity; the image of Apollo incorporates the thin line that the dream image may not cross, fearing it may impose itself on us as a crass reality.

4–5:   In the Dionysian rite, the individual forgets himself completely and, becoming reconciled with nature, experiences a mystic oneness with all of creation.

6:   Apollonian and Dionysian states, rising directly from nature, are not rendered by the human artist; thus every artist seems to be an imitator—either an Apollonian dream-artist, a Dionysian ecstatic artist, or a combination of both.

7:   In order to assess the relation of the Greek artist to his art (imitations of nature), one must discover the degree to which the two forces of nature—Apollonian and Dionysian—were developed in that artist.

8:   Dionysian and Apollonian elements, each enhancing the other in a continuous chain of creations, eventually dominated the Hellenic mind.

9–13:   From the Iron Age, with its battles of Titans and its austere popular philosophy, the Homeric world developed under the aegis of Apollo.

14–16:   The naiveté of Homeric beauty was absorbed once more by the Dionysian passions; in opposition to the Dionysian power, the Apollonian code rigidified into the majesty of Doric art and contemplation.

17:   The true end of this artistic evolution was the dramatic dithyramb (a passionate hymn delivered to Dionysus) in combination with the tragedy; this union achieved the common goal of the Apollonian and Dionysian urges.

MARTIN BUBER

From *I and Thou* (pp. 661–74)

Paragraph 1:   Overemphasizing our feeling of dependence on God leads us to misunderstand the nature of the perfect relationship.

2–3:   Our feelings are changeable, relative, and secondary to the essential fact of the relationship itself—the relationship between an I and a You.

4:   In the pure relationship, you simultaneously feel totally dependent and totally free.

5–6:   You need God, but God also needs you. Man would not exist if God did not need him. We offer ourselves to the creator as helpers and companions.

7:   Prayer and sacrifice are the two means by which we establish relationship with God. Unlike prayer and sacrifice, magic does not entail relationship with God.

8:   If we regard the pure relationship as one of total dependence, then we nullify one partner in the relationship and thereby nullify the relationship itself.

9:   We also nullify the relationship when the religious act becomes an immersion in the self. This immersion takes two forms. In the first form, the self (I) loses its individuality and merges totally with God (You); the two become one. In the second form, the self is seen as containing both the I and the You; the human and the divine are identical.

10–12:   These two "doctrines of immersion" are illustrated in epigrams—one from the Gospel of John and one from the Upanishads. These epigrams follow diametrically opposed paths, both of which are discussed here.

13:   In the Gospel of John, some find evidence to support the first doctrine of immersion—of man and God becoming one. But this Gospel as a whole affirms that man and God are two—partners in a relationship.

14–17:   While it seems to verify the reality of immersion, mysticism describes only the feeling of unity within the duality of a relationship. There are, in fact, two experiences in which we can lose awareness of this duality. First, the soul itself, within man, can be concentrated into a unity. Second, we can experience the feeling of being transported away from the world into a unity with God.

18:   But the unity achieved in such an ecstatic experience is not, in fact, a true oneness; rather, the relationship is felt so powerfully that the separate I and the You are forgotten, though never actually merged.

19–21:   The other doctrine of immersion—that the self and the universe are one—seeks a unity of being that annihilates the self and reduces the actual world to mere illusion.

22–25:   We choose to live in this world, where the strongest actuality is found not in the "pure," abstract self but in the whole, living human being in active relationship with God. The self that annihilates the actual world in order to rise above it annihilates its own actuality.

26–28:   The Buddha refuses to assert whether unity and salvation exist. Indeed, we cannot make assertions about such ultimate truths; rather, we must confront them as mystery. The Buddha teaches that there is a way toward a goal, and in this we can follow him. But we cannot accept his goal—escape from the recurrent cycle of rebirth. We do not know if there is recurrence; even if we did know, we would not try to escape from the recurrence but would choose to live fully in every existence given to us.

29–31:   For the Buddha, the world is deceptive—an illusion—but for us it is reliable. Like the Buddha, we seek unification of the soul. But unlike him, we seek to bring the unified soul into relationship (You-saying). The Buddha knows You-saying, but he does not teach it. His followers, however, have done so.

32–36: All doctrines of immersion are based on the fallacy that the spirit is fully contained within the individual rather than in the individual's relation with what he is not. The Buddha proclaims that the individual contains all the world as well as the origin and the annulment of the world. While the world is in me as a notion, in a more profound sense I am detached from the world and the world is detached from me.

37–39: The origin and annulment of the world are neither in nor outside of me but are connected with me. The world does not depend on whether I affirm or negate it within my soul; rather I influence the world by living actively in it. Living in the world leads us to God. God embraces the universe and my self; because of this, I and all people can say "You," entering into relationship with God.

ARISTOTLE

Tragedy and the Emotions of Pity and Fear (pp. 681–96)

Paragraphs 1–3: Tragedy is an imitation of an action with serious implications that is complete and has magnitude. Its language is made sensually attractive with rhythm and melody. It is presented in dialogue rather than narrative form, with some sections spoken and others sung. The performers' visual appearance is obviously important, as is the quality of the writing and music. The play is enacted by people portraying characters with certain traits who express certain opinions. Thus, tragedy has six distinctive elements—plot, characters, verbal expression, thought, visual adornment, and song-composition.

4–7: The most important element in tragedy is the plot, for tragedy is an imitation not of men but of a life, an action. The events do not occur to depict the characters; rather, the characters are a vehicle for the action. A tragedy can exist without characters but not without a plot. Its most powerful means for swaying our feelings are the peripeties and recognitions, which are elements of plot. New poets can succeed at verbal expression and character portrayal sooner than plot construction.

8–10: With plot as its heart and soul and characters coming second, a tragedy's third most essential element is thought. Springing from the arts of politics and rhetoric, thought refers to those passages in which a character tries to prove or disprove a point, or states some general principle. Fourth is verbal expression, or effective conveyance of thought through language.

11: Song-composition is the greatest of tragedy's sensuous attractions. The visual adornment of the actors can have a strong emotional effect but is least connected with the poetic art; in fact, the force of tragedy can be felt even without benefit of public performance and actors.

12–13: The tragedy's plot must be complete—that is, have a beginning, a middle, and an end. It should be short enough to be easily remembered, to hold the viewer's attention, and to be perceived as a whole; within these limits, the longer the better. More generally, its length should be whatever is required for a shift from good to bad or from bad to good fortune to take place within an unbroken sequence of events.

14–15: A plot is not unified simply because it has to do with a single person. Rather, it must have a single object—that is, it should depict a complete action in which each component event is necessary to the entire sequence and properly placed within it.

16: The poet's job, in contrast to the historian's, is not to report what has happened but what could happen given the probabilities and necessities of a certain situation. Poetry is thus a more philosophical and serious business than history, for it depicts universals, using particulars as its means.

17–18: Comic poets grasp this point, constructing their plots on the basis of general probabilities and then naming their characters arbitrarily. Tragic poets cling to historical characters because of their association with actions already known to be possible and therefore believable. When tragedians do use fictional characters, their work is just as plausible. The poet should be a maker of plots more than of verses, for his art is imitation and he imitates actions.

19–20: Among simple plots the episodic are the worst—those in which the order of the events seems arbitrary. Because the force of tragedy comes from the poignance of fear and pathos striking contrary to our expectations yet logically, the plot's sequence is crucial.

21: A simple plot is one imitating a simple action in which the reversal of fortune comes without peripety or recognition. A complex plot includes recognition or peripety or both, emerging by necessity or probability from the sequence of events.

22–24: Peripety is an unexpected ironic twist in the action; recognition is a major shift from ignorance to awareness. The finest recognition is one that happens with a peripety, exciting pity or fear in anticipation of the good and bad fortune to follow, for these are the kinds of action tragedy exists to imitate. Besides peripety and recognition, the third element of plot is the pathos, a destructive or painful act.

123

25–26:   It would be morally repugnant for virtuous men to experience a change from good to bad fortune, and unmoving for wicked men to go from bad fortune to good. Instead, the hero who is between the extremes, and who fails because of a mistake, will arouse the appropriate emotions of sympathy, pity, or fear.

27–29:   The artistically made plot involves a change from good fortune to bad—not as a result of wickedness but because of some mistake of great weight and consequence. This is the structure for technically the finest tragedy. Those plots that have opposite changes in fortune for the good and bad characters are often rated highest because audiences have a weakness for them. But this type of plot is more characteristic of comedy.

30–31:   If the plot is well structured, the audience shudders with fear and pity because of what happens and not merely because of the character's fearful or pitiable appearance. To produce pity and fear, the fearful and pitiable actions must be performed by persons who are close blood kin.

32–33:   Stories, either invented or handed down, can be handled in four different artistic modes: (1) the tragic act is performed wittingly by the character, (2) the character refrains from performing the fearful act, (3) the character performs the fearful act and only later recognizes the blood relationship, (4) while intending to perform the fearful act, the character discovers the close relationship beforehand.

34:   The worst mode is (2) because it is morally repulsive and not tragic; (1) is the second worst; (3) is better because the repulsive quality is not attached to the act, and the recognition has a shattering emotional effect; (4) is the best.

35–36:   The reason why most tragedy focuses on only a few families is that the poets searched at random for families that have suffered tragic happenings.

ALEXANDER POPE

From *An Essay on Criticism* (pp. 699–712)

Lines 1–14:   The chief cause of poor judgment among critics is pride, which blinds them to their own shortcomings.

15–32:   A second cause is lack of learning, which limits their perspective.

33–52:   A third cause is evaluating by parts rather than by whole. We should judge the overall effect of a work and not the excellence or weakness of its individual parts.

53–66:   Critics should consider that no work can be perfect in all its parts.

67–88:   A story about a critic (knight) and a playwright (bard) illustrates the error of judging by part rather than by whole.

89–104:   Some critics erroneously judge poetry for its cleverness and extravagant ornamentation (conceit) rather than for its substance.

105–136:   Others overemphasize the poet's language, favoring style over meaning, expression over sense. The best language is clear and plain, neither old-fashioned nor trendy.

137–183:   Still others overemphasize the poet's skill at versification (numbers), judging works by their sound rather than their meaning. In the best poetry, "The sound must seem an Echo to the sense."

184–193:   Critics should avoid extremes, being neither too hard to please nor too quick to admire.

194–207:   Some critics are biased toward a particular sect of writers—English or foreign, ancient or modern.

208–223:   Some are swayed by popular opinion, by an author's reputation, or by their desire to flatter a powerful author.

224–229:   Others are overly singular, shunning popular opinion even when it is right.

230–251:   Some critics constantly change their opinions, praising a work one moment, blaming it the next.

252–265:   Others value only works written by their own faction—those who share their views.

266–273:   The envious may try to dim the glory of a work of great merit, but their efforts will fail.

274–307:   A critic should be quick to praise a deserving work, for today even poetry of great merit enjoys fame but a short while.

308–325:   Some great poets jealously guard their status, giving no support to lesser poets. Poets and critics should be magnanimous and good natured in their judgments.

WILLIAM WORDSWORTH
From the preface to *Lyrical Ballads* (pp. 715–28)

Paragraph 1:   In writing these poems, I drew my subject matter from simple, common life and used ordinary—rather than artificially poetic—language. At the same time, I tried to reveal the extraordinary qualities found in simple things.

2:   I deplore the debased thought and language in some popular poetry today. My poems, unlike these, have a worthy purpose. All good poetry originates from the spontaneous outpouring of feelings, but these feelings must be modified and shaped by thought. Good poetry must enlighten the reader's mind and improve his capacity to feel.

3–4:   My poems also differ from popular poetry in their emphasis on subtle rather than coarse emotions. I believe that the human mind has the capacity to be excited without the use of crude stimulants, and my aim is to enlarge that capacity. Today, many forces, including the dreary uniformity of urban life, make people crave violent stimulation. Despite this, I believe that the higher, permanent qualities of the human mind will prevail.

5:   The style of my poems differs from that typically found in poetry. I have avoided artificial diction and conventional phrases and figures of speech, preferring instead concrete language and exact, direct description.

6–8:   Some critics claim that the language of poetry must differ from that of prose. But a sonnet by Gray shows that this is not necessarily the case. I believe, in fact, that the language of poetry is essentially the same as the language of prose. Poetic language should not be elevated or regarded as unique.

9:   For poetry, I recommend a "selection of the language really spoken by men." When chosen with taste and feeling, such language is, in itself, naturally dignified, varied, and figurative, making the addition of artificial poetic devices unnecessary.

10:   If my unconventional poetic principles were accepted, standard judgments about the works of great poets would be changed dramatically.

11:   Although he is "a man speaking to men," the poet possesses powers that exceed those of other men, including greater emotional sensitivity, greater insight into human nature, and a more powerful imagination.

12–13:   However great the poet's powers, his language must often fall short of the language that is spoken by men at moments of great emotion. The poet should strive to identify closely with the emotion of those persons he describes; he should select natural language that will capture the finest aspects of that emotion.

14:   Some advise poets to use elevated language to heighten emotion, but such advice shows little understanding of the nature of poetry. For the aim of poetry is truth, and the poet must strive to present as directly as possible the truth of the human heart.

15:   Poetry is "the spontaneous overflow of powerful feelings . . . recollected in tranquillity." The poet communicates his feelings and, in doing so, gives pleasure. Descriptions written in verse give greater, more lasting pleasure than those written in prose.

VIRGINIA WOOLF

A Letter to a Young Poet (pp. 731–49)

Paragraph 1:   There used to be an old gentleman who complained the penny post had killed the art of letter writing; but in fact that art is the child of the penny post, which, by making letters cheap to send, has freed them from their former status as important documents to be delightfully full of gossip, indiscretions, and vitality.

2:   Before replying to your question where poetry's going, or if it's dead, I must admit my lack of qualifications to answer, being unfamiliar with the various meters, and envious yet dubious (as all prose writers are) of rhyme and the other rules poets follow.

3:   You imply that poetry may be in the direst straits ever. Never believe your own case harder than other people's—difficult as this is in our drama-hungry age—for in taking yourself seriously as a leader or follower, you become a clawing animal instead of the heir to a long, rich poetic tradition.

4–6:   Imagining myself in your place, I see you seized with the rhythm of poetry, yet frustrated in your attempts to write by the intrusion of ordinary incidents and people. Unlike Chaucer, Shakespeare, and others, poets of our time leave gritty reality to the novelists. When they do try to include it in a poem, they yoke it to the moon or the nightingale, and the poem splits apart.

7–9:   I see you dismissing the sights and sounds around you and looking within yourself, the easiest subject for a poem. Present-day poets focus not on experiences and sensations we all share but on the unique, inaccessible world of their own minds. This leaves poetry gasping for breath, indeed, but not dead.

10–11:   Now that poetry has freed itself from the wreckage of the Victorian age and plumbed the mind of the poet, why should it not open its eyes and look out the window? The problem is to find the right relationship between the poetic self and the world. Your instinct of rhythm will take care of that if you saturate it with experience, enabling you to condense and synthesize as novelists cannot.

12–13:   When I read the poems of our contemporaries I am agreeably caught up, and hence optimistic, but also malcontent: I miss the beauty (which English has such power to convey) of sensory experience. The art of writing depends on knowing the language thoroughly enough to suggest as well as state, which comes from reading and even more from speaking in voices other than one's own.

14–16:   Publish nothing before you are thirty. Use these years to explore your imagination and develop your talent: the public eye will only confine and stifle you. Revel in life, and we need not worry about the death of poetry.

SUSAN SONTAG

Against Interpretation (pp. 751–67)

Paragraphs 1–3: Art began as magical, an instrument of ritual. The Greek philosophers characterized it as an imitation of reality; this mimetic theory challenges art to justify itself. Plato, seeing art as an imitation of an imitation, considered it neither useful nor true. Aristotle believed art is useful as therapy, a purge of dangerous emotions.

4–6: The defense of art as a representation of reality has led to a separation of form from content—content being essential and form accessory. This remains the case even when art is viewed as subjective expression, a statement of the artist rather than a picture of reality.

7–11: We cannot return to the innocence of simply experiencing art but are permanently committed to defending it. The concept of content has become a nuisance, giving rise to interpretation—which, conversely, sustains the idea that art has content. Interpretation means plucking a set of elements from the whole work and translating them: X really means A, and so on.

12–13: Interpretation came into being when science broke the power of myth, and the seemliness of religious symbols was questioned. Interpretation reconciled the ancient (and often coarse or unbelievable) texts with the demands of later readers. In our own more arrogant era, interpretation follows Marx and Freud in seeking the hidden meaning assumed to lie beneath the overt one.

14–18: The interpretation itself must be evaluated. In some cultural contexts it is a means of liberation from the dead past; in others—including our own—it is reactionary and stifling. Interpretation impoverishes what really exists by setting up a shadow world of meanings. It also tames works of art by reducing them to content that can be explained, declawing them for our comfort.

19–26: The philistinism of interpretation is especially rife in literature. The work of Kafka, for instance, has been read as a social allegory, a psychological allegory, and a religious allegory. Even if artists intend their work for interpretation, its merit lies elsewhere than in "meanings." "Never trust the teller," said Lawrence, "trust the tale." Driven by a wish to replace the work by something else, interpretation violates the work and turns it into an article for use.

27–29: A great deal of today's art represents a backlash against interpretation into parody, abstraction, decorative art, and nonart. Abstract painting is an attempt to have no content and hence no interpretation. In pop art the content is so blatant as to be uninterpretable. Much of modern poetry also has escaped.

30–32: Interpretation runs rampant in those American arts with a feeble and negligible avant-garde—fiction and the drama. The authors' uninspired use of form has overexposed their content. Experiments with form are one defense against interpretation; another is making unified, direct, fast-moving works. Film, which sometimes accomplishes this, is therefore the most vital art form today. Film has the advantage of having only recently entered art from mass culture and also of a diverse vocabulary of forms.

33–43: To serve the work of art rather than usurp it, criticism should pay more attention to form, becoming descriptive instead of prescriptive or interpretive. We need to experience art as it is—to see, hear, and feel more. Criticism should show how the work is that it is, or even that it is what it is and not show what it means.

SUGGESTIONS FOR FURTHER READING

HANNAH ARENDT

Arendt, Hannah. *Between Friends: The Correspondence of Hannah Arendt and Mary McCarthy, 1949–1975*. New York: Harcourt Brace, 1995.

Arendt, Hannah. *Between Past and Future: Six Exercises in Political Thought*. New York: Viking Press, 1968.

Arendt, Hannah. *The Burden of Our Time*. London: Secker & Warburg, 1951.

Arendt, Hannah. *Crises of the Republic: Lying in Politics, Civil Disobedience, on Violence, Thoughts on Politics*. New York: Harcourt Brace Jovanovich, 1972.

Arendt, Hannah. *Eichmann in Jerusalem: A Report on the Banality of Evil*. New York: Penguin Books, 1994.

Arendt, Hannah. *Essays in Understanding, 1930–1954*. Edited by Jerome Kohn. New York: Harcourt, Brace, 1994.

Arendt, Hannah. *The Human Condition*. Chicago: University of Chicago Press, 1958.

Arendt, Hannah. *The Life of the Mind*. New York: Harcourt Brace Jovanovich, 1978.

Arendt, Hannah. *Men in Dark Times*. New York: Harcourt, Brace & World, 1968.

Arendt, Hannah. *On Revolution*. Harmondsworth, Eng.: Penguin Books, 1977.

Arendt, Hannah. *On Violence*. New York: Harcourt, Brace & World, 1970.

Arendt, Hannah. *The Origins of Totalitarianism*. New York: Harcourt, Brace & World, 1966.

Aschheim, Steven E. *Culture and Catastrophe: German and Jewish Confrontations with National Socialism and Other Crises*. New York: New York University Press, 1996.

Barnouw, Dagmar. *Visible Spaces: Hannah Arendt and the German-Jewish Experience*. Baltimore: Johns Hopkins University Press, 1990.

Gottsegen, Michael G. *The Political Thought of Hannah Arendt*. Albany: State University of New York Press, 1994.

Hill, Melvyn A. *Hannah Arendt: The Recovery of the Public World*. New York: St. Martin's Press, 1979.

Kaplan, Gisela T., and Clive S. Kessler, eds. *Hannah Arendt: Thinking, Judging, Freedom*. Sydney: Allen and Unwin, 1989.

May, Larry, and Jerome Kohn, eds. *Hannah Arendt: Twenty Years Later*. Cambridge, Mass.: MIT Press, 1996.

Whitfield, Stephen J. *Into the Dark: Hannah Arendt and Totalitarianism*. Philadelphia: Temple University Press, 1980.

Young-Bruehl, Elisabeth. *Hannah Arendt: For Love of the World*. New Haven: Yale University Press, 1982.

ARISTOTLE

Adler, Mortimer. *Aristotle for Everybody: Difficult Thought Made Easy*. New York: Macmillan, 1978.

Aristotle. *A New Aristotle Reader*. Edited by J. L. Ackrill. Princeton: Princeton University Press, 1987.

Aristotle. *The Nichomachean Ethics*. Translated by Martin Ostwald. Indianapolis: Bobbs-Merrill, 1962.

Aristotle. *The Pocket Aristotle*. Edited by Justin D. Kaplan. New York: Washington Square, 1982.

Aristotle. *Poetics*. Edited by G. M. Kirkwood. New York: Norton, 1982.

Aristotle. *Poetics*. Translated by Stephen Halliwell. Cambridge, Mass.: Harvard University Press, 1995.

Aristotle. *Politics*. Rev. ed. New York: Viking Penguin, 1982.

Belfiore, Elizabeth S. *Tragic Pleasures: Aristotle on Plot and Emotion*. Princeton: Princeton University Press, 1992.

Broadie, Sarah. *Ethics with Aristotle*. New York: Oxford, 1991.

Cherniss, Harold. *Aristotle's Criticism of Plato and the Academy*. Baltimore: Johns Hopkins University Press, 1944.

Davidson, Thomas. *Aristotle and Ancient Educational Ideals*. New York: Franklin, 1969.

Davis, Michael. *Aristotle's Poetics: The Poetry of Philosophy*. Lanham, Md.: Rowman and Littlefield, 1992.

Edel, Abraham. *Aristotle and His Philosophy*. Chapel Hill: University of North Carolina Press, 1982.

Evans, John David Gemmill. *Aristotle*. New York: St. Martin's, 1987.

Ferguson, John. *Aristotle*. New York: Twayne, 1972.

Hardie, William. *Aristotle's Ethical Theory*. New York: Oxford University Press, 1980.

Kenny, Anthony. *Aristotle on the Perfect Life*. New York: Oxford, 1992.

Keyt, David, and Fred D. Miller, Jr., eds. *Aristotle's Politics: A Critical Reader*. Cambridge: Basil Blackwell, 1991.

Lear, Jonathan. *Aristotle and Logical Theory*. London: Cambridge University Press, 1980.

Lear, Jonathan. *Aristotle: The Desire to Understand*. New York: Cambridge University Press, 1988.

Lloyd, Geoffrey. *Aristotle: The Growth and Structure of His Thought*. London: Cambridge University Press, 1968.

Oates, Whitney. *Aristotle and the Problem of Value*. Princeton: Princeton University Press, 1963.

Rist, John M. *The Mind of Aristotle: A Study in Philosophical Growth*. Toronto: University of Toronto Press, 1989.

Robinson, Daniel N. *Aristotle's Psychology*. New York: Columbia University Press, 1989.

Rorty, Amlie Oksenberg, ed. *Essays on Aristotle's Poetics*. Princeton: Princeton University Press, 1992.

Veatch, Henry. *Aristotle: A Contemporary Appreciation*. Bloomington: Indiana University Press, 1974.

FRANCIS BACON

Bacon, Francis. *The Essays*. 1597. Edited with an introduction by John Pitcher. New York: Penguin, 1986.

Bacon, Francis. *Francis Bacon: A Selection of His Works*. Edited by Sidney Warhaft. Indianapolis: Odyssey, 1965.

Bacon, Francis. *New Organon and Related Writings*. Edited by H. Fulton Anderson. Indianapolis: Bobbs-Merrill, 1960.

Briggs, John C. *Francis Bacon and the Rhetoric of Nature*. Cambridge, Mass.: Harvard University Press, 1989.

Davies, Hugh Marlais. *Francis Bacon*. New York: Abbeville, 1986.

Eiseley, Loren. *The Man Who Saw Through Time*. New York: Scribner, 1973.

Epstein, Joel. *Francis Bacon: A Political Biography*. Athens: Ohio University Press, 1977.

Farrington, Benjamin. *The Philosophy of Francis Bacon*. Liverpool: University Press, 1964.

Martin, Julian. *Francis Bacon, the State, and the Reform of Natural Philosophy*. New York: Cambridge University Press, 1992.

Prez-Ramos, Antonio. *Francis Bacon's Idea of Science and the Maker's Knowledge Tradition*. New York: Oxford University Press, 1988.

Rossi, Paolo. *Francis Bacon: From Magic to Science*. Translated by Sacha Rabinovitch. Chicago: University of Chicago Press, 1968.

Snider, Alvin. *Origins and Authority in Seventeenth-Century England: Bacon, Milton, Butler*. Toronto: University of Toronto Press, 1994.

Stephens, James. *Francis Bacon and the Style of Science*. Chicago: University of Chicago Press, 1975.

Urbach, Peter. *Francis Bacon's Philosophy of Science: An Account and a Reappraisal*. La Salle, Ill.: Open Court, 1987.

Vickers, Brian. *Essential Articles for the Study of Francis Bacon*. Hamden, Conn.: Archon, 1968.

Wallace, Karl. *Francis Bacon on Communication and Rhetoric*. Chapel Hill: University of North Carolina Press, 1943.

Whitney, Charles. *Francis Bacon and Modernity*. New Haven: Yale University Press, 1986.

SIMONE DE BEAUVOIR

Bair, Deirdre. *Simone de Beauvoir: A Biography*. New York: Summit Books, 1990.

Beauvoir, Simone de. *Letters to Sartre*. Edited and translated by Quintin Hoare. New York: Arcade, 1992.

Beauvoir, Simone de. *Memoirs of a Dutiful Daughter*. 1958. New York: Harper & Row, 1974.

Beauvoir, Simone de. *The Second Sex*. 1949. New York: Knopf, 1953.

Beauvoir, Simone de. *A Very Easy Death*. 1964. New York: Pantheon, 1985.

Brosman, Catharine Savage. *Simone de Beauvoir Revisited*. Boston: Twayne, 1991.

Evans, Mary. *Simone de Beauvoir*. London: Sage, 1996.

Evans, Mary. *Simone de Beauvoir: A Feminist Mandarin*. London: Tavistock, 1985.

Hatcher, Donald L. *Understanding the Second Sex*. New York: Lang, 1984.

Leighton, Jean. *Simone de Beauvoir on Women*. Rutherford, N.J.: Fairleigh Dickinson University Press, 1975.

Marks, Elaine, ed. *Critical Essays on Simone de Beauvoir*. Boston: Hall, 1987.

Marks, Elaine. *Simone de Beauvoir: Encounters with Death*. New Brunswick, N.J.: Rutgers University Press, 1973.

Moi, Toril. *Simone de Beauvoir: The Making of an Intellectual Woman*. Oxford: Blackwell, 1994.

Okely, Judith. *Simone de Beauvoir*. New York: Pantheon, 1986.

Schwarzer, Alice. *After the Second Sex: Conversations with Simone de Beauvoir*. Translated by Marianne Howarth. New York: Pantheon, 1984.

Whitmarsh, Anne. *Simone de Beauvoir and the Limits of Commitment*. Cambridge: Cambridge University Press, 1981.

Winegarten, Renee. *Simone de Beauvoir: A Critical View*. Oxford: Berg, 1988.

RUTH BENEDICT

Benedict, Ruth. *An Anthropologist at Work: Writings of Ruth Benedict*. New York: Atherton, 1966.

Benedict, Ruth. *The Chrysanthemum and the Sword: Patterns of Japanese Culture*. 1946. Foreword by Ezra F. Vogel. Boston: Houghton Mifflin, 1989.

Benedict, Ruth. *The Concept of the Guardian Spirit in North America*. 1923. American Anthropological Association Memoirs, no. 29. New York: Kraus Reprint Corporation, 1964.

Benedict, Ruth. *Patterns of Culture*. 1934. Foreword by Mary Catherine Bateson and preface by Margaret Mead. Boston: Houghton Mifflin, 1989.

Benedict, Ruth. *Race and Racism*. London: Routledge, 1942.

Benedict, Ruth. *Race: Science and Politics*. Rev. ed. New York: Viking, 1943.

Benedict, Ruth. *Tales of the Cochiti Indians*. 1931. Introduction by Alfonso Oritz. Smithsonian Institution Bureau of American Ethnology Bulletin, no. 98. Albuquerque: University of New Mexico Press, 1981.

Benedict, Ruth. *Thai Culture and Behavior; An Unpublished War-time Study Dated September, 1943*. Ithaca: Southeast Asia Program, Department of Far Eastern Studies, Cornell University, 1952.

Caffrey, Margaret M. *Ruth Benedict: Stranger in This Land*. Austin: University of Texas Press, 1989.

Mead, Margaret, ed. *An Anthropologist at Work: Writings of Ruth Benedict*. Boston: Houghton Mifflin, 1959.

Mead, Margaret. *Ruth Benedict*. Reprint ed. New York: Columbia University Press, 1978.

Modell, Judith Schachter. *Ruth Benedict: Patterns of Life*. Philadelphia: University of Pennsylvania Press, 1984.

THE BHAGAVAD GĪTĀ

The Bhagavad Gita. Translated by J. A. B. van Buitenen. Rockport, Mass.: Element, 1997.

The Bhagavad-Gita: Krishna's Counsel in Time of War. Translated by Barbara Stoler Miller. New York: Columbia University Press, 1986.

Minor, Robert N., ed. *Modern Indian Interpreters of the Bhagavadgita*. Albany: State University of New York Press, 1986.

Sharma, Arvind. *The Hindu Gita: Ancient and Classical Interpretations of the Bhagavadgita*. La Salle, Ill.: Open Court, 1986.

Sharpe, Eric J. *The Universal Gita: Western Images of the Bhagavad Gita*. La Salle, Ill.: Open Court, 1985.

MARTIN BUBER

Berry, Donald L. *Mutuality: The Vision of Martin Buber*. Albany: State University of New York Press, 1985.

Breslauer, S. Daniel. *Martin Buber on Myth: An Introduction*. New York: Garland, 1990.

Buber, Martin. *Between Man and Man*. New York: Collier Books, 1965.

Buber, Martin. *Hasidism and Modern Man*. Translated by Maurice Friedman. New York: Horizon Press, 1958.

Buber, Martin. *Kingship of God*. Translated by Richard Scheimann. New York: Harper & Row, 1967.

Buber, Martin. *The Legend of the Baal-Shem*. Translated by Maurice Friedman. Princeton: Princeton University Press, 1995.

Buber, Martin. *Moses: The Revelation and the Covenant*. New York: Harper, 1958.

Buber, Martin. *On the Bible: Eighteen Studies*. Edited by Nahum N. Glatzer. New York: Schocken Books, 1968.

Buber, Martin. *The Origin and Meaning of Hasidism*. Translated by Maurice Friedman. New York: Horizon Press, 1960.

Buber, Martin. *The Prophetic Faith*. New York: Harper, 1949.

Buber, Martin. *Ten Rungs: Hasidic Sayings*. New York: Schocken Books, 1947.

Buber, Martin. *To Hallow This Life: An Anthology*. New York: Harper, 1958.

Buber, Martin. *Two Types of Faith*. Translated by Norman P. Goldhawk. London: Routledge & Paul, 1951.

Buber, Martin. *The Way of Man, According to the Teaching of Hasidism*. Secaucus, N.J.: Citadel Press, 1966.

Buber, Martin. *The Way of Response: Martin Buber, Selections from His Writings*. Edited by N. N. Glatzer. New York: Schocken Books, 1966.

Diamond, Malcolm Luria. *Martin Buber: Jewish Existentialist*. New York: Oxford University Press, 1960.

Friedman, Maurice S. *Martin Buber's Life and Work: The Early Years, 1878–1923*. New York: Dutton, 1981.

Friedman, Maurice S. *Martin Buber's Life and Work: The Later Years, 1945–1965*. New York: Dutton, 1983.

Friedman, Maurice S. *Martin Buber: The Life of Dialogue*. Chicago: University of Chicago Press, 1955.

Herman, Jonathan R. *I and Tao: Martin Buber's Encounter with Chuang Tzu*. Albany: State University of New York Press, 1996.

Hodes, Aubrey. *Martin Buber: An Intimate Portrait*. New York: Viking Press, 1971.

Manheim, Werner. *Martin Buber*. New York: Twayne, 1974.

Schaeder, Grete. *The Hebrew Humanism of Martin Buber*. Translated by Noah J. Jacobs. Detroit: Wayne State University Press, 1973.

Schilpp, Paul Arthur and Maurice Friedman, eds. *The Philosophy of Martin Buber*. La Salle, Ill.: Open Court, 1967.

Susser, Bernard. *Existence and Utopia: The Social and Political Thought of Martin Buber*. Rutherford, N.J.: Fairleigh Dickinson University Press, 1981.

Weinstein, Joshua. *Buber and Humanistic Education*. New York: Philosophical Library, 1975.

ÁLVAR NÚÑEZ CABEZA DE VACA

Bishop, Morris. *The Odyssey of Cabeza de Vaca*. New York: Century, 1933.

Cabeza de Vaca, Álvar Núñez. *The Account: Álvar Núñez Cabeza de Vaca's* Relación. Houston: Arte Publio Press, 1993.

Cabeza de Vaca, Álvar Núñez. *Cabeza de Vaca's Adventures in the Unknown Interior of America*. New York: Collier Books, 1961.

Cabeza de Vaca, Álvar Núñez. *Castaways: The Narrative of Álvar Núñez Cabeza de Vaca*. Edited by Enrique Pupo-Walker. Berkeley: University of California Press, 1993.

Cabeza de Vaca, Álvar Núñez. *The Journey of Álvar Núñez Cabeza de Vaca and His Companions from Florida to the Pacific, 1528–1536.* New York: Allerton, 1922.

Howard, David A. *Conquistador in Chains: Cabeza de Vaca and the Indians of the Americas.* Tuscaloosa: University of Alabama Press, 1997.

Spanish Explorers in the Southern United States, 1528–1543: The Narrative of Álvar Núñez Cabeza. New York: Scribner's Sons, 1907.

CHARLES DARWIN

Appleman, Philip, ed. *Darwin.* New York: Norton, 1970.

Bannister, Robert. *Social Darwinism: Science and Myth in Anglo-American Social Thought.* Philadelphia: Temple University Press, 1979.

Bowler, Peter J. *Charles Darwin the Man and His Influence.* Cambridge: Basil Blackwell, 1990.

Crook, D. P. *Darwinism, War, and History: The Debate over the Biology of War from the "Origins of Species" to the First World War.* New York: Cambridge University Press, 1994.

Darwin, Charles. *The Autobiography of Charles Darwin.* Edited by Nora Barlow. New York: Norton, 1969.

Darwin, Charles. *The Correspondence of Charles Darwin.* Edited by Frederick Burkhardt and Sydney Smith. New York: Cambridge University Press, 1985.

Darwin, Charles. *The Darwin Reader.* Edited by Mark Ridley. New York: Norton, 1987.

Darwin, Charles. *The Descent of Man and Selection in Relation to Sex.* Princeton: Princeton University Press, 1981.

Darwin, Charles. *On the Origin of Species.* Edited by J. W. Burrow. Baltimore: Penguin, 1968.

Darwin, Charles. *The Voyage of the Beagle: Charles Darwin's Journal of Researches.* Edited with an introduction by Janet Browne and Michael Neve. New York: Penguin, 1989.

Darwin, Charles. *The Works of Charles Darwin.* Edited by Paul H. Barrett and R. B. Freeman. New York: New York University Press, 1987.

Desmond, Adrian J. *Darwin.* New York: Warner Books, 1992.

Eiseley, Loren. *Darwin's Century: Evolution and the Men Who Discovered It.* Garden City: Doubleday, 1958.

Himmelfarb, Gertrude. *Darwin and the Darwinian Revolution.* Garden City: Doubleday, 1962.

Irvine, William. *Apes, Angels, and Victorians.* New York: McGraw-Hill, 1955.

Jastrow, Robert, and Kenneth Korey. *The Essential Darwin.* Boston: Little, Brown, 1984.

Mayr, Ernst. *One Long Argument: Charles Darwin and the Genesis of Modern Evolutionary Thought.* Cambridge, Mass.: Harvard University Press, 1991.

Miller, Jonathan. *Darwin for Beginners.* New York: Pantheon, 1982.

Russett, Cynthia. *Darwin in America.* San Francisco: Freeman, 1976.

RICHARD DAWKINS

Dawkins, Richard. *The Blind Watchmaker: Why the Evidence of Evolution Reveals a Universe Without Design.* New York: Norton, 1996.

Dawkins, Richard. *Climbing Mount Improbable.* New York: Norton, 1996.

Dawkins, Richard. *The Extended Phenotype: The Gene as the Unit of Selection.* Oxford: Freeman, 1982.

Dawkins, Richard. *River Out of Eden: A Darwinian View of Life.* New York: Basic Books, 1995.

FREDERICK DOUGLASS

Andrews, William L., ed. *Critical Essays on Frederick Douglass.* Boston: Hall, 1991.

Bontemps, Arna. *Free at Last: The Life of Frederick Douglass.* New York: Dodd, Mead, 1971.

Douglass, Frederick. *My Bondage and My Freedom.* Edited by William L. Andrews. Urbana: University of Illinois Press, 1987.

Douglass, Frederick. *Frederick Douglass on Women's Rights.* Edited by Philip S. Foner. Westport, Conn.: Greenwood, 1976.

Douglass, Frederick. *The Frederick Douglass Papers, Series One: Speeches, Debates, and Interviews.* Vol. 1. *1841–1846.* Edited by John W. Blassingame et al. New Haven: Yale University Press, 1979.

Douglass, Frederick. *The Life and Writings of Frederick Douglass.* Edited by Philip S. Foner. 5 vols. New York: International Publishers, 1950–1975.

Douglass, Frederick. *Narrative of the Life of Frederick Douglass, an American Slave.* Edited with an introduction by David W. Blight. Boston: Bedford–St. Martin's, 1993.

Douglass, Frederick. *Prose Works: Selections.* New York: Library of America, 1994.

Foner, Philip S. *Frederick Douglass.* New York: Citadel, 1964.

Gates, Henry Louis, Jr., ed. *The Classic Slave Narrative.* New York: New American Library, 1987.

Huggins, Nathan Irvin. *Slave and Citizen: The Life of Frederick Douglass.* Boston: Little, Brown, 1980.

Inge, Thomas, et al., eds. *Black American Writers: Bibliographical Essays.* Vol. 1. London: Macmillan, 1978.

Martin, Waldo E., Jr. *The Mind of Frederick Douglass.* Chapel Hill: University of North Carolina Press, 1984.

McFreely, William S. *Frederick Douglass.* New York: Norton, 1991.

Patterson, Frederick D. [Frederick Douglass]. *Chronicles of Faith: The Autobiography of Frederick D. Patterson.* Edited by Martia Graham Goodson with a foreword by Harry V. Richardson. Tuscaloosa: University of Alabama Press, 1991.

Sundquist, Eric J., ed. *Frederick Douglass: New Literary and Historical Essays.* New York: Cambridge University Press, 1990.

SIGMUND FREUD

Appignanesi, Lisa. *Freud's Women.* New York: Basic, 1992.

Arlow, Jacob. *The Legacy of Sigmund Freud.* New York: International Universities Press, 1956.

Badcock, Christopher R. *Essential Freud.* Cambridge: Basil Blackwell, 1992.

Balogh, Penelope. *Freud: A Biographical Introduction.* New York: Scribner, 1972.

Chodorow, Nancy. *Femininities, Masculinities, Sexualities: Freud and Beyond.* Lexington: University Press of Kentucky, 1994.

Clark, Ronald William. *Freud: The Man and the Cause.* London: Cape, 1980.

Fine, Reuben. *Freud: A Critical Reevaluation of His Theories.* New York: McKay, 1962.

Freeman, Lucy. *Freud Rediscovered.* New York: Arbor House, 1980.

Freud, Sigmund. *The Complete Correspondence of Sigmund Freud and Ernest Jones, 1908–1939.* Cambridge: Belknap Press of Harvard University Press, 1993.

Freud, Sigmund. *Freud on Women: A Reader.* Edited by Elisabeth Young-Bruehl. New York: Norton, 1990.

Freud, Sigmund. *The Freud Reader.* Edited by Peter Gay. New York: Norton, 1989.

Freud, Sigmund. *General Selection from the Works of Sigmund Freud.* Garden City: Doubleday, 1957.

Freud, Sigmund. *New Introductory Lectures in Psychoanalysis.* Edited by James Strachey. New York: Norton, 1965.

Freud, Sigmund. *Outline of Psychoanalysis.* Edited by James Strachey. New York: Norton, 1970.

Freud, Sigmund. *The Psychopathology of Everyday Life.* Edited by James Strachey. New York: Norton, 1971.

Freud, Sigmund. *Three Contributions to the Theory of Sex.* Translated by A. A. Brill. New York: Dutton, 1962.

Fromm, Erich. *The Crisis of Psychoanalysis.* New York: Holt, Rinehart and Winston, 1970.

Gay, Peter. *Freud: A Life of Our Time.* New York: Norton, 1988.

Gelfend, Toby, and John Kerr, eds. *Freud and the History of Psychoanalysis.* Hillsdale, N.J.: Analytic, 1992.

Hughes, Judith M. *From Freud's Consulting Room: The Unconscious in a Scientific Age.* Cambridge, Mass.: Harvard University Press, 1994.

Jones, Ernest. *The Life and Work of Sigmund Freud.* Edited by Lionel Trilling and Steven Marcus. New York: Basic, 1961.

Masson, J. Moussaieff. *The Assault on Truth: Freud's Suppression of the Seduction Theory.* New York: Farrar, Straus and Giroux, 1984.

Neu, Jerome, ed. *The Cambridge Companion to Freud.* New York: Cambridge University Press, 1991.
Reiff, Philip. *Freud: The Mind of the Moralist.* Garden City: Doubleday, 1961.
Robinson, Paul A. *Freud and His Critics.* Berkeley: University of California Press, 1993.
Rosenfeld, Israel. *Freud: Character and Consciousness.* New York: University, 1970.
Stoodley, Bartlett. *The Concepts of Sigmund Freud.* Glencoe, N.Y.: Free, 1959.
Storr, Anthony. *Freud.* New York: Oxford University Press, 1989.
Welsh, Alexander. *Freud's Wishful Dream Book.* Princeton: Princeton University Press, 1994.

JOHN KENNETH GALBRAITH

Bowles, Samuel, et al., eds. *Unconventional Wisdom: Essays on Economics in Honor of John Kenneth Galbraith.* Boston: Houghton Mifflin, 1989.
Galbraith, John Kenneth. *The Affluent Society.* Boston: Houghton Mifflin, 1978.
Galbraith, John Kenneth. *The Age of Uncertainty.* Boston: Houghton Mifflin, 1977.
Galbraith, John Kenneth. *Almost Everyone's Guide to Economics.* Boston: Houghton Mifflin, 1978.
Galbraith, John Kenneth. *Ambassador's Journal.* 1969. New York: Paragon House, 1988.
Galbraith, John Kenneth. *The Anatomy of Power.* Boston: Houghton Mifflin, 1983.
Galbraith, John Kenneth. *A Contemporary Guide to Economics, Peace, and Laughter.* Boston: Houghton Mifflin, 1971.
Galbraith, John Kenneth. *The Culture of Contentment.* Boston: Houghton Mifflin, 1992.
Galbraith, John Kenneth. *The Galbraith Reader.* Edited by the editors of Gambit. Ipswich, Mass.: Gambit, 1977.
Galbraith, John Kenneth. *A Journey Through Economic Time: A Firsthand View.* Boston: Houghton Mifflin, 1994.
Galbraith, John Kenneth. *The Nature of Mass Poverty.* Cambridge, Mass.: Harvard University Press, 1979.
Galbraith, John Kenneth. *A Short History of Financial Euphoria.* New York: Whittle Books, 1993.
Gambs, John S. *John Kenneth Galbraith.* Boston: Twayne, 1975.
Lamson, Peggy. *Speaking of Galbraith: A Personal Portrait.* New York: Ticknor & Fields, 1991.
Okroi, Loren J. *Galbraith, Harrington, Heilbroner: Economics and Dissent in the Age of Optimism.* Princeton: Princeton University Press, 1988.

HOWARD GARDNER

Gardner, Howard. *Art, Mind, and Brain: A Cognitive Approach to Creativity.* New York: Basic Books, 1982.
Gardner, Howard. *The Arts and Human Development: A Psychological Study of the Artistic Process.* New York: Wiley, 1973.
Gardner, Howard. *Creating Minds: An Anatomy of Creativity Seen Through the Lives of Freud, Einstein, Picasso, Stravinsky.* New York: Basic Books, 1993.
Gardner, Howard. *Developmental Psychology: An Introduction.* Boston: Little, Brown, 1978.
Gardner, Howard. *Extraordinary Minds: Portraits of Exceptional Individuals and an Examination of Our Extraordinariness.* New York: Basic Books, 1997.
Gardner, Howard. *Frames of Mind: The Theory of Multiple Intelligences.* New York: Basic Books, 1983.
Gardner, Howard. *The Mind's New Science: A History of the Cognitive Revolution.* New York: Basic Books, 1985.
Gardner, Howard. *Multiple Intelligences: The Theory in Practice.* New York: Basic Books, 1993.
Gardner, Howard. *The Shattered Mind: The Person After Brain Damage.* New York: Knopf, 1975.
Gardner, Howard. *To Open Minds: Chinese Clues to the Dilemma of Contemporary Education.* New York: Basic Books, 1989.
Gardner, Howard. *The Unschooled Mind: How Children Think and How Schools Should Teach.* New York: Basic Books, 1991.
Gardner, Howard, and Emma Laskin. *Leading Minds: An Anatomy of Leadership.* New York: Basic Books, 1995.

CLIFFORD GEERTZ

Carrithers, Michael, et al. "Is Anthropology Art or Science?" *Current Anthropology* 31.3 (1990): 263–272.

Geertz, Clifford. *The Interpretation of Cultures: Selected Essays*. New York: Basic, 1977.

Geertz, Clifford. *Local Knowledge: Further Essays in Interpretive Anthropology*. New York: Basic, 1985.

Geertz, Clifford. *Works and Lives: The Anthropologist as Author*. Stanford: Stanford University Press, 1989.

Handler, Richard. "An Interview with Clifford Geertz." *Current Anthropology* 32.5 (1991): 603–614.

Horgan, J. "Ethnography Art" (a profile of Clifford Geertz). *Scientific American* July 1989: 28–31.

Hutnyk, John. "Clifford Geertz as a Cultural System: A Review Article." *Social Analysis* 26 (1989): 91–107.

Lasch, Christopher. "Academic Pseudo-Radicalism: The Charade of 'Subversion.'" *Salmagundi* (Fall 1990–Winter 1991): 25–36.

Rice, Kenneth A. *Geertz and Culture*. Ann Arbor: University of Michigan Press, 1980.

Sanday, Peggy Reeves. "The Ethnographic Paradigm(s)." *Administrative Science Quarterly* 24.4 (1979): 527–538.

Schneider, Mark A. "Culture-as-Text in the Work of Clifford Geertz." *Theory and Society* 16.6 (1987): 809–839.

Shore, Bradd. "An Introduction to the Work of Clifford Geertz." *Soundings* 71.1 (1988): 15–27.

Tyson, Ruel W., Jr. "Culture's 'Hum and Buzz' of Implication: The Practice of Ethnography and the Provocations of Clifford Geertz's 'Thick Description.'" *Soundings* 71.1 (1988): 95–111.

Walters, Ronald G. "Signs of the Times: Clifford Geertz and Historians." *Social Research* 47.3 (1980): 537–556.

STEPHEN JAY GOULD

Angier, Natalie. "An Evolving Celebrity" (a profile of Stephen Jay Gould). *New York Times* 11 Feb. 1993: col. 1.

Bethell, T. "Good as Gould." *American Spectator* 24.8 (1991): 9–12.

Gould, Stephen Jay. *Bully for Brontosaurus: Reflections in Natural History*. New York: Norton, 1992.

Gould, Stephen Jay. *Eight Little Piggies: Reflections in Natural History*. New York: Norton, 1993.

Gould, Stephen Jay. *Ever Since Darwin: Reflections in Natural History*. New York: Norton, 1977.

Gould, Stephen Jay. *The Flamingo's Smile*. New York: Norton, 1985.

Gould, Stephen Jay. *Hen's Teeth and Horse's Toes*. New York: Norton, 1983.

Gould, Stephen Jay. *Illuminations: A Bestiary*. Photographs by Rosamond Purcell. New York: Norton, 1986.

Gould, Stephen Jay. *The Individual in Darwin's World: The Second Edinburgh Medal Address*. Text ed. Edinburgh: Edinburgh University Press, 1991.

Gould, Stephen Jay. *The Mismeasure of Man*. New York: Norton, 1981.

Gould, Stephen Jay. *The Panda's Thumb: More Reflections in Natural History*. New York: Norton, 1980.

Gould, Stephen Jay. *Time's Arrow, Time's Cycle: Myth and Metaphor in the Discovery of Geological Time*. Cambridge, Mass.: Harvard University Press, 1987.

Gould, Stephen Jay. *An Urchin in the Storm: Essays About Books and Ideas*. New York: Norton, 1987.

Gould, Stephen Jay, and Bernard D. Davis. "Who Has Donned Lysenko's Mantle?" (debate on *Mismeasure of Man*). *Public Interest* 75 (1984): 148–151.

Lovejoy, Derek. "The Dialectical Paleontologist: Popular Science Writings of Stephen Jay Gould." *Science and Society* 55.2 (1991): 197–207.

Purcell, Rosamund Wolff, and Stephen Jay Gould. *Finders, Keepers: Eight Collectors*. New York: Norton, 1992.

Schwartzman, David. "Evolution and Seti." *Science and Society* 56.2 (1992): 189–192.

HERODOTUS

Evans, James Allan Stewart. *Herodotus*. Boston: Twayne, 1982.

Evans, James Allan Stewart. *Herodotus, Explorer of the Past: Three Essays*. Princeton: Princeton University Press, 1991.

Fornata, Charles W. *Herodotus: An Interpretative Essay.* Oxford: Clarendon Press, 1971.

Godolphin, Francis Richard Borroum. *The Greek Historians: The Complete and Unabridged Historical Works of Herodotus.* New York: Random House, 1942.

Herodotus. *Herodotus.* Translated by J. Enoch Powell. Oxford: Clarendon Press, 1949.

Herodotus. *The Histories.* Translated by Aubrey de Selincourt. New York: Penguin Books, 1972.

Herodotus. *The Histories: New Translation, Selections, Backgrounds, Commentaries.* Translated by Walter Blanco. New York: Norton, 1992.

Herodotus. *The History.* Translated by David Grene. Chicago: University of Chicago Press, 1987.

Herodotus. *The History of Herodotus.* Translated by George Rawlinson. Everyman's Library 405–406. New York: Dutton, 1930.

Herodotus. *The History of Herodotus.* Translated by George Rawlinson. Edited by Manuel Komroff. New York: Tudor, 1947.

Herodotus. *The Persian Wars.* Translated by George Rawlinson. New York: Modern Library, 1942.

Hunter, Virginia J. *Past and Process in Herodotus and Thucydides.* Princeton: Princeton University Press, 1982.

Waters, K. H. *Herodotus, the Historian: His Problems, Methods, and Originality.* Norman: University of Oklahoma Press, 1985.

KAREN HORNEY

Horney, Karen. *Feminine Psychology.* New York: Norton, 1967.

Horney, Karen. *Final Lectures.* Edited by Douglas H. Ingram. New York: Norton, 1987.

Horney, Karen. *Neurosis and Human Growth.* New York: Norton, 1950.

Horney, Karen. *The Neurotic Personality of Our Time.* New York: Norton, 1942.

Horney, Karen. *New Ways in Psychoanalysis.* Reprint ed. New York: Norton, 1964.

Horney, Karen. *Self-Analysis.* New York: Norton, 1937.

Paris, Bernard J. *Karen Horney: A Psychoanalyst's Search for Self-Understanding.* New Haven: Yale University Press, 1994.

Quinn, Susan. *A Mind of Her Own: The Life of Karen Horney.* New York: Summit, 1987.

Rubin, Jack. *Karen Horney: Gentle Rebel of Psychoanalysis.* New York: Dial, 1978.

Sayers, Janet. *Mothers of Psychoanalysis: Helene Deutsch, Karen Horney, Anna Freud, Melanie Klein.* New York: Norton, 1991.

Westkott, Marcia. *The Feminist Legacy of Karen Horney.* New Haven: Yale University Press, 1986.

THOMAS JEFFERSON

Becker, Carl L. *The Declaration of Independence: A Study in the History of Political Ideas.* Rev. ed. New York: Knopf, 1966.

Bedini, Silvio A. *Thomas Jefferson: Statesman of Science.* New York: Macmillan, 1990.

Brodie, Fawn M. *Thomas Jefferson: An Intimate History.* New York: Norton, 1974.

Cunningham, Noble E., Jr. *In Pursuit of Reason: The Life of Thomas Jefferson.* Baton Rouge: Louisiana State University Press, 1987.

Dewey, Frank L. *Thomas Jefferson, Lawyer.* Charlottesville: University Press of Virginia, 1986.

Fliegelman, Jay. *Declaring Independence: Jefferson, Natural Language and the Culture of Performance.* Stanford: Stanford University Press, 1993.

Huddleston, Eugene L. *Thomas Jefferson, A Reference Guide.* Boston: Hall, 1982.

Jefferson, Thomas. *Notes on the State of Virginia.* Edited with an introduction and notes by William Peden. New York: Norton, 1972.

Jefferson, Thomas. *A Summary View of the Rights of British America.* 1774. Introduction by Lawrence W. Towner. A facsimile of the 1st ed. as amended by the author in his own hand. Chicago: Caxton Club, 1976.

Jefferson, Thomas. *The Viking Portable Thomas Jefferson.* Edited by Merrill D. Peterson. New York: Viking Penguin, 1977.

Jefferson, Thomas. *Writings.* The Library of America 17. New York: Viking, 1984.

Malone, Dumas. *Jefferson and His Time*. 6 vols. Boston: Little, Brown, 1948–1981.

Matthews, Richard K. *The Radical Politics of Thomas Jefferson: A Revisionist View*. Lawrence: University Press of Kansas, 1984.

Mayer, David N. *The Constitutional Thought of Thomas Jefferson*. Charlottesville: University Press of Virginia, 1994.

McLaughlin, Jack. *To His Excellency Thomas Jefferson: Letters to a President*. New York: Norton, 1991.

Peterson, Merrill D., ed. *Thomas Jefferson: A Reference Biography*. New York: Scribner, 1986.

Randall, Willard Sterne. *Thomas Jefferson: A Life*. New York: Holt, 1993.

Risjord, Norman K. *Thomas Jefferson*. Madison, Wis.: Madison House, 1994.

Sheldon, Garrett Ward. *The Political Philosophy of Thomas Jefferson*. Baltimore: Johns Hopkins University Press, 1991.

Shuffelton, Frank. *Thomas Jefferson: A Comprehensive Annotated Bibliography of the Writings about Him*. New York: Garland, 1983.

Wills, Garry. *Inventing America: Jefferson's Declaration of Independence*. Garden City: Doubleday, 1978.

CARL JUNG

Aziz, Robert. *C. G. Jung's Psychology of Religion and Synchronicity*. Albany: State University of New York Press, 1990.

Bennet, E. A. *What Jung Really Said*. Introduction by Anthony Storr. New York: Pantheon Books, 1983.

Clarke, John J. *In Search of Jung: Historical and Philosophical Enquiries*. New York: Routledge, 1992.

Dyer, Donald. *Cross-Currents of Jungian Thought: An Annotated Bibliography*. Boston: Shambhala, 1991.

Fordheim, Frieda. *An Introduction to Jung's Psychology*. Baltimore: Penguin, 1954.

Hall, Calvin Springer. *A Primer of Jungian Psychology*. New York: New American Library, 1973.

Hannah, Barbara. *Jung: His Life and Work*. New York: Putnam, 1976.

Jung, Carl. *Aspects of the Feminine*. Translated by R. F. C. Hull. Princeton/Bollingen ed. Princeton: Princeton University Press, 1982.

Jung, Carl. *The Essential Jung*. Princeton: Princeton University Press, 1983.

Jung, Carl. *The Gnostic Jung*. Princeton: Princeton University Press, 1992.

Jung, Carl. *Man and His Symbols*. New York: Dell, 1968.

Jung, Carl. *Memories, Dreams, Reflections*. New York: Random House, 1965.

Jung, Carl. *The Viking Portable Jung*. Edited by Joseph Campbell. New York: Viking Penguin, 1976.

Moreno, Artorio. *Jung, God, and Modern Man*. Notre Dame: University of Notre Dame Press, 1970.

Pauson, Marian L. *Jung the Philosopher: Essays in Jungian Thought*. New York: Lang, 1988.

Prograff, Ira. *Jung's Psychology and Its Social Meaning*. New York: Dialogue House Library, 1985.

Robertson, Robin. *C. G. Jung and the Archetypes of the Collective Unconscious*. New York: Lang, 1987.

Sanford, John. *The Invisible Partners: How the Male and Female in Each of Us Affects Our Relationships*. New York: Paulist, 1980.

Smith, Curtis D. *Jung's Quest for Wholeness: A Religious and Historical Perspective*. Albany: State University of New York, 1990.

Stevens, Anthony. *On Jung*. New York: Routledge, 1990.

Ulanov, Ann Bedford. *The Feminine in Jungian Psychology and in Christian Theology*. Evanston: Northwestern University Press, 1971.

Wehr, Gerhard. *Carl Gustav Jung*. Boston: Shambhala, 1987.

MICHIO KAKU

Kaku, Michio. *Hyperspace: A Scientific Odyssey Through Parallel Universes, Time Warps, and the Tenth Dimension*. New York: Oxford University Press, 1994.

Kaku, Michio. *Quantum Field Theory: A Modern Introduction*. New York: Oxford University Press, 1993.

Kaku, Michio, and Daniel Axelrod. *To Win a Nuclear War: The Pentagon's Secret War Plans*. Boston: South End Press, 1987.

Kaku, Michio, and Jennifer Trainer, eds. *Nuclear Power, Both Sides: The Best Arguments for and Against the Most Controversial Technology*. New York: Norton, 1982.

MARTIN LUTHER KING, JR.

Albert, Peter J., and Ronald Hoffman, eds. *We Shall Overcome: Martin Luther King, Jr., and the Black Freedom Struggle*. New York: Pantheon, 1990.

Branch, Taylor. *America in the King Years*. New York: Simon & Schuster, 1988.

Branch, Taylor. *Parting the Waters*. New York: Simon & Schuster, 1988.

Downing, Frederick L. *To See the Promised Land: The Faith Pilgrimage of Martin Luther King, Jr.* Macon, Ga.: Mercer University Press, 1986.

Erskine, Noel Leo. *King Among the Theologians*. Cleveland: Pilgrim Press, 1994.

King, Martin Luther, Jr. *I Have a Dream: Writings and Speeches That Changed the World*. Edited by James Melvin Washington. San Francisco: Harper, 1992.

King, Martin Luther, Jr. *I've Been to the Mountaintop*. San Francisco: Harper, 1994.

King, Martin Luther, Jr. *The Papers of Martin Luther King, Jr.* Edited by Clayborne Carson et al. Berkeley: University of California Press, 1992.

King, Martin Luther, Jr. *Strength to Love*. Philadelphia: Fortress, 1981.

King, Martin Luther, Jr. *A Testament of Hope: The Essential Writings of Martin Luther King, Jr.* Edited by James M. Washington. New York: Harper & Row, 1986.

King, Martin Luther, Jr. *Where Do We Go from Here: Chaos or Community?* Boston: Beacon, 1968.

King, Martin Luther, Jr. *Why We Can't Wait*. New York: New American Library, 1965.

King, Martin Luther, Jr. *The Wisdom of Martin Luther King, Jr.* Edited by Alex Ayers. New York: Meridian, 1993.

King, Martin Luther, Jr. Papers Project. *A Guide to Research on Martin Luther King, Jr., and the Modern Black Freedom Struggle*. Stanford: Stanford University Libraries, 1989.

Lewis, David. *King: A Critical Biography*. New York: Praeger, 1970.

Lyght, Ernest Shaw. *The Religious and Philosophical Foundations in the Thought of Martin Luther King*. New York: Vantage, 1972.

Miller, Keith D. *Voice of Deliverance: The Language of Martin Luther King, Jr., and Its Sources*. New York: Free Press, 1992.

Oates, Stephen B. *Let the Trumpet Sound: The Life of Martin Luther King, Jr.* New York: Harper & Row, 1982.

Ramachandram, G., and T. K. Mahadevan. *Nonviolence After Gandhi: A Study of Martin Luther King*. New Delhi: Gandhi Peace Foundation, 1968.

Walton, Hanes. *The Political Philosophy of Martin Luther King*. Westport, Conn.: Greenwood, 1971.

Zepp, Ira G. *The Social Vision of Martin Luther King, Jr.* Brooklyn: Carlson, 1989.

THE KORAN

Avverroes. *On the Harmony of Religions and Philosophy*. London: Luzac, 1961.

Bell, Richard. *Bell's Introduction to the Qur'an*. Edinburgh: Edinburgh University Press, 1970.

Chodkiewicz, Michel. *An Ocean Without Shore: Ibn 'Arabi, the Book, and the Law*. Albany: State University of New York Press, 1993.

Cragg, Kenneth. *The Event of the Qur'an: Islam in Its Scripture*. Oxford: Oneworld, 1994.

Gatje, Helmut. *The Qur'an and Its Exegesis: Selected Texts with Classical and Modern Muslim Interpretations*. Berkeley: University of California Press, 1976.

Rahman, Fazlur. *Major Themes of the Qur'an*. Minneapolis: Bibliotheca Islamica, 1980.

Siddiqi, Mazheruddin. *The Qur'anic Concept of History*. Karachi: Central Institute of Islamic Research, 1965.

Tabataba'i, Muhammad Husayn. *The Qur'an in Islam: Its Impact and Influence on the Life of Muslims*. London: Zahra, 1987.

Wadud-Muhsin, Amina. *Qur'an and Woman*. Kuala Lumpur: Fajar Bakti, 1992.

LAO-TZU

Finazzo, Gioancarlo. *The Notion of Tao in Lao-Tzu and Chuang Tzu.* Taipei, Taiwan: Mei Ya, 1968.

Heider, John. *The Tao of Leadership: Lao-Tzu's Tao Te Ching Adapted for a New Age.* Atlanta: Humanics New Age, 1985.

Ho-Shang-Kung. *Commentary on Lao-Tzu.* Translated by Eduard Erkes. Ascona, Switzerland: Artibus Asiae, 1958.

Kaltenmark, Max. *Lao-Tzu and Taoism.* Translated by Roger Greaves. Stanford: Stanford University Press, 1969.

LaFargue, Michael. *Tao and Method: A Reasoned Approach to the Tao Te Ching.* Albany: State University of New York Press, 1994.

Lagerway, John. *Taoist Ritual in Chinese Society and History.* New York: Macmillan, 1987.

Lao-Tzu. *Hua Hu Ching.* Translated by Brian Walker. Livingston, Mont.: Clark City Press, 1992.

Lao-Tzu. *Tao Te Ching.* Translated by Ni Hua-Ching. Santa Monica, Calif.: Sevenstar Communications Group, 1993.

Lao-Tzu. *Tao Te Ching.* Translated with an introduction by D. C. Lau. Baltimore: Penguin, 1964.

Lao-Tzu. *Tao Te Ching: The Classic Book of Integrity and the Way.* New York: Bantam, 1990.

Liu, Hsiao-kan. *Classifying the Zhuangzi Chapters.* Ann Arbor: Center for Chinese Studies, University of Michigan, 1994.

Maspero, Henri. *Taoism and Chinese Religion.* Translated by Frank A. Kierman, Jr. Amherst: University of Massachusetts Press, 1981.

Mitchell, Stephen, tr. *Tao Te Ching.* New York: Harper & Row, 1988.

McNaughton, William. *The Taoist Vision.* Ann Arbor: University of Michigan Press, 1971.

Welch, Holmes. *Taoism: The Parting of the Way.* Rev. ed., 1964. Boston: Beacon, 1957.

Wing, R. L., tr. and ed. *The Tao of Power: A Translation of the Tao Te Ching.* Garden City: Doubleday, 1986.

NICCOLÒ MACHIAVELLI

Anglo, Sydney. *Machiavelli: A Dissection.* New York: Harcourt, Brace, and World, 1970.

Bock, Gisela, et al., eds. *Machiavelli and Republicanism.* New York: Cambridge University Press, 1990.

Bondanella, Peter. *Machiavelli and the Art of Renaissance History.* Detroit: Wayne State University Press, 1973.

Butterfield, Herbert. *The Structure of Machiavelli.* New York: Collins, 1962.

Hulliung, Mark. *Citizen Machiavelli.* Princeton: Princeton University Press, 1983.

Jay, Anthony. *Management and Machiavelli: An Inquiry into the Politics of Corporate Life.* New York: Holt, Rinehart and Winston, 1968.

Jensen, De Lamar. *Machiavelli: Cynic, Patriot or Political Scientist?* Lexington, Mass.: Heath, 1960.

Kahn, Victoria Ann. *Machiavellian Rhetoric: From the Counter-Reformation to Milton.* Princeton: Princeton University Press, 1994.

Machiavelli, Niccolò. *The Prince: A Revised Translation, Backgrounds, Interpretations, Marginalia.* New York: Norton, 1992.

Machiavelli, Niccolò. *The Viking Portable Machiavelli.* Edited and translated by Peter Bondanella and Mark Musa. New York: Viking Penguin, 1979.

Olschki, Leonard. *Machiavelli the Scientist.* Berkeley: Gallick, 1945.

Parel, Anthony. *The Machiavellian Cosmos.* New Haven: Yale University Press, 1992.

Parel, Anthony, ed. *The Political Calculus: Essays on Machiavelli's Philosophy.* Toronto: University of Toronto Press, 1972.

Pearce, Edward. *Machiavelli's Children.* London: Victor Gollancz, 1993.

Procock, John. *The Machiavellian Moment.* Princeton: Princeton University Press, 1974.

Ridofi, Roberto. *The Life of Machiavelli.* Translated by Cecil Grayson. Chicago: University of Chicago Press, 1963.

Ridowski, Victor Anthony. *The Prince: A Historical Critique.* New York: Twayne, 1992.

Ruffo-Fiore, Silvia. *Niccolò Machiavelli: An Annotated Bibliography of Modern Criticism and Scholarship.* New York: Greenwood, 1990.

MOSES MAIMONIDES

Fox, Marvin. *Interpreting Maimonides: Studies in Methodology, Metaphysics, and Moral Philosophy.* Chicago: University of Chicago Press, 1990.

Heschel, Abraham Joshua. *Maimonides: A Biography.* Translated by Joachim Neugroschel. New York: Image Books, 1991.

Keller, Menachem Marc. *Maimonides on Judaism and the Jewish People.* Albany: State University of New York Press, 1991.

Maimonides, Moses. *The Code of Maimonides.* New Haven: Yale University Press, 1949.

Maimonides, Moses. *The Essential Maimonides: Translations of the Rambam.* Edited by Avraham Yaakov Finkel. Northvale, N.J.: Aronson, 1996.

Maimonides, Moses. *The Guide of the Perplexed.* Translated by Shlomo Pines. Chicago: University of Chicago Press, 1963.

Maimonides, Moses. *Rambam: Readings in the Philosophy of Moses Maimonides.* New York: Viking Press, 1976.

Maimonides, Moses. *Treatise on Poisons and Their Antidotes.* Edited by Suessman Muntner. Philadelphia: Lippincott, 1966.

Maimonides, Moses. *Treatise on Resurrection.* Translated by Fred Rosner. New York: Ktav, 1982.

Minkin, Jacob Samuel. *The World of Moses Maimonides, with Selections from His Writings.* New York: Yoseloff, 1957.

Silver, Daniel Jeremy. *Maimonidean Criticism and the Maimonidean Controversy.* Leiden: Brill, 1965.

Twersky, Isadore, ed. *Studies in Maimonides.* Cambridge, Mass.: Harvard University, Center for Jewish Studies, 1990.

KARL MARX

Adamson, Walter L. *Marx and the Disillusionment of Marxism.* Berkeley: University of California Press, 1985.

Avineri, Schlomo. *The Social and Political Thought of Karl Marx.* London: Cambridge University Press, 1968.

Callinicos, Alex. *Marxism and Philosophy.* New York: Oxford University Press, 1983.

Carver, Terrell, ed. *The Cambridge Companion to Marx.* New York: Cambridge University Press, 1991.

Clarke, Simon. *Marx's Theory of Crisis.* London: Macmillan, 1994.

Conway, David. *A Farewell to Marx: An Outline and Appraisal of His Theories.* New York: Penguin, 1987.

Cowling, Mark, and Lawrence Wilde. *Approaches to Marx.* Philadelphia: Open University Press, 1989.

Dupre, Louis. *The Philosophical Foundations of Marxism.* New York: Harcourt, Brace, and World, 1966.

Elster, John. *An Introduction to Karl Marx.* New York: Cambridge University Press, 1986.

Felix, David. *Marx as Politician.* Carbondale: Southern Illinois University Press, 1983.

Fetscher, Irving. *Marx and Marxism.* New York: Herder and Herder, 1971.

Forbes, Ian. *Marx and the New Individual.* Boston: Unwin Hyman, 1990.

Gottlieb, Roger S. *Marxism, 1844–1990: Origins, Betrayal, Rebirth.* New York: Routledge, 1992.

Graham, Keith. *Karl Marx: Our Contemporary.* New York: Harvester Wheatsheaf, 1992.

Lichtheim, George. *Marxism: An Historical and Critical Study.* New York: Praeger, 1961.

Lukacs, Gyorgy. *History and Class Consciousness: Studies in Marxist Dialectics.* Cambridge, Mass.: MIT Press, 1971.

Marx, Karl. *Capital.* 3 vols. New York: International, 1976.

Marx, Karl. *The Communist Manifesto.* Edited by A. J. Taylor. Baltimore: Penguin, 1968.

Marx, Karl. *Karl Marx, A Reader.* Edited by John Elster. New York: Cambridge University Press, 1986.

Marx, Karl, and Friedrich Engels. *The Communist Manifesto.* Translated by Samuel Moore. Edited and annotated by Friedrich Engels. Chicago: Kerr, 1978.

Mazlish, Bruce. *The Meaning of Karl Marx.* New York: Oxford University Press, 1984.

Meister, Robert. *Political Identity: Thinking Through Marx.* Cambridge: Basil Blackwell, 1991.

Meszaros, Istvan. *Marx's Theory of Alienation.* New York: Harper & Row, 1972.

Ollman, Bertell. *Alienation: Marx's Conception of Man in Capitalist Society.* New York: Cambridge University Press, 1976.

Parkinson, G. H. R. *Marx and Marxisms*. New York: Cambridge University Press, 1982.

Rubel, M., and M. Mamale. *Marx Without Myth: A Chronological Study of His Life and Work*. New York: Harper & Row, 1975.

Shortall, Felton C. *The Incomplete Marx*. Aldershot: Avebury, 1994.

Thomas, Paul. *Alien Politics: Marxist State Theory Retrieved*. New York: Routledge, 1994.

Tucker, Robert C. *The Marxian Revolutionary Idea*. New York: Norton, 1968.

Van den Berg, Axel. *The Immanent Utopia: From Marxism on the State to the State of Marxism*. Princeton: Princeton University Press, 1988.

ST. MATTHEW

Barton, Stephen C. *Discipleship and Family Ties in Mark and Matthew*. Cambridge: Cambridge University Press, 1994.

Cooper, Robin. *The Synoptic Gospels: An Interpretation for Today*. London: Hodder and Stoughton, 1990.

Evans, Craig A, and Stanley Porter, eds. *The Synoptic Gospels*. Biblical Seminar 31. Sheffield, Eng.: Sheffield Academic Press, 1995.

Guy, Harold A. *A Critical Introduction to the Gospels*. London: Macmillan, 1955.

Guy, Harold A. *The Gospel of Matthew*. London: Macmillan, 1971.

Guy, Harold A. *New Testament Prophecy: Its Origin and Significance*. London: Epworth Press, 1947.

Kunkel, Fritz. *Creation Continues: A Psychological Interpretation of the Gospel of Matthew*. New York: Paulist Press, 1987.

Jones, Alexander. *The Gospel According to St. Matthew: A Text and Commentary for Students*. London: Chapman, 1965.

Luz, Ulrich. *The Theology of the Gospel of Matthew*. Cambridge: Cambridge University Press, 1995.

Malina, Bruce J. *Calling Jesus Names: The Social Value of Labels in Matthew*. Sonoma, Calif.: Polebridge Press, 1988.

Menninger, Richard E. *Israel and the Church in the Gospel of Matthew*. New York: Lang, 1994.

Montague, George T. *Companion God: A Cross-Cultural Commentary on the Gospel of Matthew*. New York: Paulist Press, 1989.

Riches, John Kenneth. *Matthew*. New Testament Guides. Sheffield, Eng.: Sheffield Academic Press, 1996.

Shuler, Philip L. *A Genre for the Gospels: The Biographical Character of Matthew*. Philadelphia: Fortress Press, 1982.

Stendahl, Krister. *The School of St. Matthew and Its Use of the Old Testament*. Philadelphia: Fortress Press, 1968.

Wainwright, Elaine Mary. *Towards a Feminist Critical Reading of the Gospel According to Matthew*. New York: De Gruyter, 1991.

Wilder, Amos Niven. *Early Christian Rhetoric: The Language of the Gospel*. Cambridge, Mass.: Harvard University Press, 1971.

MARGARET MEAD

Bateson, Mary Catherine. *With a Daughter's Eye: A Memoir of Margaret Mead and Gregory Bateson*. New York: Morrow, 1984.

Cassidy, Robert. *Margaret Mead: A Voice for the Century*. New York: Universe, 1982.

Freeman, Derek. *Margaret Mead and Samoa: The Making and Unmaking of an Anthropological Myth*. New York: Penguin, 1986.

Goodman, Richard A. *Mead's Coming of Age in Samoa: A Dissenting View*. Oakland: Pipperine, 1983.

Gordon, Joan. *Margaret Mead: The Complete Bibliography*. The Hague: Mouton, 1976.

Howard, Jane. *Margaret Mead: A Life*. New York: Simon & Schuster, 1984.

Mead, Margaret. *Anthropology, A Human Science: Selected Papers, 1939–1960*. Princeton: Van Nostrand, 1964.

Mead, Margaret. *Blackberry Winter: My Early Years*. 1972. Gloucester: Peter Smith, 1989.

Mead, Margaret. *Coming of Age in Samoa: A Psychological Study of Primitive Youth for Western Civilization*. 1961. Foreword by Franz Boas. Gloucester: Peter Smith, 1973.

Mead, Margaret. *Growing Up in New Guinea: A Comparative Study of Primitive Education.* Reprint ed. New York: Morrow, 1975.

Mead, Margaret. *Letters from the Field, 1925–1975.* New York: Harper & Row, 1977.

Mead, Margaret. *The School in American Culture.* Cambridge, Mass.: Harvard University Press, 1951.

Mead, Margaret. *Some Personal Views.* Edited by Rhoda Metraux. New York: Walker, 1979.

Mead, Margaret, and Ken Heyman. *Family.* New York: Macmillan, 1965.

Mead, Margaret, and Martha Wolfenstein, eds. *Childhood in Contemporary Cultures.* Text ed. Chicago: University of Chicago Press, 1963.

FRIEDRICH NIETZSCHE

Clark, Maudmarie. *Nietzsche on Truth and Philosophy.* New York: Cambridge University Press, 1990.

Danto, Arthur C. *Nietzsche as Philosopher.* New York: Macmillan, 1965.

Gillespie, Michael Allen, and Tracy B. Strong, eds. *Nietzsche's New Seas: Explorations in Philosophy, Aesthetics, and Politics.* Chicago: University of Chicago Press, 1988.

Heller, Erich. *The Importance of Nietzsche: Ten Essays.* Chicago: University of Chicago Press, 1988.

Heller, Otto. *Prophets of Dissent.* New York: Knopf, 1918.

Hollingdale, R. J. *Nietzsche: The Man and His Philosophy.* Baton Rouge: Louisiana State University Press, 1965.

Jaspers, Karl. *Nietzsche and Christianity.* Translated by E. B. Ashton. Chicago: Regnery, 1961.

Kaufmann, Walter A. *Nietzsche: Philosopher, Psychologist, Antichrist.* Princeton: Princeton University Press, 1950.

Makarushka, Irena S. M. *Religious Imagination and Language in Emerson and Nietzsche.* New York: St. Martin's Press, 1994.

Nietzsche, Friedrich. *The Viking Portable Nietzsche.* Edited by Walter A. Kaufmann. New York: Viking Penguin, 1977.

Pfeffer, Rose. *Nietzsche: Disciple of Dionysus.* Lewisburg: Bucknell University Press, 1972.

Salter, William. *Nietzsche the Thinker.* London: Cecil, Palmer, and Hayward, 1917.

Schacht, Richard. *Nietzsche.* London: Routledge and Kegan Paul, 1983.

Solomon, Robert C., and Kathleen M. Higgins, eds. *Reading Nietzsche.* New York: Oxford University Press, 1988.

Staten, Henry. *Nietzsche's Voice.* Ithaca: Cornell University Press, 1990.

Tanner, Michael. *Nietzsche.* Oxford: Oxford University Press, 1994.

Westphal, Merold. *Suspicion and Faith: The Religious Uses of Modern Atheism.* Grand Rapids, Mich.: Eerdmans, 1993.

Wilcox, John. *Truth and Value in Nietzsche.* Ann Arbor: University of Michigan Press, 1974.

Zeitlin, Irving M. *Nietzsche: A Re-Examination.* Cambridge: Polity Press, 1994.

PLATO

Barrow, Robin. *Plato, Utilitarianism, and Education.* London: Routledge and Kegan Paul, 1975.

Brickhouse, Thomas C. *Plato's Socrates.* New York: Oxford University Press, 1994.

Brumbaugh, Robert Sherrick. *Plato for the Modern Age.* New York: Crowell-Collier, 1962.

Clegg, Jerry. *The Structure of Plato's Philosophy.* Lewisburg: Bucknell University Press, 1976.

Cornford, Francis MacDonald. *Before and After Socrates.* Cambridge: Cambridge University Press, 1958.

Fox, Adam. *Plato for Pleasure.* London: Westhouse, 1945.

Grube, Georges. *Plato's Thought.* Boston: Beacon, 1958.

Gulley, Norman. *Plato's Theory of Knowledge.* New York: Barnes and Noble, 1962.

Kraut, Richard, ed. *The Cambridge Companion to Plato.* New York: Cambridge University Press, 1992.

McCrone, John. *The Myth of Irrationality: The Science of the Mind from Plato to Star Trek.* London: Macmillan, 1993.

Melling, David J. *Understanding Plato.* Oxford: Oxford University Press, 1987.

Plato. *The Dialogues of Plato.* Edited by Justin D. Kaplan. New York: Washington Square, 1982.

Plato. *Plato's Sophist.* Translated by William S. Cobb. Savage: Rowand & Littlefield, 1990.

Plato. *The Republic of Plato.* Translated by Allan Bloom. New York: Basic Books, 1991.

Plato. *The Viking Portable Plato.* Edited by Scott Buchanan. New York: Viking Penguin, 1977.

Rankin, H. D. *Plato and the Individual.* New York: Barnes and Noble, 1964.

Rowe, C. J. *Plato.* New York: St. Martin's, 1984.

Taylor, Alfred. *Plato: The Man and His Work.* London: Methuen, 1960.

Tuana, Nancy, ed. *Feminist Interpretations of Plato.* University Park: Pennsylvania State University Press, 1994.

Vlastos, Gregory. *Plato's Universe.* Seattle: University of Washington Press, 1975.

Zeitlin, Irving M. *Plato's Vision: The Classical Origins of Social and Political Thought.* Englewood Cliffs, N.J.: Prentice-Hall, 1993.

ALEXANDER POPE

Brower, Reuben Arthur. *Alexander Pope: The Poetry of Allusion.* Oxford: Clarendon Press, 1959.

Brownell, Morris R. *Alexander Pope and the Arts of Georgian England.* Oxford: Clarendon Press, 1978.

Erskine-Hill, Howard. *The Social Milieu of Alexander Pope: Lives, Example, and the Poetic Response.* New Haven: Yale University Press, 1975.

Fraser, George Sutherland. *Alexander Pope.* London: Routledge and Paul, 1978.

Knight, George Wilson. *The Poetry of Pope, Laureate of Peace.* New York: Barnes and Noble, 1965.

Mack, Maynard. *Alexander Pope: A Life.* New Haven: Yale University Press, 1985.

Mack, Maynard. *Collected in Himself: Essays Critical, Biographical, and Bibliographical on Pope.* Newark: University of Delaware Press, 1982.

Mack, Maynard. *Essential Articles for the Study of Alexander Pope.* Hamden, Conn.: Archon Books, 1964.

Nicolson, Marjorie Hope, and G. S. Rousseau. *"This Long Disease, My Life": Alexander Pope and the Sciences.* Princeton: Princeton University Press, 1968.

Parkin, Rebecca Price. *The Poetic Workmanship of Alexander Pope.* New York: Octagon Books, 1966.

Pope, Alexander. *Correspondence.* Oxford: Clarendon Press, 1956.

Pope, Alexander. *The Dunciad.* Edited by James Runcieman Sutherland. London: Methuen, 1943.

Pope, Alexander. *An Essay on Man.* Twickenham ed. London: Methuen, 1951.

Pope, Alexander. *The Poems of Alexander Pope.* Edited by John Butt. Twickenham ed. London: Routledge, 1993.

Pope, Alexander. *The Prose Works of Alexander Pope.* Edited by Norman Ault. Oxford: Blackwell, 1936.

Pope, Alexander. *The Rape of the Lock and Other Poems.* Edited by Geoffrey Tillotson. Twickenham ed. New York: Oxford University Press, 1942.

Rogers, Pat. *An Introduction to Pope.* London: Methuen, 1975.

Russo, John Paul. *Alexander Pope: Tradition and Identity.* Cambridge, Mass.: Harvard University Press, 1972.

Spacks, Patricia Ann Meyer. *An Argument of Images: The Poetry of Alexander Pope.* Cambridge, Mass.: Harvard University Press, 1971.

Tillotson, Geoffrey. *On the Poetry of Pope.* Oxford: Clarendon Press, 1938.

Tillotson, Geoffrey. *Pope and Human Nature.* Oxford: Clarendon Press, 1958.

ROBERT B. REICH

Henkoff, Ronald. "An Interview with Robert Reich." *Fortune* 127 (1993): 11.

Litchfield, Randall. "New Dealer: Interview with Robert B. Reich." *Canadian Business* 66 (1993): 38–39.

Magaziner, Ira C., and Robert B. Reich. *Minding America's Business: The Decline and Rise of the American Economy.* 1982. New York: Vintage, 1983.

Reich, Robert B. *Education and the Next Economy.* Washington, D.C.: National Education Association, Professional and Organizational Development, Research Division. West Haven, Conn.: Order from NEA Professional Library, 1988.

Reich, Robert. *Locked in the Cabinet.* New York: Knopf, 1997.

Reich, Robert B. *The Next American Frontier.* New York: Viking Penguin, 1984.

Reich, Robert B., ed. *The Power of Public Ideas.* 1988. Cambridge, Mass.: Harvard University Press, 1990.

Reich, Robert B. *The Resurgent Liberal: And Other Unfashionable Prophecies.* 1989. New York: Vintage, 1991.

Reich, Robert B. *The Work of Nations: Preparing Ourselves for Twenty-first-Century Capitalism.* New York: Knopf, 1991.

JEAN-JACQUES ROUSSEAU

Blanchard, William. *Rousseau and the Spirit of Revolt.* Ann Arbor: University of Michigan Press, 1967.

Broome, Jack Howard. *Rousseau: A Study of His Thought.* New York: Barnes and Noble, 1963.

Cassirer, Ernst. *The Question of Jean-Jacques Rousseau.* Translated and edited by Peter Gay. New York: Columbia University Press, 1954.

Chapman, John William. *Rousseau: Totalitarian or Liberal?* New York: Columbia University Press, 1956.

Dent, N. J. H. *A Rousseau Dictionary.* Cambridge, Mass.: Blackwell Reference, 1992.

Dobinson, Charles Henry. *Jean-Jacques Rousseau: His Thought and Its Relevance Today.* London: Methuen, 1969.

Fermon, Nicole. *Domesticating Passions: Rousseau, Woman, and Nation.* Hanover, N.H.: University Press of New England, 1997.

Grimsley, Ronald. *Jean-Jacques Rousseau.* Totowa, N.J.: Barnes and Noble Books, 1983.

Huizinga, Jacob Herman. *Rousseau: The Self-Made Spirit.* New York: Grossman, 1976.

Masters, Roger. *The Political Philosophy of Rousseau.* Princeton, N.J.: Princeton University Press, 1968.

Morgenstern, Mira. *Rousseau and the Politics of Ambiguity: Self, Culture, and Society.* University Park: Pennsylvania State University Press, 1996.

Murry, John Middleton. *Heroes of Thought.* New York: J. Messner, 1938.

Orwin, Clifford, and Nathan Tarcov. *The Legacy of Rousseau.* Chicago: University of Chicago Press, 1997.

Perkins, Merle. *Jean-Jacques Rousseau on the Individual and Society.* Lexington, Mass.: University Press of Kentucky, 1974.

Riesenberg, Peter N. *Citizenship in the Western Tradition: Plato to Rousseau.* Chapel Hill: University of North Carolina Press, 1992.

Rousseau, Jean-Jacques. *The Annotated Social Contract.* Edited by Charles M. Sherover. New York: New American Library.

Rousseau, Jean-Jacques. *Confessions.* Translated by John M. Cohen. Baltimore: Penguin, 1953.

Wokler, Robert. *Rousseau.* Oxford: Oxford University Press, 1995.

SIDDHĀRTHA GAUTAMA, THE BUDDHA

Batchelor, Stephen. *Alone with Others: An Existential Approach to Buddhism.* New York: Grove, 1983.

Batchelor, Stephen. *The World of Buddhism: Buddhist Monks and Nuns in Society and Culture.* New York: Facts on File, 1984.

Bercholz, Samuel, and Sherab Chödin Kohn, eds. *Entering the Stream: An Introduction to the Buddha and His Teachings.* Boston: Shambhala, 1993.

Carmody, Denise Lardner. *In the Path of the Masters: Understanding the Spirituality of Buddha, Confucius, Jesus, and Muhammad.* New York: Paragon House, 1994.

Conze, Edward. *Buddhist Scriptures.* 1959. Selected and translated by Edward Conze. Baltimore: Penguin, 1960.

Eckel, Malcom David. *To See the Buddha: A Philosopher's Quest for the Meaning of Emptiness.* Princeton: Princeton University Press, 1994.

Gross, Rita. *Buddhism After Patriarchy: A Feminist History, Analysis, and Reconstruction of Buddhism.* Albany: SUNY Press, 1993.

Herbert, Patricia M. *The Life of the Buddha.* London: British Library, 1993.

Jacobson, Nolan Pliny. *Buddhism and the Contemporary World: Change and Self-Correction.* Carbondale: Southern Illinois University Press, 1983.

Kohn, Sherab Chödzin. *The Awakened One: A Life of Buddha.* Boston: Shambhala, 1994.

Lefebure, Leo D. *The Buddha and the Christ: Explorations in Buddhist and Christian Dialogue.* Maryknoll, N.Y.: Orbis Books, 1993.

Mizuno, Kogen. *Basic Buddhist Concepts.* Translated by Charles S. Terry and Richard L. Gage. Tokyo: Kosei, 1987.

Pardue, Peter A. *Buddhism: A Historical Introduction to Buddhist Values and the Social and Political Forms They Have Assumed in Asia.* New York: Macmillan, 1971.

Prebish, Charles S. *Buddhism: A Modern Perspective.* University Park: Pennsylvania State University Press, 1975.

Robinson, Richard H., and Willard L. Johnson. *The Buddhist Religion: A Historical Introduction.* 3d ed. Belmont: Wadsworth, 1982.

Stambaugh, Joan. *The Real Is Not the Rational.* Albany: State University of New York Press, 1986.

Wright, Arthur F. *Studies in Chinese Buddhism.* New Haven: Yale University Press, 1990.

Yoo, Yushin. *Books on Buddhism: An Annotated Subject Guide.* Metuchen: Scarecrow, 1976.

ADAM SMITH

Aspromourgos, Tony. *On the Origins of Classical Economics: Distribution and Value from William Petty to Adam Smith.* London: Routledge, 1996.

Brown, Vivienne. *Adam Smith's Discourse: Canonicity, Commerce, and Conscience.* London: Routledge, 1994.

Campbell, Thomas Douglas. *Adam Smith's Science of Morals.* London: Allen and Unwin, 1971.

Copley, Stephen, and Kathryn Sutherland, eds. *Adam Smith's Wealth of Nations: New Interdisciplinary Essays.* Manchester, Eng.: Manchester University Press, 1995.

Fitzgibbons, Athol. *Adam Smith's System of Liberty, Wealth, and Virture: The Moral and Political Foundations of the Wealth of Nations.* Oxford: Clarendon Press, 1995.

Fry, Michael. *Adam Smith's Legacy: His Place in the Development of Modern Economics.* London: Routledge, 1992.

Lindgren, J. Ralph. *The Social Philosophy of Adam Smith.* The Hague: Marinus Nijhoff, 1973.

Minowitz, Peter. *Profits, Priests, and Princes: Adam Smith's Emancipation of Economics from Politics.* Stanford: Stanford University Press, 1993.

Muller, Jerry Z. *Adam Smith in His Time and Ours: Designing the Decent Society.* New York: Free Press, 1993.

Rae, John. *Life of Adam Smith.* New York: Kelley, 1965.

Smith, Adam. *The Early Writings of Adam Smith.* Edited by J. Ralph Lindgren. New York: Kelley, 1967.

Smith, Adam. *The Essential Adam Smith.* Edited by Robert L. Heilbroner. New York: Norton, 1986.

Smith, Adam. *An Inquiry into the Nature and Cause of the Wealth of Nations: A Selected Edition.* Oxford: Oxford University Press, 1993.

Smith, Adam. *Lectures on Jurisprudence.* Edited by R. L. Meek, D. D. Raphael, and P. G. Stein. Indianapolis: Liberty Classics, 1982.

Smith, Adam. *The Theory of Moral Sentiments.* Edited by D. D. Raphael and A. L. Macfie. Indianapolis: Liberty Classics, 1982.

SUSAN SONTAG

Brooks, Peter. "Death of/as Metaphor." *Partisan Review* 46 (1979): 438–444.

Jeffords, Susan. "Susan Sontag." *Modern American Critics Since 1955.* Edited by Gregory Jay. Detroit: Bruccoli-Clark-Layman, 1988.

Kennedy, Liam. *Susan Sontag: Mind as Passion.* Manchester, Eng.: Manchester University Press, 1995.

Phillips, William. "Radical Styles." *Partisan Review* 36 (1969): 388–400.

Poague, Leland, ed. *Conversations with Susan Sontag.* Jackson: University Press of Mississippi, 1995.

Rubin, Louis D., Jr. "Susan Sontag and the Camp Followers." *Sewanee Review* 82 (Summer 1974): 503–510.

Sayres, Sohnya. *Susan Sontag: The Elegaic Modernist.* New York: Routledge, 1990.

Sontag, Susan. *Against Interpretation and Other Essays.* New York: Farrar, Straus & Giroux, 1966.

Sontag, Susan. *AIDS and Its Metaphors.* New York: Farrar, Straus & Giroux, 1988.

Sontag, Susan. *Illness as Metaphor.* New York: Farrar, Straus & Giroux, 1978.
Sontag, Susan. *Styles of Radical Will.* New York: Farrar, Straus & Giroux, 1969.

ST. TERESA OF AVILA

Ahlgren, Gillian T. W. *Teresa of Avila and the Politics of Sanctity.* Ithaca: Cornell University Press, 1996.
Bilinkoff, Jodi. *The Avila of Saint Teresa: Religious Reform in a Sixteenth-Century City.* Ithaca: Cornell University Press, 1989.
Gross, Francis L., Jr., and Toni Perior. *The Making of a Mystic: Seasons in the Life of Teresa of Avila.* Albany: State University of New York Press, 1993.
Lincoln, Victoria. *Teresa, a Woman: A Biography of Teresa of Avila.* Albany: State University of New York Press, 1984.
Teresa of Avila. *The Collected Works of St. Teresa of Avila.* Translated by Kieran Kavanaugh. Washington: Institute of Carmelite Studies, 1976–1980.
Teresa of Avila. *The Interior Castle.* Translated by Allison Peers. New York: Doubleday, 1989.
Teresa of Avila. *The Life of Saint Teresa of Avila.* Translated by J. M. Cohen. London: Penguin Books, 1957.
Walsh, William Thomas. *Saint Teresa of Avila: A Biography.* Milwaukee: Bruce, 1943.
Weber, Allison. *Teresa of Avila and the Rhetoric of Femininity.* Princeton, N.J.: Princeton University Press, 1990.

HENRY DAVID THOREAU

Borst, Raymond. *Henry David Thoreau: A Reference Guide.* Boston: Hall, 1987.
Derleth, August William. *Concord Rebel: A Life of Henry David Thoreau.* Philadelphia: Cholton, 1962.
Fink, Steven. *Prophet in the Marketplace: Thoreau's Development as a Professional Writer.* Princeton: Princeton University Press, 1992.
Hamilton, Franklin W. *Thoreau on the Art of Writing.* Flint, Mich.: Walden, 1967.
Harding, Walter Roy. *Henry David Thoreau: A Profile.* New York: Hill and Wang, 1971.
Gayet, Claude. *The Intellectual Development of Henry David Thoreau.* Stockholm: Almqvist and Wikseu, 1981.
Myerson, Joel, ed. *The Cambridge Companion to Henry David Thoreau.* New York: Cambridge University Press, 1995.
Richardson, Robert D., Jr. *Henry Thoreau: A Life of the Mind.* Berkeley: University of California Press, 1986.
Salt, Henry. *Life of Henry David Thoreau.* Urbana: University of Illinois Press, 1993.
Sattelmeyer, Robert. *Thoreau's Reading: A Study in Intellectual History.* Princeton: Princeton University Press, 1988.
Sayre, Robert F., ed. *New Essays on Walden.* New York: Cambridge University Press, 1992.
Schneider, Richard J. *Henry David Thoreau.* Boston: Twayne, 1987.
Thoreau, Henry David. *The Annotated Walden: Walden, or Life in the Woods.* New York: Potter, Crown, 1970.
Thoreau, Henry David. *The Best of Thoreau's Journal.* Edited by Carl Bode. Carbondale: Southern Illinois University Press, 1971.
Thoreau, Henry David. *Collected Poems.* Edited by Carl Bode. Baltimore: Johns Hopkins University Press, 1964.
Thoreau, Henry David. *The Thoreau Log: A Documentary Life of Henry David Thoreau.* Compiled by Raymond Borst. New York: Hall, 1992.
Thoreau, Henry David. *Walden.* Edited by J. Lyndon Shanley. Princeton: Princeton University Press, 1971.
Thoreau, Henry David. *Walden and Resistance to Civil Government.* Edited by William Rossi. New York: Norton, 1992.
Thoreau, Henry David. *A Week on the Concord and Merrimack Rivers.* Edited by Carl Howde. Princeton: Princeton University Press, 1980.

VIRGINIA WOOLF

Beer, Gillian. *Virginia Woolf: The Common Ground*. Ann Arbor: University of Michigan, 1996.

Bell, Quentin. *Virginia Woolf: A Biography*. New York: Harcourt, Brace, Jovanovich, 1973.

Bishop, Edward. *Virginia Woolf*. New York: St. Martin's Press, 1991.

Gordon, Lyndall. *Virginia Woolf: A Writer's Life*. London: Oxford University Press, 1984.

Gorsky, Susan Rubinow. *Virginia Woolf*. Boston: Twayne, 1989.

Hussey, Mark. *Virginia Woolf A to Z: A Comprehensive Reference for Students, Teachers, and Common Readers to Her Life, Work, and Critical Reception*. New York: Facts on File, 1995.

King, James. *Virginia Woolf*. London: Norton, 1995.

Lee, Hermione. *Virginia Woolf*. New York: Knopf, 1997.

Poole, Roger. *The Unknown Virginia Woolf*. Cambridge: Cambridge University Press, 1995.

Reid, Panthea. *Art and Affection: A Life of Virginia Woolf*. New York: Oxford University Press, 1996.

Rose, Phyllis. *A Woman of Letters: The Life of Virginia Woolf*. New York: Oxford University Press, 1981.

Woolf, Virginia. *The Captain's Deathbed and Other Essays*. New York: Harcourt, Brace, 1950.

Woolf, Virginia. *The Death of the Moth and Other Essays*. New York: Harcourt, Brace, 1942.

Woolf, Virginia. *Moments of Being: Unpublished Autobiographical Works*. Edited by Jeanne Schulkind. New York: Harcourt, Brace, Jovanovich, 1973.

Woolf, Virginia. *Night and Day*. New York: Harcourt, Brace, Jovanovich, 1973.

Wussow, Helen. *New Essays on Virginia Woolf*. Dallas: Contemporary Research Press, 1995.

WILLIAM WORDSWORTH

Baker, Jeffrey. *Time and Mind in Wordsworth's Poetry*. Detroit: Wayne State University Press, 1980.

Beer, John B. *Wordsworth in Time*. London: Faber, 1979.

Bewell, Alan. *Wordsworth and the Enlightenment: Nature, Man, and Society in the Experimental Poetry*. New Haven: Yale University Press, 1989.

Davies, Hunter. *William Wordsworth: A Biography*. New York: Atheneum, 1980.

Durrant, Geoffrey. *Wordsworth and the Great System: A Study of Wordsworth's Poetic Universe*. London: Cambridge University Press, 1970.

Ellis, Amanda Mae. *Rebels and Conservatives: Dorothy and William Wordsworth and Their Circle*. Bloomington: Indiana University Press, 1967.

Galperin, William H. *Revision and Authority in Wordsworth: The Interpretation of a Career*. Philadelphia: University of Pennsylvania Press, 1989.

Garber, Frederick. *Wordsworth and the Poetry of Encounter*. Urbana: University of Illinois Press, 1971.

Gill, Stephen Charles. *William Wordsworth: A Life*. Oxford: Clarendon Press, 1989.

Hartman, Geoffrey H. *The Unremarkable Wordsworth*. Minneapolis: University of Minnesota Press, 1987.

Jacobus, Mary. *Tradition and Experiment in Wordsworth's Lyrical Ballads*. Oxford: Clarendon Press, 1976.

Lacey, Norman. *Wordsworth's View of Nature and Its Ethical Consequences*. Hamden, Conn.: Archon Books, 1965.

Moorman, Mary Trevelyan. *William Wordsworth: A Biography*. Oxford: Clarendon Press, 1957–1965.

Owen, Warwick Jack Burgoyne. *Wordsworth as Critic*. Toronto: University of Toronto Press, 1969.

Purkis, John Arthur. *A Preface to Wordsworth*. New York: Scribner, 1972.

Salvesen, Christopher. *The Landscape of Memory: A Study of Wordsworth's Poetry*. London: Arnold, 1965.

Scoggins, James. *Imagination and Fancy: Complementary Modes in the Poetry of Wordsworth*. Lincoln: University of Nebraska Press, 1966.

Sheats, Paul D. *The Making of Wordsworth's Poetry, 1785–1798*. Cambridge: Harvard University Press, 1973.

Sherry, Charles. *Wordsworth's Poetry of the Imagination*. Oxford: Clarendon Press, 1980.

Williams, John. *William Wordsworth: A Literary Life*. New York: St. Martin's Press, 1996.

Wordsworth, William. *The Letters of William and Dorothy Wordsworth*. Edited by Ernest de Selincourt. Oxford: Clarendon Press, 1967–1988.

Wordsworth, William. *Lyrical Ballads and Other Poems, 1797–1800*. Edited by James Butler. Ithaca: Cornell University Press, 1992.

Wordsworth, William. *Poems*. Edited by John O. Hayden. Harmondsworth, Eng.: Penguin Books, 1977.

Wordsworth, William. *The Prelude: A Parallel Text*. Edited by J. C. Maxwell. Harmondworth, Eng.: Penguin Books, 1972.

Wordsworth, William. *The Prose Works of William Wordsworth*. Edited by W. J. B. Owen and Jane Worthington Smyser. Oxford: Clarendon Press, 1974.

Wordsworth, William. *Wordsworth's Literary Criticism*. Edited by W. J. B. Owen. London: Routledge and Paul, 1974.

APPENDIX

Two Student Papers

Bedford Books recently asked instructors who used the previous edition of *A World of Ideas* to submit student essays written in response to selections in the book. Here we offer two of those essays.[1] The first writer applies Lao-tzu's principles to the government of the family; the second examines Martin Luther King, Jr.'s use of emotion as a persuasive tool. You may use these actual student papers in any way you wish. The assignments for these essays also follow.

---

1. I want to thank Michael Hennessy, Professor of English at Southwest Texas State University, who submitted the following assignments and essays

Assignment 1

Take any group structure within our society — family, classroom, workplace, community, and so on — and imagine that the leader of that particular group is a Taoist. How could Lao-tzu's principles of government be applied to the group? How would the leader have to adapt those principles to fit contemporary circumstances?

Paul Nelson   Nelson 1

Professor Michael Hennessy

English 1320.264

5 February 1995

Losing Control: Good Family Advice

The ancient Chinese philosopher Lao-tzu writes: "The people are difficult to govern: It is because those in authority are too fond of action." I see this as Lao-tzu's assertion that too much government control will breed resentment in the people and thus make them difficult to handle. The act of controlling suddenly brings about uncontrollability, much to the leader's surprise. John Wayne might express this idea differently: "Pull the reins too tight--horse'll buck!" This lesson also lends itself readily to the "government" of a family. Picture the "leaders" as the mother and father (or either one separately) and the "people" they govern as the children, whether one child or many. When a parent exerts too much control over a child, the action initiates a pattern of resentment, which can create distance between the two and eventually leave the relationship devoid of respect and love.

I believe that people, for the most part, do not like being told what to do. Lao-tzu seems to think so too. He explains that he prefers people in their simple, unmeddled-with form, like that of an "uncarved block." For him, people in this form are truer to their nature and perhaps closer to a basic goodness; it is when people are continually acted upon or "controlled" that they exhibit undesirable behaviors. "Win the empire by not being meddlesome," advises Lao-tzu. He also writes, "The better known the laws and edicts, the more thieves and robbers there are." I translate this as, "More control results in uncontrollability." One could argue, of course, that children not only need but also feel more comfortable with some predetermined boundaries. Perhaps this is true of adults as well. We feel safer knowing that all of our desires will not be permitted to run recklessly through the world in a laissez-faire fashion. Therefore, I think it is important to clarify that "less" control does not necessarily mean a complete absence of control, rather that a little personal freedom must be granted to individuals in order to bring about healthy behaviors in them. To give credibility to this statement, I can cite a personal experience.

When I moved to Texas three years ago, I began a relationship with a woman who already had a young son. After a year or so, we began living together and operating as a family. Both the child and I had no idea how we were going to begin our relationship, but I knew I wanted to be the father, and I knew I wanted him to listen to me. At first I observed a respectful distance between us, hoping to give birth slowly to a long and beautiful friendship. I thought to myself, "Pretty soon this kid will be crazy about me and will do all the things I ask out of profound admiration and undying love." After a while I realized the foolish error of my reasoning and then made my second mistake. To get the cooperation I wanted out of this six-year-old boy, I tried to control him with a host of rules, close observation, and timely punishment, which I regret included a few spankings. I found that not only did I start a pattern of fear and resentment, but that I was less happy with myself. I sought absolute power and felt the by-product of corruption eating away at my own well-being. To paraphrase Lao-tzu, I lost the empire with too much meddling. I took the "uncarved block" and whittled an angry, frustrated, rebellious figure. Lao-tzu teaches that people will be hard to govern if those in authority are too fond of action. It was only after I realized the mess I helped create that I made the decision to do less. I reasoned that constant action implies constant fixing, which is not only bothersome but unnecessary.

I have given up a great deal of desire to control. By accepting my stepson, now eight, as he is, I discovered that he's quite a wonderful person, and by not telling him what to do so often, I have discovered that most of the time he *knows* what to do and takes pride in doing it. He now enjoys a little bit of personal freedom. This personal freedom has manifested itself as self-esteem, which in turn has generated respect for me and inspired a little bit of love. Our relationship has strengthened considerably, and the family is happier.

As I suggested earlier, I believe the desire to control someone tends to make that person more uncontrollable. It happened with my stepson. History is also full of good examples: England tried to control the religious practices of its people and ended up in a revolution; Prohibition was an attempt to control the use of alcohol, and we found that the cure was more problematic than the problem. These situations more than likely could have been avoided. By decreasing the amount of control over our children, perhaps we can become parents whom they love and respect. Love and respect may be the masks of what Lao-tzu considered the "second best ruler," but I believe they make a first-rate parent.

Assignment 2

Martin Luther King, Jr. uses both reason and emotion to make his ideas convincing. Locate a key passage in the letter that is primarily rational and one that is primarily emotional. Briefly discuss the two passages, focusing on why you think each is or is not effective. In general, are people today more easily persuaded by appeals to reason or appeals to emotion? Cite examples and explain.

Angie Calder

Professor Michael Hennessy

English 1310.264

21 February 1995

Calder 1

The Use of Emotion in Martin Luther King, Jr.'s
"Letter from Birmingham Jail"

Through the media and in our daily interaction with others, we are bombarded by a steady stream of "arguments" persuading us to adopt a political position, to follow a certain course of action, or to buy a particular brand of car or deodorant. These arguments are both reasonable and emotional, but I believe that people are more responsive to arguments that appeal to their emotions than those that appeal to their reason. When someone backs a position for emotional reasons, he or she is more likely to have a strong commitment to that position. Politicians know this and make heavy use of emotional appeals to sway voters and constituents. However, in terms of emotional intensity, today's political battles pale in comparison to those of the civil rights struggles of the 1960s. At the most stirring points in the classic "Letter from Birmingham Jail," for example, Martin Luther King, Jr., uses emotion to point out the horror of segregation and to explain why it must be ended immediately. Although King uses sound reason to make many of his points, his most moving arguments persuade by triggering his audience's emotions.

In King's "Letter," he rationally makes the point that he and the members of the Southern Christian Leadership Conference (SCLC) have tried everything possible, within reason, to end segregation. To King, public demonstrations are the last resort. He says, "In any nonviolent campaign there are four basic steps: collection of the facts to determine whether injustices exist; negotiation; self-purification; and direct action." King assures his audience that he and the other sit-in participants have gone through these steps. He states that the number of unsolved bomb-ings of African-American homes and churches in Birmingham is higher than in any other city in the United States. Clearly, he and his colleagues have done their research. In the next few paragraphs of his "Letter," King recounts how he and the SCLC attempted to negotiate with city officials, how this failed, and how he and the other protesters underwent a process of self-purification in order to be ready for direct action: the planned sit-ins. Here King clearly and rationally states his views, his actions, and his reasons for his actions. This method of making his case is effective in communicating facts and clarifying opinions. Reasonable argument aptly carries King's points; however, it alone does not move people to action the way that emotional argument might.

King is indeed very talented at evoking the kinds of emotions that do move people to action. In paragraph 14, where he describes in vivid detail what segregation is like and what it means to be oppressed, he transports the reader into his life and the life of everyone who has ever felt oppressed. King draws on emotions that many people try to ignore, such as fear, hate, pity, frustration--the emotions that go along with oppression. King explains why it is so difficult

153

for African Americans to wait for equality when faced with what they must live through. He tells of watching "vicious mobs lynch . . . mothers and fathers at will"; of trying "to explain to [a] six-year-old daughter why she can't go to the public amusement park . . . and see[ing] tears well up in her eyes when she is told that Funtown is closed to colored children"; of trying to find "an answer for a five-year-old son who is asking 'Daddy, why do white people treat colored people so mean?'"; and of feeling humiliated "when your first name becomes 'nigger,' your middle name becomes 'boy' (however old you are) and your last name becomes 'John,' and your wife and your mother are never given the respected title 'Mrs.'" These insults that King and other African Americans have had to endure are horrible. These horrors, more powerful and compelling than arguments based solely on reason, have the ability to arouse strong emotions in his audience.

I believe it to be as true today as it was when King wrote: emotion is generally more powerful than logic and reason. In today's politics, appeals to people's emotions form the basis of most effective political debates. One has simply to look at any of Newt Gingrich's or Rush Limbaugh's speeches to see how emotion is used to influence the public. Further, many current and controversial political questions concern emotionally charged issues such as abortion, morality, the homeless, and health care; issues such as foreign affairs, the national debt, and the constitutionality of government policies, on the other hand, are often left to the lawmakers and their various committees. In the past, emotions played a much stronger role than logic in stirring public reaction. Many of the most influential people in history relied almost entirely on the power of emotions, and for the most part they were successful in persuading people to follow them. For example, Joan of Arc convinced the French to follow her because of the strong emotions--religious and patriotic--with which she spoke of her cause. Four centuries later, Adolph Hitler succeeded in part because of his ability to whip a crowd into an emotional frenzy. With such overwhelming examples, how can one argue the power of the emotional argument?

Martin Luther King, Jr., was well aware of the appeal of emotion. I believe he was wise to use emotion in his "Letter" because of its power to persuade. However, King also knew when to be reasonable and rational. Had he not known how to use emotion and reason in balance, not only in his "Letter" but in his entire campaign, the American civil rights struggle might have turned out very differently. King was willing to fight for what he believed in because of his emotions, and he appealed to this side of his audience in searching for help in his struggle for equality. Most stirring debates, past and present, have been fought on deeply felt emotional, not logical, grounds. When logic is no longer useful, people turn to emotional tactics. I doubt that this will change in the future; after all, think about what persuades you to adopt a political position, follow a certain course of action, or buy a particular product. I believe that Martin Luther King, Jr., knew that he had to touch people's emotions in order to persuade his audience and win his battle for civil rights.